Practical Advocacy in th

Practical Advocacy in the Crown Court

Editors:
Mary Cowe, Barrister
Susan Cavender, Barrister

Contributors:
Ian Fenny
Grace Flynn
Anjali Gohil
Gregory Gordon
Alistair Haggerty
Andrew Langdon QC
Nick Lee
Ramin Pakrooh
Christopher Quinlan QC
David Scutt
Charles Thomas
Ray Tully
Anna Vigars QC
Tara Wolfe

All barristers at Guildhall Chambers, Bristol

Bloomsbury Professional

LONDON · DUBLIN · EDINBURGH · NEW YORK · NEW DELHI · SYDNEY

BLOOMSBURY PROFESSIONAL

Bloomsbury Publishing Plc

41–43 Boltro Road, Haywards Heath, RH16 1BJ, UK

BLOOMSBURY and the Diana logo are trademarks of Bloomsbury Publishing Plc

© Bloomsbury Professional 2020

Reprinted 2021

British Library Cataloguing-in-Publication Data

A catalogue record for this book is available from the British Library.

ISBN:	PB:	978 1 52651 632 9
	Epdf:	978 1 52651 634 3
	Epub:	978 1 52651 633 6

Typeset by Compuscript Ltd, Shannon
Printed and bound by CPI Group (UK) Ltd, Croydon, CR0 4YY

To find out more about our authors and books visit www.bloomsburyprofessional.com. Here you will find extracts, author information, details of forthcoming events and the option to sign up for our newsletters

Foreword

The most attractive advocacy I have seen during my time as a barrister and recorder, and latterly as a judge, has been in the Crown Court. Why should this be?

A sound knowledge of the applicable law is a pre-requisite: I note with considerable respect the authors' systematic reference to key cases, as well as to *Archbold* and *Blackstone's*. Although at the time I chafed (often) when instructed by my pupil supervisor to read the cases before setting out the law in an advice or a pleading, I have never regretted it since. The cases are where the clearest exposition of legal principle is to be found, articulated by reference to real factual situations. Occasionally the facts of a case will match – be 'on all fours' with – the problem immediately facing the advocate, in which case the answer is clear, but even if not the process of reasoning will frequently show the way through. Good advocates go to case law, using it to derive and apply the relevant legal principles, laying down a bedrock of knowledge which will guide and direct their route through even the most complex cases. For a busy advocate, attention to the detail of past cases takes resolution, and industry, but the returns lie in increased confidence at court.

After knowledge of the law, there is the audience: in the Crown Court advocates are performing and presenting not only to the judge but also, and crucially, to a jury of 12 ordinary people drawn from a wide cross-section of the public. These lay judges want to be spoken to directly, using language they can understand. They are dismissive of legalese, quick to see through insincerity or waffle, eager to be pointed to relevant material and responsive to atmosphere. They are, in short, a keen, responsible, and demanding audience who want to be guided by the law, but not to be a slave to it. Judges, although they may not want to be addressed in full jury mode, are human too, and welcome focused submissions in plain English.

Next there is the range of trial skills which advocates in the Crown Court are daily required to use. Whilst a practitioner in the civil or family courts may go for weeks without setting foot in a courtroom, never mind conducting a full trial, busy advocates in the Crown Court will be on their feet every day. Moreover in a trial they are required to deploy the full range of witness skills: asking questions in chief of their own witnesses (a process which is generally by-passed in other courts via witness statements prepared and served well before trial) and cross-examining a very wide range of witnesses and experts as well as the defendant. All this against a backdrop where the stakes are exceptionally high, involving the potential for a finding of criminal liability and sanction including, in the most serious cases, lengthy terms of imprisonment. The depths of courage and resolve required to visit a client in the cells after they have been tried, convicted and deprived of their liberty should never be underestimated.

But a good knowledge of the law, an ability to speak to an audience and developing a range of witness management skills is only the start. Chapter 1 of this excellent book emphasises advocacy as a skill that can be learned. Any judge who has watched young practitioners progress as they reappear in their courts over the years will confirm this. The authors refer here to the views of the ancients. I would add this, from Socrates: to know yourself is the beginning of wisdom. The process of a Crown Court trial, during which 12 ordinary people sit as judges upon the actions of another human being, drives all participants to a better understanding of humanity in general, and of themselves in particular.

In a Crown Court, where real-life dramas are deconstructed and examined, it is impossible to come away without new insights into people, how they think and what they do. All of life is there, under the microscope, coming at you from every corner of the court. Not just from the complainant, defendant and witnesses, but also from police, press, public gallery, other counsel, court staff and jurors. How should the judge respond to a note from a juror saying that the person next to them smells? Or that they must go now to a close relative who is mortally ill? How can counsel elicit the best evidence from a young witness with autism who will only speak from under a blanket in the next room? Examples such as these (of which I could give many more) challenge everyone in court to a fresh understanding of humanity, encouraging a creative response to difficult situations in the interests of justice.

The very best advocates note and absorb all of this, thereby advancing their knowledge of others, and of themselves, growing in wisdom as a result. They have developed a tolerance and understanding of human frailty. They have learned to recognise their own strengths and weaknesses, to challenge their own prejudices, the better to advise their clients and, at a trial, to probe and test evidence in a properly disinterested way. Justice is famously blind, but to be properly unsighted an independent advocate needs to be able to declutter their part of the stage, leaving it to be filled by the case against and for this defendant. Clean shoes, non-distracting suiting, as (correctly) recommended by the authors, provide an apt metaphor. Strong advocates know, as the authors so rightly point out, that the process is never about them. The best speeches to the jury are rarely flamboyant; effective advocates do not parade their own activities or experience. Instead they demonstrate, through their analysis of the issues and the evidence, a profound understanding of people's thoughts, motives and actions. Submissions which come from this place are irresistibly persuasive, since they articulate manifest truths derived from a clear appreciation of our common humanity.

Good advocacy is not necessarily always successful advocacy, in terms of result at trial. These authors, empathic, observant and intelligent advocates themselves, understand this. They know that there is much to be learned from coming second. The proper view of success lies in a true appreciation of the advocate's task in an adversarial system: presenting opposing sides of the case, sharpening the pencil to get to the point – has the prosecution proved the case to the necessary (high) standard? The more skilfully the opposing sides present the evidence and argue for their conclusions, the more closely the pencil will be shaved and the better Justice is served. That is the true success.

Understanding the legal principles relating to the criminal charges and the evidence, eliciting and marshalling that evidence, then formulating the most persuasive arguments for the jury's consideration are the fundamentals of a criminal advocate's job. These fundamentals are easily articulated but very much more difficult to execute. As judges sitting on the bench observing we do well to remember that. In reading the chapters of this book I have been reminded once more of the colossal industry that goes into presenting any case. And of the huge service to the rule of law that independent advocates provide each time they step into court.

This book will be welcomed by all new practitioners in the Crown Court, and by many experienced ones too. It is a highly useful, practical guide to all types of pre-trial mentions and case management hearings, trials and sentencing procedures, also appeals. It assists with tips for behind-the-scenes dealings with instructing solicitors and clients prior to and during such hearings. Above all it appreciates the value to an advocate of observing and learning about our fellow human beings, in all their fascinating diversity.

The Hon. Mrs Justice May DBE
September 2020

Preface

This book is aimed at aspiring and junior criminal advocates. It does not set out to explain the law or to give abstract guidance. It provides practical advice about advocacy in the real world of Crown Court work. This advice is the product of the authors' many years of experience as specialist criminal practitioners, but you will not find their anecdotes within these pages; that would be a very different book. Instead, those practitioners have drawn on their experiences to provide you with concrete advice about how to improve your advocacy now.

The many different voices you will encounter in this book should be an encouragement to find your own voice. Their shared concerns should demonstrate that whilst there is no single right way to conduct effective advocacy, some things will be common to all good approaches.

The book starts with a survival guide aimed at the very new, and then takes the reader through the different stages in the lifecycle of a Crown Court case, from bail and legal applications through to witness handling, addressing a jury in closing and (if necessary) sentencing. There is also a section dealing with the appellate jurisdiction of the Crown Court to assist new practitioners who are frequently called on to conduct this work. Not all advocacy is oral, and not all of it is directed at the judge or jury; so we have included the sometimes neglected topic of effective communication with lay and professional clients, and how to produce persuasive written advocacy.

A good advocate must have a clear understanding of their role in the criminal justice system. We have interspersed the main chapters with short reflective pieces about the purpose of advocacy, your place in the adversarial system, your ethical obligations, and how you can best dust yourself off after trying times and strive again for excellence.

We have varied the use of 'he' and 'she' throughout the book in relation to defendants and judges, as an acknowledgement that one may encounter males and females within both groups, without reverting to 'his/her'.

References within the book to *Archbold*, *Blackstone's* and the Criminal Procedure Rules all relate to these works, and the legislation in force, as at June 2020.

Although this book has been written with junior advocates in mind, we editors have found that our colleagues' insights have generated many stimulating conversations between us. We hope that practitioners of all vintages will find it refreshing to read this book and reflect on their approach to advocacy. We believe that any advocate could find something useful and inspiring within these pages.

On behalf of all the authors of this book, we would like to record our gratitude to our families who have lived through the process of its production with us.

We would also like to acknowledge the debt we owe to all those many colleagues and friends who have shaped our professional development and shared with us the occasional sorrows and many joys of life as a criminal advocate.

Mary Cowe
Susan Cavender
Guildhall Chambers
June 2020

Contents

Contents

Contents

Contents

Contributors

Guildhall Chambers' Crime Team is based in Bristol; we work primarily on the Western Circuit.

As a set we prosecute and defend all types of criminal cases; individuals also have their own specialities.

EDITORS AND CONTRIBUTORS

Susan Cavender (call 2004): In addition to crime and regulatory work also a liquor licensing specialist, a continuation from 15 years as a solicitor in Soho with a niche licensing and entertainment practice.

Mary Cowe (call 2006): Fraud specialist, prosecutes complex and multi-handed cases, often defends in cases with psychiatric element: MPhil dissertation on mental health and crime. Advocacy trainer.

CONTRIBUTORS

Ian Fenny (call 1978): A senior specialist criminal practitioner with extensive experience of rape and serious sexual offences, offences against those with vulnerability and crimes of violence and drug supply.

Grace Flynn (call 2015): Has also worked for The Criminal Cases Review Commission and Court of Justice of the European Union.

Anjali Gohil (call 2000): A sex offences specialist; a member of the Bristol BAME Criminal Lawyers Group, heads up the Western Circuit Diversity Forum 'Bar None' and sits on the Bristol Lammy Review.

Gregory Gordon (call 2010): A recognised specialist in animal welfare, hunting and raptor persecution legislation who represents local authorities and national charitable organisations.

Alistair Haggerty (call 2012): Has an established practice in health and safety and environmental law. Worked in Mississippi for the Office of Post-Conviction Counsel for individuals on Death Row.

Andrew Langdon QC (call 1986, silk 2006): Homicide, Fraud and Regulatory Crime. Crown Court Recorder. Western Circuit Leader 2014–2016. Chairman of the Bar 2017.

Nick Lee (call 2018): Previously worked in finance, including a brief stint in the legal department of the European Central Bank.

Christopher Quinlan QC (call 1992, silk 2011): Crown Court Recorder, crime, sport and environmental law. Bencher, Inner Temple; Judicial Panel Chairman World Rugby and Football Association. Head of Crime Team.

Ramin Pakrooh (call 1996): Leading junior, wide experience in drugs and firearms conspiracies, violent crime and homicide, police disciplinary hearings.

David Scutt (call 1989): Experienced Specialist Criminal Practitioner. An advocacy trainer, both in the UK and abroad (including the International Criminal Court in The Hague).

Charles Thomas (call 1990): Crown Court Recorder; sits as a Legally Qualified Chair at the Medical Practitioners Tribunal Service and also for Sport Resolutions UK.

Ray Tully (call 1987): Experienced Specialist Criminal Practitioner. Former Head of Crime team 2013-2018. Specialist Organised Crime Prosecutor. Member CBA National Exec.

Anna Vigars QC (call 1996, silk 2017) Head of Chambers: Particular expertise in the prosecution of multi-defendant sexual exploitation cases. Crown Court Recorder; Western Circuit Director of Education.

Tara Wolfe (call 2000) Experienced criminal practitioner with a background in immigration and asylum law and a Masters in International Law. Taught Advocacy and Opinion Writing and Drafting on the BPTC.

PROOF-READERS

With grateful thanks to our proof-readers:

Mark Worsley (call 1994) (chief proof-reader): Recorder (Family), Member of the New York Bar (called 1989).

James Haskell (call 2004) (assistant): Specialist Criminal Advocate; professional disciplinary hearings. Advocacy Trainer BPTC; Joint Head of Chambers' Pupillage Committee.

Part I

Starting out

Chapter 1

Survival guide

Gregory Gordon

Each stage of a career at the Bar offers different advantages. While those in their prime have wells of experience and wisdom from which to draw, those of you fresh out of the box have the freedom to ask anything without anyone questioning your aptitude.

In a profession where knowledge is key, of course no-one wants to ask a stupid question: but if you've done your research and you still don't know what to do, the chances are that you're not the only one who wants to ask that question. A healthy robing room, and chambers' common room, is one where barristers of all levels of call are asking questions and bouncing ideas off one another; self-employed, but in it together. So, while this chapter hopes to address some of the 'too frightened to ask …' topics which may arise in practice, the first lesson is the most important one of all: *Never be too afraid to ask*. You'll rarely regret that you did.

WHAT TO WEAR

You step out onto Chancery Lane with your shiny new wig, and what is the first thing you want to do with it? Drag it backwards through a hedge to give it that 'ready worn' look – because arriving in a foreign robing room with your headpiece illuminated like a lighthouse shows everyone just how inexperienced you are. Well, consider yourself let-in on a secret: everyone already knows, and it's got nothing to do with the wig.

The judge knows, solicitors and paralegals know, every other barrister knows, and the defendants, witnesses, juries, clerks, ushers, police officers, cleaners and security staff – they all know. So please don't soil your wig. It doesn't work and they're expensive to repair or replace. Also, you don't need a wig tin with your name embossed on the lid in order to fit in. If you want one, great, look after it – it'll make a nice heirloom, or cremation tin. But if you want to save money, a biscuit tin or Tupperware box does the trick.

Polish your shoes – it gets noticed – and only wear colourful socks or snazzy tights if you're happy for people to comment on them. If you can afford it, it can help to have a spare suit, shirt and pair of shoes in chambers, so that when you are faced with the inevitable wardrobe malfunction on the train, or a gull decides to bestow upon you its good luck, you won't need to scour the charity shop rails over lunch for a replacement. Gentlemen: always buy more collar studs than you need as they have a habit of disappearing. In an emergency, treasury tags make serviceable collar studs or cufflinks, so keep a handful in your wig tin. Ladies: an extra collarette is handy to have and a spare pair of tights kept in your desk drawer can be invaluable.

For those times when you leave home in a rush with the wrong bag, find out who in chambers has the same collar size as you, and ask your clerks whether there is a spare set of robes around. Also, keep a spare phone charger in your bag, and have photo ID on you at all times – if you're called to a prison for a conference, it is embarrassing to be turned away with your instructing solicitor watching.

If you notice someone else leaving the robing room without their tabs, tell them; turn their collar down; brush the flaking baby sick from their cuff. Looking smart is important, as it shows everyone – judge, jury, client and opponent – that you take the job seriously. You would want someone else to tell you if your laces were untied, so help out your colleagues too. People will judge you on appearances. If you only realise after the hearing that you've been wearing your brightest pink tie throughout, having forgotten to change into your tabs (and the judge was gracious enough not to pass comment), then return to the courtroom and apologise. You won't get a dressing down, it's just good manners.

So, you're looking smart, professional, and you've got a clean set of robes. Unfortunately, in the magistrates' court, where you're likely to begin your practice, your wig and gown stay in the bag. Gentlemen, it's probably a good idea to pick an unadventurous tie, and ladies, button conservatively – you want the bench focused on your advocacy, not your dandy fashion sense. The same goes for the Youth Court.

In the Crown Court, robes on – mostly

Some judges will still hear bail applications 'in chambers' – usually in a closed courtroom, rather than actually in their own private room in the court building – and will take off their wigs for such hearings. It's wise though not to assume that this will be the case. If you are unsure, ask the court's clerk, before the hearing, whether the judge will be wearing their wig. As a rule of thumb, if you're not certain, wear it – when the judge walks in, it is easier to take yours off than have to apologise for being unable to put it on.

Also, if you're waiting in court for the judge to come in, and chatting with colleagues, keep your wig on – judges can reappear with alarming haste, and it doesn't look good to be scrabbling at your clothing.

Approach virtual hearings as if you were in the same room as the judge. It might feel strange, sitting in a TV room no bigger than a shoe cupboard next to the courtroom in your wig and gown, but for that hearing, that is your courtroom. Treat it as such.

It shouldn't happen, but there may be an occasion when you have to go into court in just a suit: perhaps you left your robes at a court some distance away, knowing that you're due to return the next day, but on arriving back in chambers you're asked to deal with a defendant at your local court who was arrested that morning on a warrant. First, let your clerks know and ask them to check with the court: is it alright that you turn up without robes? When you get there, double check with the court's clerk: is the judge content that you appear unrobed? Never assume. Never say, 'I'm sorry, I will be appearing in just my suit.' Ask: 'I hope that the court will not object if I appear in just my suit?' Let's face it, the judge is unlikely to say no, but it is their court, and you win no friends by being presumptuous.

If you're fortunate, you will practise from courts with functioning heating and air-conditioning systems; however, with the present state of the HMCTS estate, that's unlikely. Hot summer days can be unbearable if the air-conditioning malfunctions – if it becomes so uncomfortable that it is affecting your work, don't be afraid to raise it with the judge. They might let you take off your wig and robes.

How you present yourself doesn't just affect you. During pupillage, you are an extension of your pupil supervisor, and what you do reflects upon them – so if you are feeling under the weather and walk around chambers in a scarf and beanie hat, that will be noted. Also, don't wear your robes when in your first six months of pupillage unless specifically required to do so by your pupil supervisor. If you're not yet 'on your feet', keep to business-suit smart. In tenancy, you are an extension of your chambers and, while you may be self-employed, what you do may reflect on everyone and can have consequences for others, let alone yourself. So while you might occasionally see other (usually more experienced) practitioners making a bold fashion choice, or smoking outside the court whilst still robed, or walking between court and chambers with their tabs still on, don't copy them; be aware that some in your chambers may find that highly unprofessional. Dress smartly, simply. The criminal bar is such a fantastically fun career, and you want to enjoy it – not have to worry about why everyone is staring at your socks.

FORMS OF ADDRESS

Up! When talking to the judge, stand up.

If the judge is talking to you, stand up.

If the judge is talking to you and your opponent, stand up, even if your opponent doesn't.

Never allow the judge to face an empty row. Always remain until the next advocate takes their seat, unless the judge notices, thanks you (generally) and tells you not to wait.

The only exceptions are when you are appearing on a videolink (never stand – not even when the judge is coming into court – the court won't thank you for a crotch shot), or when another person is appearing on the videolink (check the practice with court beforehand, but most courts will expect you to remain seated when speaking, so that your voice is captured by the microphones).

Opening with, 'May it please Your Honour …' might not set the tone as you hope if the judge interjects with 'We'll see.' Don't panic, smile, carry on.

When prosecuting, always start by introducing yourself (not by name – just, 'Your Honour, I prosecute') and then your opponent ('and my learned friend Ms Perriwig defends').

If you are holding the case for someone else and you want the judge to know that, you can say, 'I prosecute for today's purposes.' It's not a get out of jail free card – you should always be on top of the case, even if it is someone else's – but it is a subtle indication to the judge that you won't necessarily know all the ins and outs. If holding the case for someone else, make sure to have their diary with you so that you can ensure that the next hearing is on a date that suits them.

Your opponent should always be 'My *learned* friend,' even if they are a Higher Court Advocate. It's frankly rude these days to distinguish between barristers and solicitors in that way; don't be that person.

Sometimes, when defending, it might be appropriate to be the one to rise first, introduce the parties, and make the opening submissions – but if you want to do that, it's polite to check with your prosecuting opponent first.

Sometimes, when you are prosecuting, your opponent might catch you off guard and push in – there can be a tactical benefit to setting the agenda, after all. It's more likely to happen to you when you are new. Don't be fazed – if you are well prepared, and there is something you need to say, you will have your opportunity.

Get to know your judge. Do they have any pet peeves? A particular approach to certain issues? Any words or phrases they dislike, or submissions they encourage or discourage? Will they require all the detail, or expect you to get to the point? If you don't know your judge, ask around chambers. If something went wrong during a hearing (perhaps you made a submission that was received icily) and you don't know why, put your big girl/boy pants on and be brave – ask to speak with the judge in chambers, and politely enquire whether it was something you said. There are precious few opportunities for feedback and constructive criticism at the Bar, so find them where you can.

Circuit Judges and Recorders are always 'Your Honour'. Lords Justices of Appeal, High Court Judges, and Senior Circuit Judges (anyone wearing red and/ or frills) are 'My Lady/Lord' or 'Your Ladyship/Lordship'. Don't worry if you mix a Lordship with an Honour, it happens; apologise, carry on.

District Judges (DJs), Deputy DJs and magistrates are simply 'Madam/ Sir,' but a magistrate can also be addressed as 'Your Worship' – a reasonable compromise is to address the bench as 'Your Worships' the first time, and then 'Madam/Sir', addressed to the Chair, thereafter. Never say 'Good morning' unless (as can happen in the magistrates' courts) you are addressed in that way by the bench first. You don't have obsequiously to pepper every sentence with 'Your Honour'/'My Lady'/'Your Worship' – it is perfectly acceptable to say 'you' and 'your' sometimes.

Always be polite, to *everyone*. Security guards, clerks, ushers, probation officers, custody guards, mental health nurses, cleaners – all of them can make your life so much easier, or harder, so be nice. Left your laptop in a locked court? Forgotten the key-code to the robing room? Urgently need that indictment printed? No-one will go out of their way to be unhelpful to you, but will they go out of their way to help? If that sounds a shamefully self-serving motive for doing what you should be doing anyway, it is, but here's the more important reason: none of them needs a barrister looking down their nose at them. Hopefully you are in the business of criminal justice because you want to make a positive difference in peoples' lives – well, that starts with you and the way you behave. Of course, you will become frustrated with others and their foibles – that happens in every workplace – but remember, they have difficult and stressful jobs too, so what can you do to make their lives easier? There are a plethora of wonderful and decent and interesting people working in all different parts of the criminal justice system; if you're lucky, and you treat them with kindness and as your equal, you'll make a few friends along the way.

LEARNING THE LANGUAGE

It takes time to develop your own tone and register – something that sounds like you, that isn't forced, but comes naturally. In the meantime, it's worth paying close attention to your opponent for what works well, and what doesn't, and then practising what you want to incorporate into your own spiel. Steal shamelessly, and work it until it feels like you own. When you're setting out it's better to be too serious than too jokey, especially when addressing the bench – making the right points and making them well is much more important than showing the judge you have a winning personality. Well-pitched humour, in the right case, can work – with jury advocacy in particular – but it can also fall painfully flat, so until you get a feel for what works, perhaps run your zingers by someone you trust.

Always prepare your remarks in advance, no matter how brief or trivial the point. Be clear and concise. You should never be too scared to pursue a point that you think needs to be made, and you don't want to leave a courtroom wishing you had made the argument that you intended to make, so by all means argue passionately, but try not to be overbearing or argumentative. Learning when to press on, and when to give ground and step back from a point you have lost will gain you respect in the long run, as will learning which points not to pursue in the first place.

Certain unfortunate words and phrases that you use will burn themselves on your mind – perhaps you mentioned your client's 'story' to the police, instead of his 'account'. It will happen. Embrace the embarrassment – it's your brain's way of ensuring those moments are never to be repeated.

Beware acronyms in oral advocacy. Beware Americanisms, abbreviations, and slang. You may feel like an initiate into a secret club when you can reassure the judge that the CPS will upload the PNC record and ABE transcript to the CCDCS, but some judges won't thank you for your informality. At least until you are confident that you know your tribunal, it is best to be scrupulously sober and formal. Your first contact with many of your professional clients will be in writing, whether drafting advices or emailing thanks and questions to your instructing solicitors, so set the right tone – until you know them well, formality and politeness are paramount.

If you email a judge directly, always be formal, always start with 'Dear Judge', and cc your opponent unless there is an exceptional reason not to do so, such as a 'without notice' application of some kind.

Keep a note of people who have praised your work and the case you were doing; you will need a bank of potential referees for all manner of applications. Remember always to email/phone/text your instructing solicitor and your clerks after a hearing, so that they know what's going on. Keep your website profile professional and up-to-date and sell yourself confidently – but do it honestly and keep within the Code of Conduct. Beware the dangers of social media. Have in mind issues such as court-imposed reporting restrictions, your duty of confidentiality, and your duty not to bring the profession into disrepute. Never write anything on a public platform that you wouldn't be happy for a judge to read.

PRE-HEARING PREPARATION

Be proactive. Some of an advocate's best work can be done before the hearing starts, but only if you're prepared. For that, you will need to know what is expected of you.

If prosecuting a Pre-Trial Preparation Hearing (PTPH), you will need to have completed the form on the Digital Case System in good time before the hearing – at least the working day before. If prosecuting, have suggested 'stage dates' ready and be able to say whether there will likely be any special measures, bad character or hearsay applications. It is your duty to know the custody time limit where applicable: reminding the court what it is, even if not asked, is something the CPS expects of you.

If defending, you need to know if there are concerns about the defendant's fitness to plead, or to be ready to say that you are considering an application to dismiss – in which case, do not allow the defendant to be arraigned. Will the defendant offer any pleas, and are they acceptable to the prosecution? Are you ready to proceed to sentence straight away or is there a proper reason to ask for a pre-sentence report or to gather other important information that will help the sentencing tribunal? If the defendant is having a trial, be able to say what the defence is and what are the key issues in dispute; know which witnesses will be required; be able to suggest a sensible trial length; be ready to raise any potential disclosure or legal issues; make sure that the defendant has been advised about potential credit for guilty pleas, and the consequences of failing to attend the trial.

If a Further Case Management Hearing (FCMH) or other mention hearing has been listed, ensure you know why – what is the court expecting you to have done? Diarise any actions that should have been completed a week before, and set an alert, so that you can follow them up in good time before the hearing.

If you are dealing with a bail application, have you seen the application – does it address any issues that the court might have; have the police considered it, and have they visited any proposed bail address to ensure that it is suitable? Whether prosecuting or defending, find the court liaison officer on the morning of the hearing and speak with them – what concerns do the police have, if any?

If you are 'holding' cases for senior members of chambers, what do they expect and want to happen? They should speak with you, or ideally provide you with a written note; if they don't, ask – never go into a hearing blind. If someone else is holding one of your briefs, they will expect to find it in good order – and you should have a note ready for them which is specific to the hearing.

If holding a defence case, introduce yourself to the lay client, and reassure them that you have had a detailed conversation with their barrister, and that you know what needs to happen in this hearing. Provide a detailed note for the barrister after the hearing. If holding a trial while the jury is in retirement, have you been given a note of the evidence and a summary of the main issues that arose during the trial; if the jury ask a question, do you know how to deal with it, or how to contact the barrister for whom you are holding the case? If the jury comes back with a verdict, do you know what orders need to be made? Will sentence be expected straight away, or is a pre-sentence report requested? Are there any ancillary matters to consider such as Sexual Harm Prevention Orders or Proceeds of Crime Act applications?

Far in advance of any trial that you are conducting, you should be working with your opponent: to identify and narrow the issues; to address disclosure and witness requirements; to agree edits to documents such as transcripts. Even from the earliest stage – at the first hearing in the Crown Court – you will save yourself a lot of time and hassle by dealing with as much as possible without the need for judicial intervention. Still, don't be afraid to say to your opponent when you can't agree and will need the judge to decide.

If you're not sure who your opponent is, check the 'people' tab of the digital case system. If you need to talk, phone them in chambers – if it's urgent and they're not in, ask for a call back, or ask the clerk if you can have their mobile number. (Store *everyone's* number in your contacts, along with any direct dial phone numbers – being kept on hold on a switchboard while a judge is waiting for you to come back to court is a sweat-inducing frustration.) All hearings run much more smoothly when the advocates have been in contact, so keep lines of communication open; but do remember, your opponent is a busy advocate as well and won't thank you for hundreds of emails each day.

Whatever the hearing, you need to have anticipated the issues. What is the judge likely to ask of you? What will your opponent want? Where can you give, and where do you need to stand firm? Get to the robing room in plenty of time and find your opponent – you may have nothing to talk about, but ask them, in case they've thought of something you haven't. If you are caught off guard by your opponent who comes with an offer or is applying pressure, there's no need to make a snap decision, even if your case is about to be called on. It's OK to be sceptical, and it's OK to request time to take advice and/or instructions.

If prosecuting a litigant in person, have you spoken with them before the hearing? You are not required to, but it is usually helpful and, in any event, courteous. Find a private area or room, but keep the door open. Explain your role and why you can't give them legal advice and explain that they shouldn't divulge anything to you that they would not want the prosecution to know. Set out what will happen in the hearing, what you will ask for, and ask them if they are willing to tell you how they are likely to respond. Explain to them that the judge may ask them if they want a lawyer and what steps they have taken to find one. If the case is listed for sentence and the defendant says that he will represent himself, explain what you are saying about any guidelines. You can also use this as an opportunity to consider if this is an appropriate case for a court-appointed advocate if there is to be a trial.

Remember that you owe your duty to the court and to the administration of justice: if you are worried that a defendant is just not with it, make sure the judge knows about it.

SAYING SORRY, PLEASE AND THANK YOU

When facing the consequences of an inevitable error of judgement, there is really only one way to go: candour. Say sorry and mean it. Don't try to explain it away.

A genuine and disarming apology is one of the most potent tools in the advocate's toolbox. Don't dress it up with fancy language: 'I'm very sorry,' are often the three best words to use. Just try not to get yourself into the habit of needing to use it too often. Missed a deadline? Late to court? Forgot to mention an important point? Apologise sincerely, and promise to put it right straight away (and then do it). There will sometimes be no apology that can wipe the slate clean, but it will still be the best way to salvage something from a bad situation.

You may be double-courted and, for reasons beyond your control, if one hearing takes longer than expected you may be late for another court. Apologise, even if it is technically not your fault. A judge may take a dim view of your diary management, and no-one likes to be kept waiting. Apologise to the judge, the court staff, and your opponent. (If you are double-courted, always, at the start of the day, visit both courts and explain to the usher/clerk and your opponent(s) which other court you will be in and when.)

If you're lucky, you will be criticised by judges – pulled into their room for a hard talk, or even find a letter sent to your head of team or chambers. It is a deeply humbling, and humiliating, experience. But be thankful for it. No advocate is perfect, although some of us behave as if we are, and being told where our faults lie is a gift. You may not agree with criticism that is levelled at you, but even if you are certain it is unjustified, it's worth remembering that there may be others who would not agree – in a job where your presentation is paramount, you might want to think about what you are doing wrong.

You may even want to go looking for criticism. Was your opponent someone from your chambers, or was someone else sitting in court during that challenging submission you dealt with? Did someone you trust watch your closing speech? They're unlikely to tell you what they really thought unless you ask them. Invite the criticism, or you won't grow as an advocate.

In the heat of battle, relationships with opponents can become extremely strained, even if you went into the trial as friends from the same chambers. If you've been unpleasant, unprofessional, snapped at or been sarcastic to them (it shouldn't ever happen, but days in court can be intensely stressful and emotional, and lapses in temperament can happen to the best of us), find them as soon as your temper has calmed and apologise. It sounds basic, but some people don't; the resentment that can fester may mean that the next time you see that person on the other side of the courtroom it may not be a pleasant or productive experience.

Relationships with your own side ought to be better. If being led, work really hard – you really want to shine – and don't be afraid to give your opinion. Use your antennae: jumping into a debate between leader and senior investigating officer may be unhelpful, but an email to your leader the night before conference with your thoughts and research may be very welcome. Even the most eminent silk should value a sounding board, and don't be disheartened if they reject your ideas or suggestions. It's a fantastic learning process for you, to see how a case is assembled and tactically driven, so enjoy it. And if you mess up – apologise!

If you do make a mistake in court, the temptation may be not to advertise the fact to your client – whether professional or lay. Who wants to risk your solicitors or the Crown Prosecution Service stopping further instructions, or being shouted at by an angry defendant? Well, being a coward isn't justification for failing to do the right thing, and frankly they may well find out another way anyway. You do need to report accurately what happened in a hearing: if there is something you conceded that needs to be un-done or something you forgot to do that needs to be fixed, be honest. Your duty is to do the best for your client not for yourself. People also tend to value honesty. Just try not to repeat your mistakes.

Never be afraid to ask for time. If you need time because you are unprepared, or hadn't properly considered the point, you will have to own up, and apologise – but better that than rushing in. If the time is for something you couldn't have anticipated, but need to ask others for instructions, or for advice, say so.

You will never finish carving out your reputation until you retire, but with one misplaced stroke it could be permanently disfigured. Either way, it will stay with you.

The Bar is a small world and people talk; judges talk to each other; solicitors and paralegals talk. You shouldn't lose much of the good credit you build if you apologise for a mistake, but you could destroy it if you don't. That said, it is worth remembering not to be too swayed by what you are told about the reputations of others; try to make up your own mind. Reputations are rarely wholly justified, and if you really want to get on at the Bar, you ought to give everyone a chance.

OTHER GUIDEBOOKS ARE AVAILABLE

You've already made the most important purchase for your legal library in this book, but annual outlays on other volumes will still be necessary. *Archbold* or *Blackstone's* is a must. Both have strengths and weaknesses, but whichever you find easier to use is the one for you.

Then, actually read it. Not front-to-back like a novel, but get to know it, and what topics are covered in which chapters – the burning glare of the judicial stare as you fail to find the right chapter is painful.

Check whether your chambers has an online subscription through Westlaw or LexisNexis; your arms will thank you if you can leave the tome out of your bag. Online highlighting/tabbing tools, and click-through links to case law, make referencing much easier than in the hardback books. One major benefit of the physical *Archbold* is the reference for model indictments at the very front – more times than you would expect, you will be called upon to draft a new count for the indictment at short notice, sometimes while the judge is waiting. Keeping a collection of indictments that you have previously drafted, for easy copy-and-pasting, also helps. For guides you will need less often, such as *Banks on Sentence*, consider sharing the cost with a colleague in chambers.

Websites such as legislation.gov.uk and bailii.org are useful free resources but are not always current. When referring to the sentencing guidelines, use the sentencingcouncil.org.uk website, not the PDFs, for the most up-to-date guidelines. The Crown Prosecution Service's website can be a helpful reference point for many topics, and don't be afraid to google a question – many barristers, solicitors and legal scholars write helpful articles and blogs. The key to relying on secondary sources is always to check and double check.

The key to survival at the Bar? In truth, it's nothing very difficult. Try to be nice to people, avoid eating fish in the robing room, get some well-being seminars in, and try and live together in peace and harmony with barristers of all circuits.

Look closely, and you will find that most of your colleagues are not out to get you. They want to help you survive, and thrive. Work hard and be kind, and you cannot hope for a more exciting, rewarding career.

Chapter 2

What is advocacy?

Mary Cowe

ADVOCACY IS A SKILL THAT CAN BE TAUGHT

More than 2,300 years ago Aristotle knew that advocacy can be taught: he wrote *Rhetoric* because he feared that others were teaching it in the wrong way. His theory of rhetoric concerned a type of persuasion that was aimed at the public and designed to resolve civic issues; practical advocacy as opposed to philosophical debate. If wrongly taught, public advocacy had the capacity to create demagogues who could persuade through false argument.

He was in no doubt that advocacy mattered, and that it could be taught. His ideas about what an aspiring advocate should learn were harnessed to his belief that rhetoric was a branch of philosophy, aimed at logically revealing likely underlying truths. As it was aimed at a lay audience dealing with real-life problems, this logical analysis had to engage public emotion and focus on realistic rather than ideal outcomes.

This is all less distant than it may seem. Practical advocacy is still largely directed at the public and it still has a resolutely civic function in terms of its focus on matters such as individual culpability and good public order. Hopefully, your advocacy will demonstrate some of the skills Aristotle identified, such as logic, empathy, and, where appropriate, pragmatism. Your skills as a jury advocate, however, will not be used in the service of revealing all truths, but *a* truth: whether the prosecution can prove its case.

This apparently modest-sounding aim is fundamental to our judicial system, and as you will see when you read **Chapter 4** on the adversarial system, it is also essential to your understanding of your role as an advocate. The system in which our practical advocacy happens is one which prioritises our individual liberty, our right not to be removed from society unless the state can convince our fellow citizens that they are sure we have broken the rules. We are all so familiar with the burden and standard of proof that it is easy to forget that it encapsulates something vital about where the balance of power lies between the individual and the state.

The fact that as advocates we do not imagine ourselves to be in the business of revealing universal truths, the fact that our justice system has no higher aim than convicting the guilty and acquitting the innocent, is a considerable human achievement. It represents the vindication of a belief that individual liberty and other human rights remain important in a system designed to promote the collective good.

If advocacy is a skill which can play such an important part in a good society, why is there such cynicism about the work of advocates? Consider how well you could explain to a friend from a non-legal background why it is that an advocate does not refuse to help a client who it appears has committed a crime. Would you describe it simply in terms of how the system *happens* to work, or would you talk about the values and aims that are inherent in our system of justice: the right to legal representation, the right to a fair public hearing of the evidence rather than the condemnation of private judgement?

Practical advocacy is a purposive activity that is designed to achieve certain goals. Unless we can explain what the goals are and how our professional codes help to achieve them, the public will understandably wonder why advocates seem to play by different rules from the rest of society. If you stop believing in those goals yourself, this will become apparent in your own advocacy. A cynical advocate may simply play to win, desirous of securing a conviction or an acquittal at all costs with no regard for their broader duties to the court; or they may lazily go through the motions of presenting a case without proper preparation because they are no longer focused on achieving a just result. Advocates who show symptoms of either variant of cynicism rarely persuade.

This book is not designed to teach you a series of tricks to win arguments irrespective of the evidence. It treats advocacy as a set of skills that you can develop to present your case in the best possible way within the rules, so that you can fully perform your role in the administration of justice. You will notice that various authors throughout this book reiterate the importance of having a proper understanding of both your role and the nature of the task you are performing. You need to think carefully about what a prosecutor can and should try to achieve in cross examining a defendant or what defence counsel's task is in relation to a closing speech before you put pen to paper: you need to know where you are trying to end up before you embark on your journey.

Aristotle's book was known in Latin as *Ars Rhetorica* or *The Art of Rhetoric* and whilst 'Art' in the Roman world meant something more like our idea of science, there has been a long history of great advocates being described as artists. Resist that classification: calling advocacy an art makes it sound important, but it has the tendency to mystify and exclude. It also ignores the fact that an essential part of your job is to be the voice of someone else. This may involve creativity in terms of your language or approach to the case, but your role is not fundamentally about self-expression.

This may sound less than glamourous, but it is a hugely responsible role: consider the enormous trust placed in you and in your abilities as a communicator. A vulnerable defendant or complainant who has never met you before trusts that you will listen carefully to their account, present a case on their behalf, and inspire confidence in that case with both a learned judge and a lay jury. They trust you to do all this because you tell them that you are an advocate. They understand this means that you can talk for anyone to anyone about anything: that is your skill, and your privilege.

Beyond logic, empathy and a good grasp of professional ethics, what is it about a really good advocate that gives them fluency at this task of putting forward someone else's point of view; what is it that makes them compelling?

Cicero's *On the Orator* is a fictional dialogue between famous advocates discussing what personal qualities someone should possess if their words are to have power. This discussion is located at a time when all advocacy was political: Cicero had just returned from exile and perhaps wished to demonstrate that oratorical skills were invaluable to the state. In his vision, orators were to Rome what philosophers had been to Athens, and they needed to have a broad grasp of human affairs.

Is Cicero still relevant when considering that extra spark that gives life to the best advocacy? Although you will not be advocating for or against social or political change in the Crown Court as orators did in the Senate, you will still have a client who needs your eloquence and your understanding. The fact that representing your client is an end in itself and not a means to some other end, such as repealing a law or embarrassing a foe, in no way diminishes the importance of your task. Each individual complainant or defendant deserves justice, irrespective of their social position or their ability to further your career. Working in a system where advocacy is free of politics means that your duties are clear: fearless pursuit of your client's interests subject only to your duty to the court. You need to be able to understand and articulate those interests.

The conception of the ideal advocate as a person who has familiarity with all fields of human endeavour remains important in our system. You are an advocate and nothing human should be alien to you. Being widely read or having broad cultural knowledge does not mean that you can really know how another person experiences their own life, but it might give you some insight into other ways of being. A greater understanding of the human condition will give you an advantage in acting as the professional intermediary between two groups of people – your client and the jury – neither of whom may be much like you. Reading can also only enhance your facility with language, which is, after all, the tool of your trade.

This short chapter refers to writers from the ancient world because whoever you are, as an advocate, you are their heir. This does not mean that reading their work is either necessary or sufficient. Aristotle did not write about child witnesses nor Cicero about representing those with psychiatric conditions. In your job, you will encounter people who have experienced racism or sexual trauma; people who feel marginalised because they were brought up in care, or are Deaf, or suffer from addiction; people whose trust you may struggle to gain. They may be either witnesses or defendants. They will all be individuals and not just the sum

16

of the labels applied to them. How will you speak for them? What should your bookshelf look like?

You have many different teachers available to you: colleagues, training courses, books like this one. To say that experience is the greatest teacher does not mean that you have to wait to become a good advocate: it means that you can draw on every aspect of your own life, as well as every case that you undertake, to help you know what to say and how to say it well.

Advocacy is a skill you can learn.

Part II

Bail

Chapter 3

Bail hearings

Alistair Haggerty and Grace Flynn

Key references

- *Archbold: Criminal Pleading, Evidence and Practice 2020*, 3-51 and 3-52

- *Blackstone's Criminal Practice 2020*, D7.70

- Criminal Procedure Rules 2015, SI 2015/1490 (CPR 2015)

- Criminal Practice Directions, III, 14F: Forfeiture of monies lodged as security or pledged by a surety/estreatment of recognizances

---

Case law

- *Kent Crown Court, ex parte Jodka* [1997] EWHC 346 (Admin)

- *R (Gibson) v Winchester Crown Court* [2004] EWHC 361 (Admin)

- *R (Malik) v Central Criminal Court* [2006] EWHC 1539 (Admin)

- *R v Ipswich Crown Court ex p CPS* [2010] EWHC 1515 (Admin)

- *R v Manchester Crown Court, ex p McDonald* [1999] 1 WLR 841, 847

- *R v Scott* [2007] EWCA Crim 2757

INTRODUCTION

A busy morning list will typically feature a number of bail applications buried amongst sentences, mentions and pre-trial preparation hearings. The advocate prosecuting or defending a bail application will often be doing several of those other hearings in the list. It is also rare for the defendant to be present in court when their bail application is being heard. It will therefore be tempting for both the judge and advocates to rattle through the application as quickly as possible so that more attention can be devoted to weightier and seemingly more interesting hearings.

However, bail applications have serious repercussions. For a defendant, the refusal to grant bail could mean the immediate loss of employment, accommodation, and their family and social network. For a vulnerable complainant, the decision to grant bail could mean the immediate release of a violent and vengeful domestic abuser. Whether you are prosecuting or defending, making and responding to bail applications requires careful preparation and attention to detail. The hearing may be short, but the stakes are high.

Depriving someone of their liberty before they stand trial is a serious step. There is therefore a general presumption in favour of bail, which is codified in the Bail Act 1976, s 4. This presumption continues from the time of arrest up until the time of conviction. However, if, after conviction, the court adjourns for a report before sentencing, the presumption continues up to the sentencing hearing (see the Bail Act 1976, s 4(2), (4)).

The Criminal Justice and Public Order Act 1994, s 25 sets out situations in which this general presumption to bail does not apply: defendants charged with offences of homicide or serious sexual offences who have previous convictions for such offences will only be granted bail in exceptional circumstances.

For all other defendants, there are some exceptions to the general right to bail and these are set out in the Bail Act 1976, Sch 1. You must be familiar with this list. Bail can only be refused if one or more of these exceptions applies. It cannot be withheld for any other reason. An unusual exception is that a defendant can be refused bail if the court is satisfied that they should be kept in custody for their own protection: such a prosecution application is likely to require evidence of vigilante activity for example.

The most commonly encountered are the three exceptions contained in the Bail Act 1976, Sch 1, para 2. This provision stipulates that the defendant need not be granted bail if the court is satisfied that there are substantial grounds for believing that the defendant, if released on bail, would:

- fail to surrender to custody;

- commit an offence whilst on bail; or

- interfere with witnesses or otherwise obstruct the course of justice

The nature and seriousness of the alleged offence, the strength of the evidence, and the defendant's previous convictions are not exceptions which justify refusing bail. They can inform the statutory exceptions – for example, a defendant with a substantial list of previous convictions may well be more likely to commit an offence whilst on bail, and, where the evidence is strong and the alleged offence is a serious one, the defendant may be more likely to abscond – but they do not, in themselves, provide exceptions to bail.

PREPARATION FOR THE HEARING

The magistrates' court can make the preliminary determination on the issue of bail in all cases except murder, which must be dealt with by the Crown Court. It follows that in the vast majority of cases, by the time a bail application is made in the Crown Court, the magistrates will have already decided not to grant the defendant bail. Their reasons for refusing bail are typically set out in the sending sheet uploaded on the digital system. Before the bail hearing, an application for bail will need to be made in writing and served at least two days in advance of the hearing (CPR 2015, r 14.7). This is usually drafted by the instructing solicitors and also uploaded onto the digital system. When preparing for a bail application, your starting point, whether you are defending or prosecuting, should be these documents.

The other important document in a bail hearing is the defendant's list of previous convictions. This list will not only set out their previous offences, but will also highlight which ones were committed whilst on bail and the occasions on which the defendant failed to surrender to custody.

In addition to receiving a copy of the bail application, the prosecution should be provided with a police memo which sets out their views on the application. This will outline the reasons why they object to bail and may also contain some useful information about the views of the complainants and any specific fears they might have.

The police are also responsible for making enquiries at any proposed bail address to check whether it is suitable. The location of the proposed bail address and its proximity to the home of the complainant should always be checked. It is also not unknown for defendants to put forward bail addresses without checking with the home owner if they are truly welcome. The police can also assess issues such as whether an electronic monitoring box could be installed at the address and whether there are any other reasons the address is not suitable: is it regularly used by drug addicts, or overcrowded, or the home of an erstwhile criminal associate, or is the occupant vulnerable? In some cases, the age of the occupant's children may be a significant factor, depending on the offence.

If you are prosecuting a bail application and have not been sent a police memo, one should be requested urgently from the CPS. If you are defending and you see that the application does not contain a full address including a postcode and a telephone number for the occupant, check with your solicitors whether that information is available. If the police say they cannot check the address, you will have to decide whether to ask for an adjounrment until it has been checked; the application is unlikely to succeed without this information.

A note on those cases where the police can't check the address: some judges will invite you to continue with your application 'in principle' on the basis that if they were minded to grant bail, an address could later be found: whether this is a sensible invitation to accept will depend on the case. Bear in mind that unless there is a change of circumstances, you will only be allowed to make one application to the Crown Court for bail: a new address may provide such a change, but if a Circuit Judge has said, 'Even if there was a new address, I do not see how bail could be granted' you will have an uphill struggle. If there is a suggestion that your client has in some way been less than wholly truthful about an address, you may want to consider withdrawing the application to work out what has gone on and generate a new, clearly suitable address, rather than letting the judge you are in front of consider bail with the general impression your client is a liar as well as anything else he is charged with.

The final important set of documents, which you will need to consider for every hearing, are the case papers. As bail hearings often come at an early stage, the full papers may not yet have been served. However, the case summary and the important witness statements should be available. Read these carefully in advance of the hearing and note down the strengths and weaknesses of the competing cases.

BAIL CONDITIONS

Where bail has been refused by the magistrates' court, the Crown Court is highly unlikely to grant a defendant unconditional bail. It will therefore be necessary for the advocate making the application to advance conditions which will reassure the court that the risks regarding bail can be overcome.

Typical bail conditions include:

- Prevention of contact with prosecution witnesses and/or co-defendants.

- Residential requirement (to live and sleep at a specified address).

- Curfew (if this curfew is for a minimum of nine hours per day and is electronically monitored it becomes a qualifying curfew. This means that, for each day of qualifying curfew whilst on bail, half a day will be deducted from the eventual prison sentence if the defendant is convicted).

- Regular reporting to a local police station.

- Being excluded from a particular geographical location or specific premises.

- Surrender of passport.

- Standing a surety.

A surety is an individual who is prepared to guarantee a sum of money that becomes payable if the defendant does not surrender to bail (see the Bail Act 1976, s 8 and of *Archbold* 3-51 and 3-52). It can therefore be effective in reassuring the judge that the defendant is not a flight risk. The court is entitled to consider the suitability of the proposed surety by having regard to his financial resources, his character and any previous convictions, and his proximity (in terms of relationship and geographical location) to the defendant. Details regarding the proposed surety are to be set out in the bail application and served on the court two days before the hearing (CPR 2015). The surety should also ideally be present at the bail hearing so that he can be questioned (CPR 2015, r 14.2 requires the surety to be present or to have had the opportunity to make representations).

Sureties should be reliable, in a reasonably strong financial position, and have no criminal convictions (or at least no recent convictions). They will need to prove that they have the means to pay a significant amount of money, (typically by producing relevant bank statements) which will be stated in the application and then confirmed by the court, should the defendant abscond. Once the amount of financial security is set the judge is entitled to refuse an application for the amount to be reduced and to insist on a replacement being found who can stand as surety for the same amount, see *Kent Crown Court, ex parte Jodka* [1997] EWHC Admin 346 (*Archbold* 3-15). Standing a surety is not to be taken lightly (see Criminal Practice Direction III 14F.1). There are many examples, including amongst the rich and famous (such as those who provided sureties for Julian Assange), of people losing substantial sums of money when they have offered to be a surety for a friend or relative who has subsequently breached their bail.

If defending, be aware that the offer of a surety will likely prompt the police to examine the source of that money, particularly if the offer comes in a case relating to drug trafficking, money laundering or other organised crime: if a financial investigator concludes that there is a link between the money offered as surety and the crime, further bank accounts may be restrained.

Whether or not it is part of the package you put forward, a judge may ask about the possibility of the defendant reporting to a local police station, so make sure you know the nearest station to the proposed bail address and its opening hours. If part of the reason for applying for bail is so the defendant can take up a job offer or return to employment, or to provide support to a member of their family, consider how curfew hours and reporting times will work alongside the avowed reason they want bail in the first place.

THE BAIL HEARING

The rules for the conduct of bail hearings are outlined in the CPR 2015, Part 14. There is a discretion for the judge to hear bail applications in chambers, in which case the court will be closed to the public, but the presumption is in favour of them being heard in open court (see *R (Malik) v Central Criminal Court* (*Archbold* 3-24)). There are no clear rules as to the order in which advocates are heard in a bail hearing. In some cases, it might be more logical for the defence to start as they are making the application. However, the judge will often want to hear a brief summary of the facts first, in which case he will ask the prosecution to open.

When prosecuting a bail application it is important to have a thorough grasp of the facts of the alleged offence and to be in a position to open with them succintly. The judge will probably ask for them at some point during the hearing or will, at the very least, ask some questions about particular facts. If asked to give a summary, it should be brief and draw the judge's attention to the most salient points. The judge will not be impressed if you give a full opening speech. An effective way to end the summary is to outline to the judge, almost like bullet points, the strongest pieces of prosecution evidence and then conclude by stating the reasons why the prosecution object to bail being granted, or you may wish to start with a short statement of those objections. However you structure it, make sure you clearly state the nature of the objections and link them to your summary of the facts: is this about the strength of the evidence, or do the facts suggest he is likely to interfere with a particular witness?

In many cases, further prosecution evidence will be in the pipeline at the point the bail application is being made. If you are aware of the nature of this evidence and how it will strengthen the prosecution case you can mention it to the judge when resisting the application.

The prosecuting advocate should also bring the defendant's previous convictions to the judge's attention. It is important to identify any previous offences which are of a similar nature to the present allegation and to highlight any offending on bail and previous failures to surrender. However, it carries greater weight if you summarise these, rather than laboriously taking the judge through the defendant's list line by line. Telling a judge, for example, that 'the defendant has committed ten previous offences whilst on bail, and has failed to surrender to custody on eight previous occasions, most recently in May of last year' has all the impact which you need.

For the defence advocate making the bail application, your submissions need to be persuasive. You start the hearing on the back foot. The magistrates' court refused bail in the first instance. The judge will have read the case papers before the hearing. If the prosecution have opened, the judge will have heard how they put their case and the details of your client's criminal history. He will therefore be understandably concerned about the consequences of releasing the defendant. Although you will want to keep your submissions brief, it is important that they are well structured and it can be helpful to look at the application in four parts:

• The objections to bail and the conditions to offset this.

• Your client's circumstances (including any family ties that mean they are unlikely to abscond or misbehave).

• Your client's antecedents (noting any gaps in offending, but being careful they weren't in custody during those gaps!).

• The prosecution evidence (but see the need for realism below).

A good way to start an application is by dealing with the prosecution's objections to bail. If there is more than one objection, address them in turn and highlight how the proposed bail conditions will assuage the judge's concerns. Keep submissions focused and on point. If the prosecution's concern is the risk of the defendant committing further offences, talking at length about how your client is willing to surrender his passport is unlikely to impress the judge.

Remember that the test for refusing bail is one of 'substantial risk' and that only if the proposed conditions are incapable of minimising this risk to an acceptable level should the application be refused. Although you start on the back foot when defending, the presumption is in your favour: weave these concepts about risk and the general right to bail into your submissions; don't give the judge a lecture on the Bail Act which will be all too familiar! You need to make what you are saying sound fresh and focused.

Make sure that the proposed bail conditions are realistic and that your client is willing to abide by them. If any of the conditions set out in the application are ambiguous, unrealistic or seem to be inappropriate, discuss them with your instructing solicitor before the hearing.

Try to provide the judge with a positive impression of your client and highlight the stabilising factors which might persuade the judge to grant bail. The most important of these factors are stable accommodation, employment, dependents (especially young children), and positive familial and social influences, especially if they live locally and are therefore likely to reduce the risk of the defendant absconding.

Judges are often told that 'prison has been a salutary experience for the defendant'. Although there is often the germ of a good submission here, you need to expand on it, or else the judge may say 'great, he can have some more'. If you want to talk about how the client's circumstances are different from when they was originally remanded into custody, keep it focused. If they are now clean, how will they stay clean? Do they have help from a group or drugs support worker lined up? If custody is damaging their mental health, is there a package of support for them in the community that will mean they won't just feel better but will also be supervised to some extent? If it is their first time in custody, perhaps after a breach of bail, and you are really saying they have learned their lesson about compliance, be direct about this and consider if you can suggest further requirements that may bring home to the client the fact that complying with bail conditions is not optional.

You will also need to deal with your client's antecedents. If they have a bad record, the judge will be all the more concerned about releasing them on bail. Look at the dates of the previous offences and, if you can, try to obtain some information about them. They may have been committed some time ago, your client may have been very young at the time and has since matured, and there may have been particular mitigating circumstances. There might also be gaps in their offending during the times when they have stable accommodation or are in work. Perhaps your client has a poor record of offending whilst in the throes of a drug addiction, but at the time of the application has been clean for several months. If this is the case, be sure to highlight these features.

Although the strength of the prosecution case is not determinative, the judge will be more inclined to grant bail where there are inherent weaknesses in the case. These weaknesses should be outlined to the judge in your oral submissions when making the bail application. Again, keep the submissions succinct, but if the identification evidence is weak and unreliable, or the complainant has since retracted the allegations, it is important that these factors are drawn to the judge's attention. Make it clear that you are not saying 'he isn't taking this seriously' but that you are saying the current evidential position is not such that he is likely to abscond. Expressing this needs careful thought, particularly if the judge is suspicious that releasing your client on bail will turn a wobbly witness into an absent one.

Do not give the judge your closing speech to the jury at this stage: unless there is a genuine weakness in the case, trawling through the evidence at length may be counter-productive. This part of your submission may be very short or indeed non-existent in an obviously strong case. Remember, the fact the evidence is strong doesn't mean by itself your client should not get bail. If your point is that their ties to their family are more important to them than the idea they could abscond, acknowledge the strength of the evidence, but make your submission on the basis that this is not the only factor affecting your client's behaviour.

Frankly, some defendants do not have the resources to abscond and are so well known to the police, they know there is no point. If your client falls into this category, a very minor addict/dealer perhaps, a submission that has at its heart 'where are they going to go?' can sometimes be persuasively if correctly pitched.

If the case has changed such that it looks like, for example, the section 20 offence is now an ABH, submissions on the basis that, in reality, they have already served a significant proportion of any likely sentence can be effective in the right case.

Once the judge has heard arguments from both sides, she will announce whether bail has been granted and, if so, which conditions are to be attached. If the judge decides against granting bail she has to give reasons for this decision and announce which of the statutory exceptions to bail apply.

APPEALS IN RELATION TO BAIL

A defendant who has been refused bail may make a renewed application at the next hearing, regardless of whether this repeats the arguments which were previously heard. Therefore, if the magistrates refused bail at the first hearing, the bail application can be renewed in the first hearing in the Crown Court, provided that the required notice has been given. However, should the second application fail, the court may not hear a subsequent bail application in the same case unless there has been a change in circumstances that might have affected the earlier decision (*Archbold* 3-25 and *Blackstone's* D7.70).

Under the Senior Courts Act 1981, s 81 a defendant may appeal the decision of the magistrates' court to withhold bail or refuse to vary a bail condition. As a bail application can be renewed in the Crown Court, having been refused at first instance by the magistrates' court, this provision also applies to cases which will remain in the magistrates' court but which have been adjourned for specified reasons (*Archbold* 3-208 (SCA 1981, s 81(g))).

Where the prosecution has applied for a defendant to be remanded in custody at the magistrates' court, but bail has been granted, there is a right of appeal to the Crown Court under the Bail Amendment Act 1993, s 1. The timetable set is extremely tight. These cases are always a priority for the CPS so be aware!

- Notice must be given to the court at the conclusion of the bail hearing and before the defendant is released, at which point the defendant will be remanded in custody pending the hearing before the Crown Court.

- The defendant will also be served with a written notice of appeal within two hours of the conclusion of the bail hearing before the magistrates (see CPR 2015, r 14.9).

- The appeal hearing in the Crown Court must then take place within 48 hours of the end of the day on which the bail application was heard (excluding weekends and bank holidays).

- A bail appeal hearing is a complete re-hearing of the application but before a Crown Court judge.

There is also provision, under the Bail Amendment Act 1993, s 1(1B) for the prosecution to appeal the decision of a Crown Court judge to grant bail. This would only arise in situations where the Crown Court had granted bail after it had initially been refused by the magistrates' court. Such appeals are heard by the High Court and the procedure for serving notice on the defence and court is the same as that for appeals to the Crown Court. There is no equivalent provision for defendants, but there is the possibility of seeking judicial review by the High Court.

Chapter 4

Bench warrants and custody time limit applications

Alistair Haggerty and Grace Flynn

Key references

- *Archbold: Criminal Pleading, Evidence and Practice 2020*

- Bail Act 1976

- Senior Courts Act 1981

- Prosecution of Offences Act 1985

- Prosecution of Offences (Custody Time Limits) Regulations 1987, SI 1987/299

Case law

- *R (Gibson) v Winchester Crown Court* [2004] EWHC 361 (Admin)

- *R v Ipswich Crown Court ex p CPS* [2010] EWHC 1515 (Admin)

- *R v Manchester Crown Court, Ex p McDonald* [1999] 1 WLR 841

- *R v Scott* [2007] EWCA Crim 2757

BENCH WARRANTS

Having been granted bail, defendants must in due course 'surrender to the custody of the court' and attend all future hearings. Failure to do so is an offence under the Bail Act 1976, s 6, unless the defendant can establish that they had a 'reasonable cause' not to attend. The burden of establishing this is on the defendant (Bail Act 1976, s 6(3)).

Should a defendant not attend a hearing, if prosecuting, you will need to allow defence counsel some time to make enquiries. It may be that a defendant has missed their bus, telephoned to apologise and will be at court soon, in which case it would be sensible to wait for their arrival. Alternatively, there could be some medical reason for non-attendance. If defending, try to contact your client or instructing solicitor to confirm the position. Should these efforts prove fruitless, the prosecution will make an oral application to the judge for a warrant to be issued.

It should be remembered that the court is not expected to wait indefinitely for a defendant to arrive. In *Scott* Toulson LJ expressed his view that arriving at court even half an hour late could justify a bail act charge. A culture of tardiness will not be tolerated.

In these circumstances, the court will use its power to issue a warrant for the defendant's arrest under the Bail Act 1976, s 7(1). This is commonly referred to as a 'bench warrant' in practice. The 'bench' refers to the judge's position in court. There are two types of warrant between which the court has the discretion to choose – either 'backed for bail' or 'not backed for bail'.

A warrant 'backed for bail' orders that the defendant, once arrested, will be released on bail with the requirement to attend their next court hearing (Senior Courts Act 1981, s 81(4)). The vast majority of warrants are, however, 'not backed for bail'. As the name suggests, there is no automatic re-admission to bail.

Once arrested, a defendant is taken into custody and brought before the court as soon as possible. The warrant is executed and the hearing that they missed will take place. It should be noted that these hearings take place at short notice and require swift action by all parties. It may be that it has been many weeks, months, or even years since the warrant was issued.

Given this sudden loss of liberty, the question of bail needs revisiting. It is likely that you will have only a short amount of notice before this hearing, whether prosecuting or defending. It is highly unlikely that the same counsel who dealt with the original hearing will be available.

If prosecuting, you will need to familiarise yourself with the papers quickly. Firstly, identify the hearing that led to the issuing of the warrant. You need to be prepared for an effective hearing to happen now. If it was a sentencing hearing, be ready to open the facts to the judge and have the sentencing guidelines at your fingertips. If it was a PTPH, be ready to confirm next steps for trial and be aware that if the defendant pleads guilty, the court may wish to move to sentence. There is also the matter of whether a Bail Act offence will be put to the defendant as a new charge.

When defending, it is highly likely that this will be a defendant whom you have never met before. That is immaterial: they are your client now. You need to head over to court to take their instructions in the cells. Topics you will want to cover include:

• Why did they not attend court last time? Is there a valid reason? Should they admit a bail act charge?

31

- In what circumstances were they arrested? Did they voluntarily attend a police station? Have they been arrested for new offences which you need to be aware of?

- If they are likely to be arraigned on the indictment today, what is their plea?

- If they are likely to be sentenced today, what mitigation is there? Do you need a pre-sentence report?

- If relevant, what additional conditions would they agree to comply with if they were granted bail again?

Having suddenly lost their freedom, a defendant will understandably be anxious to know whether they will be released on bail again. You may well need to re-apply for bail in the hearing, somewhat hampered by the fact that your client has already once failed to surrender; an uphill task but not an impossible one.

Consider what additional conditions you can propose to reassure the judge that the defendant merits being re-admitted to bail. This could include a signing-on requirement at a police station or an electronically monitored curfew.

The execution of a bench warrant, whether prosecuting or defending, is an exercise in both quick thinking and thoroughness. As a prosecutor, it may feel as if you are preparing the case in examination conditions – experience and practice will make this easier. For defence counsel, these hearings by their very nature involve picking up a new case at short notice, without the luxury of a lengthy conference and a solicitor in attendance. Do not be afraid to let the court know if you need a little more time to cover all topics; they will be grateful if you can make real progress in the case. If in any doubt, obtain a signed endorsement to confirm that your client has understood your advice and appreciates the consequences. Time may be of the essence, but everyone wants both progress to be made and the next steps to run smoothly.

CUSTODY TIME LIMIT APPLICATIONS

The Custody Time Limit (CTL) is a safeguard which sets out the amount of time that a defendant can be kept in custody awaiting the start of their trial. It is an important protection for those who have their liberty removed whilst awaiting trial. The CTL expiration date must be born in mind at every stage of the proceedings, particularly if you are prosecuting the case.

The key rules governing CTLs are:

- the Prosecution of Offences (Custody Time Limits) Regulations 1987, SI 1987/299; and

- the Prosecution of Offences Act 1985, s 22.

Vigilance is needed to ensure that this deadline is not breached. The CPS see a CTL breach as a major corporate risk; if they conclude that the instructed advocate has not been on the ball this can have serious professional consequences. You must ensure that you know the CTL for each count in each case you are prosecuting (they may be different depending on issues such as joinder). In the Crown Court, the maximum amount of time that a defendant can spend on remand before the first day of their trial is 182 days (SI 1987/299, reg 5(6B)). CTLs cease to apply to a count when a jury is sworn or a guilty plea is entered to the count (even if that plea is later vacated).

Whilst a trial within six months is of course the ideal scenario, circumstances can arise which are out of anyone's control and delay becomes inevitable. For example, what if a defendant falls ill the week before their trial, or if a defendant decides to dispense with their legal representatives on the morning of their trial, or if the judge decides that a mental health assessment is required, and the CTL expires the following week before it can be completed?

Whatever the situation, if there is a risk that the CTL will be breached, the prosecution must make a written and oral application to the court to formally request an extension under the Prosecution of Offences Act 1985, s 22(3) and SI 1987/299, reg 7(2) (*Archbold* 3-85).

Under s 22(3), to grant an extension, the court must be satisfied:

(a)   that the need for the extension is due to—

      (i)   the illness or absence of the accused, a necessary witness, a judge or a magistrate;

      (ii)   a postponement which is occasioned by the ordering by the court of separate trials in the case of two or more accused or two or more offences; or

      (iii)   some other good and sufficient cause; and

(b)   that the prosecution has acted with all due diligence and expedition.

There are therefore two elements that need to be satisfied. Namely, a good and sufficient reason for the extension and, crucially, evidence that the prosecution has been suitably diligent in its preparation. Note that if, for example, the particular Crown Court to which the case has been sent is unable to try the case within the CTLs, it is incumbent upon the prosecution to ask the listing office of that Crown Court to contact other local Crown Courts to see if the trial can be accommodated elsewhere.

The prosecution submits a written application, identifying the steps that they have taken to be ready for trial within the CTL. A chronology is also often submitted to supplement this. This is followed by a hearing at which you will need to explain the position to the judge, effectively taking them through the application and expanding with extra details if appropriate. You also have to identify a specific date you want the CTL to expire: as CTLs expire at midnight on the expiry day, it is usual to ask for a new CTL to expire on the second day of trial to cater for a delay in the jury being sworn.

You will need to establish, on the balance of probabilities, that the grounds for the court to grant the application are met. You are effectively demonstrating due diligence. Prior to the hearing, should you require additional information, contact the CPS and/or the officer in the case to ask for further details. Bear in mind the elements of the statutory test of which the judge will need to be satisfied. You will need to be able to answer questions about the efficiency of the police, the CPS and counsel. Each case is unique and what amounts to a satisfactory reason to extend the CTL is a case by case decision.

Factors for the court to consider when assessing whether the standard has been met may include:

• the nature and complexity of the case;

• what efforts have been made to avoid the delay;

• whether there has been any delay due to the conduct of the defence; or

• whether the prosecution is reliant on other agencies or parties beyond their control.

Some practical commentary, eminently quotable, is provided by Bingham CJ in *R v Manchester Crown Court, Ex p McDonald* at:

> 'To satisfy the court that this condition is met the prosecution need not show that every stage of preparation of the case has been accomplished as quickly and efficiently as humanly possible. That would be an impossible standard to meet, particularly when the court which reviews the history of the case enjoys the immeasurable benefit of hindsight. Nor should the history be approached on the unreal assumption that all involved on the prosecution side have been able to give the case in question their undivided attention. *What the court must require is such diligence and expedition as would be shown by a competent prosecutor conscious of his duty to bring the case to trial as quickly as reasonably and fairly possible.*' [Emphasis added]

A couple of other wrinkles to bear in mind: *R (Gibson) v Winchester Crown Court* suggests that even in cases where the Crown have not acted with due diligence, the CTL may be extended if there is a good and sufficient reason so to do, and the real reason the trial cannot happen is unrelated to prosecutorial delay, eg the trial could not have happened anyway because of a pending defence psychiatric report. Lack of due diligence is not therefore immediately fatal to an application to extend the CTL. It was accepted in this case that lack of judicial resources, such as the unavailability of a High Court judge and a courtroom until a date after the CTL, were appropriate considerations.

R v Ipswich Crown Court ex p CPS is a useful authority to have in mind in those cases where a defendant had been released under investigation or on bail for a significant period pre-charge: although the court may look at the case holistically, the question of due diligence relates to the CTL period itself. Whether, for example, a defendant could have been tried alongside co-conspirators in an earlier trial had they been charged sooner is irrelevant. Delays in arrest and charge are immaterial and pose no bar to the extension of the CTL.

DO

- think about realistic conditions to offer

- read the PNC printout of previous convictions carefully

- be prepared for a bench warrant to turn into plea and sentence

- think about custody time limits

DON'T

- gloss over the problems or risks that are present, instead deal with them head on

- get drawn into an argument about the strength of the evidence

- give the judge a law lecture

- forget to keep an eye on CTLs!

Part III

Clients

Chapter 5

Talking to clients

Susan Cavender

Key references

- *Archbold: Criminal Pleading, Evidence and Practice 2020*, 4-175, 5A-111, 5A-290, 12-64

- Bar Standards Board Code of Conduct, Part 2B Bar Standards Board Code of Conduct; Core Duties & Guidance

- Advocates Gateway 'Toolkits' 18 invaluable 'toolkits' provide guidance for cases involving a witness or defendant with communication needs. https://www.theadvocatesgateway.org/toolkits

- Criminal Procedure Rules 2015, SI 2015/1490

- Criminal Procedure and Investigations Act 1996, ss 6A-6E

- http://prisonuk.blogspot.com/2014/10/off-to-prison-my-packing-list.html

- https://www.doingtime.co.uk/first-things-first/before-sentencing/

Case law

- *R v Goodyear* [2005] 2 Cr App R 20, CA

- *R v Newton* 77 Cr App R 13

- *R v Smith and Others* [2011] EWCA Crim 1772

First meetings with clients differ. In more complicated cases it will often be in a calm pre-arranged conference in chambers a day or two before the Plea and Trial Preparation Hearing (PTPH). The solicitor will be with you to take notes and assist, if need be, in explaining things to the client. But that scenario is often not practical, and usually reserved for trickier clients, or complicated and serious cases.

In practice that first meeting is often right outside the court door (or in the cells if they are on remand) on the day of the PTPH.

It can be stressful; you are waiting to be called on, often without a solicitor as back-up and perhaps with other cases to be heard that morning. You need to juggle various competing demands; to make sure that the court usher knows that your client has arrived, and (presuming that you can find an interview room) where you can both be found. Trying to find a vacant room can be tricky; you may have to make do with a quiet corner of the building. Be very aware of anyone (a co-defendant? prosecutor?) who might be in ear-shot.

Some clients are old hands at the criminal justice system and will know exactly what to expect, for others this may be their first time in court which is extremely daunting; you need to make a series of quick and detailed assessments as well as ensure you communicate key information:

• Does the client understand exactly what they face? You may need to explain the charges, which can even in low level cases seem complicated to a non-lawyer. That an 'assault' can be the mere threat of violence makes no sense to most people; be prepared to explain in simple terms that what the client thought was only a gentle shove would amount, in law, to an assault.

• If it seems that they do not understand, ask yourself whether they need specialist assessment? Very often Crown Courts have mental health practitioners on site who can sometimes see a client that day (see below).

• Explain credit for plea in every case ('I know that you are going to plead Not Guilty, but I must explain ...')

• Set out, in simple language, what will happen in court; for example see below the example about what happens at PTPH

• Make absolutely sure that the importance of staying in touch with the solicitors is understood – a full defence statement will be required and only the defendant can give the detailed instructions needed. Do your solicitors have the defendant's mobile number? If not, take it and pass it on.

Whether in chambers or outside the door of the court you will, of course, have read the papers carefully, noted the evidence against your client (which, for example in a multi-handed pub brawl might involve making a table of who said what and against whom so that you can see at a glance what each witness says about them), gleaned what their case seems to be in answer to the allegations, and made a list of the things that you need to discuss.

This will include:

• How does she answer the allegations made by the various witnesses?

• Does she agree any of the allegations?

- Did she really say what the police quote her as saying upon arrest?

- What'is her reaction to the CCTV footage (watch the important bits frame by frame, together)?

- If she made admissions in interview, was she sure that she understood the questions? Did she mean the answers to come out as they did?

- Do her previous convictions reveal any problems – eg, a suspended order which has now been breached (had she been complying with the order?) or perhaps this case would make her a 3rd strike burglar?

- She will need to understand what is at stake, so explain the potential sentence she may get after any trial as well as credit. Cover ancillary matters – likely restraining orders even on acquittal – so the client is forewarned.

Wherever you are, and however tricky the circumstances, your first job is to build trust between yourself and the client as quickly as possible. If your instructing solicitor is with you they can be a vital bridge with the client. They may know the client of old, will almost certainly have met them when making an application for Legal Aid, or (if you are lucky enough to be privately paid) arranged payment.

That trust should enable your client to explain to you what he says actually happened, quite how complicated the background relationships are, just what he does admit to having said or done, and how much he wants to admit at this stage.

Your assessment of the client at this first meeting is crucial. Does he really understand the complexities of the court system, or perhaps need additional support? Quite often clients will turn up at court with a support or key worker who can be invaluable in helping with communicating those things which are rather embarrassing to explain – no money, supported housing, drug withdrawal etc.

Do you need an expert psychiatric report, either now or at a later stage? Some clients are perfectly capable of taking full part in the court process, but may be greatly assisted by a specialist report when it comes to sentencing. Identifying these matters early is important.

Beware the overly helpful friend or family member who can inhibit proper instructions being taken. No-one will have a frank conversation with you about what the police found on their computer with their mum in the room. Gently explain that is the client's conference, so they need to be comfortable. They also need to do the talking: they won't have their mum with them in the witness box, so they need to explain it themselves.

As an advocate you exist to give a voice to your client's instructions, and in order to obtain those instructions the rapport that you build with the client at this early stage is crucial. They do not need to like you, but they do need to believe that you are really listening, and that you understand what they are trying to say. You want the client to have confidence in the advice which you give.

The advocate advises the client, but it is the client who instructs the advocate.

You will be the person standing up in court and acting upon those instructions – which is much easier to do if they are realistic and make sense!

You must point out where instructions are at odds with the evidence, and where they are totally unrealistic.

Sometimes it is necessary to remind the client that you cannot – under any circumstances – mislead either the court or your opponent.

Act as devil's advocate by testing the defence which they want to run, point out the holes in it and encourage them to think carefully about how to plead.

In other words, as long as you have built sufficient rapport pretty quickly, you are then in a position to give robust advice which – with any luck – the client will follow. But, having given that advice, you then take instructions and act accordingly – however peculiar those instructions may seem!

THE PTPH

The Plea and Trial Preparation Hearing is necessary for the court and the Crown to find out whether the defendant wants a trial, and if so to set a timetable and ensure that any other matters that need to be in place before trial are flagged up and suitable orders made.

Explain to the client that they will be standing in the dock, they will be asked their name and nationality but that you will speak for them after that.

If they really need to get your attention during the hearing then they can raise a hand – although you will have your back to them, the judge will see them.

The defendant should refer to the judge as 'Your Honour' unless you are before a 'red judge' when it's 'Your Lordship or Ladyship'. Write 'Your Lordship' at the top of your page in big letters as an aid.

The court then needs to set the Stage dates for progress of the trial.

The usual Stage Dates are as follows:

- Stage 1 – Service of the Prosecution case – either 50 or 70 days after the sending of the case from the magistrates' court, depending on whether the defendant is in custody.

- Stage 2 – Defence response (Defence Statement including requests for further disclosure plus list of witnesses required to attend) 28 days after Stage 1.

- Stage 3 – Prosecution response to the Defence Statement with disclosure: 14–28 days after Stage 2.

- Stage 4 – for defence to provide further requests/applications – 14–28 days after Stage 3. Often not a set date.

This is your chance to let the court know if there is anything at all which may need to be considered in order to make the trial run more smoothly. So just think about all the practical things needed, for example (and in no particular order):

- An interpreter. For multi-handed cases the court will need enough interpreters to go around. Often you will need the court to supply an interpreter even if you have your own defence interpreter for conferences, to avoid the court interpreter becoming a witness.

- An intermediary if a witness, or the defendant, is going to struggle without. If no report has been done yet, just tell the court that you think it may be necessary and will keep everyone informed if an intermediary is needed.

- Special Measures and similar – a witness who wants screens/live link/lots of breaks because of physical or mental health issues.

- An order for disclosure of social services' records, where a complainant has known history with social services and there is a possibility that a different account may have been given or different facts emerged.

- If there is very bad feeling between parties or high emotions in the case (for example in a case of death by careless or dangerous driving the family of the defendant needs to be kept apart from the witnesses) a bit of warning can help the court to make arrangements to keep the factions separate.

If you are without a solicitor and your client gives specific instructions about taking a particular course of action, then write out what they want you to do and get them to sign it. This is crucial, especially when the instructions are contrary to your best advice.

The most obvious example is when someone says, 'I didn't do it but I want to plead guilty anyway'.

Perhaps the client has been charged with fraud. They tell you that the transfer of money repeatedly moved from their employer's account to their personal bank account was an error and therefore not dishonest. But they may also recognise that a jury are unlikely to believe them, and want to avail themselves of maximum credit. This is especially the case where that crucial credit (33% in the magistrates' court, diminishing from then until 10% on the day of trial) can bring a sentence down into the range that can be suspended.

In such a case you must get signed instructions which should include the following points:

1   The client understands that it is their choice whether to have a trial or plead guilty. They have been told that they should not plead guilty to something they have not done. It is a choice they must make freely.

2   If what the client says amounts to a defence, this fact should be recorded, along with any specific advice about that defence, eg 'I understand that if I was not dishonest this is a defence. However, I accept a jury are very unlikely to believe that all 72 transfers happened because of my poor IT skills'.

3   A record of the client's decision, a reason for the decision, and their understanding of the consequences of their decision, eg 'I want to plead guilty to this charge because I accept I am likely to be convicted and I want to obtain maximum credit. I understand that this means I cannot tell the judge at sentence that I am not guilty.'

That written endorsement will serve to ensure that the client really does understand the decision that they have taken, and give you security when – at sentence with an unhelpful Pre- Sentence Report (PSR) – the client suddenly says that they want a trial and that they only pleaded guilty because you made them.

Ensuring effective participation

One of the things to be aware of when first meeting the client is being prepared to make an off-the-cuff assessment about whether the client has mental health needs.

This can cover a wide variety of issues and personalities. If the client (or a witness) is vulnerable the Toolkits found on the Advocate's Gateway are invaluable.

You need to be highly attuned to your client's presentation and be prepared to take control if they dominate the conference too much.

Some clients are nervous and can't stop talking; some are nervous and don't know where to start. Some are bullies, but the vast majority are grateful for your desire to help them and will be keen to help you in return.

Don't be afraid of politely but firmly saying 'Stop! I know that you are keen to tell me everything, but I assure you I have read the papers and I need to ask you some specific things. We don't have much time', or 'I have read everything, but it would really help me to hear you describe what actually happened to bring it to life, I'll ask you questions and take notes as we go along'.

If you are concerned about a client's understanding, asking them to explain things back to you rather than asking 'Do you understand that?' will give you more insight. Try instead: 'Can I just check I explained that properly? If you pushed me and I put you on the floor and kicked you, do you think that would be self -defence?'

Some clients will clearly need more help; you will come across a vast range of different personality types and will learn to spot signs as you read the papers for the first time.

Arson, for example, is a red-flag offence. It used to be said that it was unwise to sentence a case of arson without a psychiatric report. Take advice from the mental health screening service at court, or ask for a GP's report.

A charge of harassment can be another warning sign – this person may be obsessive or controlling (not something that a report can often help with).

You will become adept at reading between the lines when looking at a list of previous convictions; a long history of shop-lifting and convictions for possession of drugs often indicates Class A addiction.

Quite a surprising number of clients can't read or write; if they seem to be reluctant just ask them if they'd rather you read out important parts of the statements.

Although all these signs can help you work out if there is a participation issue, keep an open mind and remember that everyone is an individual. If you are worried about someone's understanding, mood, or ability to communicate, don't let the absence of a clear indicator like a previous hospital order/support worker put you off from pursuing your instinct. Some people fall through the net many, many times before anyone identifies that their anger or unresponsiveness is a coping mechanism for a psychological or psychiatric condition.

In order to ensure they can participate effectively you may need to consider:

–   Adapting your own language: sentence structure, pace.

–   Getting sufficient evidence together to convince the court that adaptations are needed: getting permission to contact the client's GP is a useful starting point.

–   Getting a screening report (which the court pays for and will see) to give you a steer.

–   Getting a psychological or psychiatric report (or both – which normally the Legal Aid Agency will pay for, and you decide whether to serve it). Psychological reports can not only be used as part of a package of reports in relation to fitness/specific intent/disposal but can be a helpful preliminary to getting an intermediary report, or a stand-alone report to encourage the court to look at the issue of participation more broadly.

If you do need a report, sensitively explain to the client why you are asking them to speak with an expert. Describe how this will improve their experience of court and possibly help their case more generally.

Clients will show up for court in all sorts of conditions and sometimes the worse for wear; the court will often be accommodating if told that someone has arrived early and waited all morning but really must be heard soon in order to keep a doctor's appointment or to collect a methadone 'script'.

All prisoners are screened when first remanded to see if they need to be assessed by a Health Care Practitioner. If your client agrees, hand over all the medical reports you obtained that flag up any issues.

Alcoholics are the most concerning. Whilst a heroin addict unmedicated in custody will have an unpleasant time of it, a chronic alcoholic can die without medical attention. It is important to act as your client's 'voice' with the custody staff and prison officers just as much as with a judge. Make sure that a message goes with the client into custody that this person will need immediate medical attention for alcohol withdrawal – the prison service know to take such people very seriously.

CODE OF CONDUCT

You must know and understand the Code of Conduct Rules and how they relate to your practice; to understand what amounts to a conflict of interest, and what is coyly known as 'Professional Embarrassment'.

Put in basic terms the Code of Conduct Rules cover the following:

1   You first duty is to the court and the administration of justice: your duty to your client is subject to this primary responsibility (Rules 1–3).

2   You must fearlessly promote your lay client's interests by all lawful and proper means, including when it is deeply embarrassing for you (Rules 15 and 16). This means not talking in code with the judge about a hopeless looking bail application being made 'on instructions'. It also means that you must tell your client if you discover post-conviction that your solicitor forgot to proof a key defence witness. Talk to others, including clerks, about how to be diplomatic, but you can't duck it.

3   You are personally responsible for your own conduct and work, regardless of the views of others (Rule 20).

4   You cannot act for someone if:

   a   you do not have enough experience for the case; or

   b   you don't have enough time; or

   c   if this case conflicts with that of another client; or

   d   if you have confidential information from another case which prevents you from acting in the best interests of this client; or

   e   if this client's interests conflict with previous work (you can't defend someone if you prosecuted the same person last year): Rule 21 contains 10 such examples.

5   You must cease to act if you discover that Legal Aid has been wrongly obtained and your client refuses to put this right, or if the client refuses to let you disclose to the court a document which your duty to the court requires to be disclosed (Rule 25).

6   You can return instructions if:

    a   Your professional conduct is called into question – ie the client tells you that you are doing a rotten job, he has lost faith in you – you are sacked. This occasionally happens on the day of trial, and quite often because of supposedly 'better' advice than yours which has been given to your client by his mates or other prisoners on remand. Most judges will ask the defendant if they really want to represent themselves; they may decide that you are not so bad after all …

    b   If you are self-employed and there is an un-avoidable work-diary clash.

    c   Illness, injury, pregnancy, bereavement, etc make it impossible for you to act.

    d   You become aware of confidential information which relates to the case. This can often be as simple as 'Well, yes, I did do it, but I won't admit it and want to carry on and have a trial'. That is confidential information which you cannot tell the court, but which – as a result of your over-riding duty to the court – means neither can you continue to represent the defendant as you had been planning to do. You may not put a positive case on the basis he is not guilty, but you are permitted to test the prosecution case; once the client realises how limited a job you can do, they will usually decide it's time for a fresh pair of eyes (Rule 26).

7   If you do withdraw from a case, you must explain why to the client (Rule 27). Don't leave the client alone at court without having told the judge what is going on.

8   Rules 28–30 set out the requirement not to discriminate and the 'cab rank' rule.

Further discussion about why these rules matter and how they should inform your advocacy are in The Good Advocate section.

DRAFTING DEFENCE STATEMENTS

Once the PTPH is over and a timetable has been set the next stage is to wait for the full prosecution papers to arrive, and then arrange a conference for drafting of the defence statement. When you come out of court you make sure that the defendant will stay in close touch with your instructing solicitors, and impress upon him the Stage 2 date – the date by when his defence statement must be served.

Before that date, the solicitors should prepare a full proof of evidence. That will be the basis for the Defence Statement.

The Defence Statement must include the following information:

- The nature of the defence – 'I did hit him that night at the pub, but it was in self-defence'.

- Which matters of fact are disputed with the prosecution 'I did not use a glass, I only used my fist'.

- And why 'The injuries are not consistent with glassing' or, perhaps 'no other witness saw me with a glass in my hand'.

- Any matters of fact upon which he does rely 'the complainant started the fight, I was trying to stop him from hitting my girlfriend'.

- Indicate any matters of law – 'I want to make a non-defendant bad character application because I am of good character but the complainant has previous convictions for violence.'

Bear in mind that an adverse inference can be drawn against your client if the defence statement does not mention something that the rules require it to mention. A sensibly detailed defence statement is more likely to generate disclosure.

The Statement should also include:

- Any requests for further disclosure –

  'There is CCTV covering that part of the pub which needs to be disclosed'.

  'The complainant's medical records are requested'.

  'Have there been house-to-house enquiries? It is believed that several neighbours were watching what happened'.

- If an alibi is put forward ('I was not at the pub that night, I was driving to Swansea with my boss') then as many details as possible must be given about the person who can provide confirmation of the alibi including name, address and date of birth. This will enable the police to speak to that person and ask for a statement.

  NB: 'I was at home with my girlfriend' is not the most convincing of alibis!

THINGS YOUR CLIENT NEEDS TO KNOW

Not every client wants to go to trial. Many are a bit unsure about the pros and cons of pleading guilty.

Plea to a lesser offence

Where the prosecution evidence is not that strong it is always worth asking whether a plea to a lesser offence may suffice. Charges of possession with intent to supply where there is only a relatively small amount of drugs may be reduced to simple possession if the prosecutor can see the sense in resolving the case. Or if the injuries are borderline, a plea to common assault may be acceptable in the place of an ABH. It can't hurt to ask, as long as you can make a sensible suggestion and justify the question by reference to the evidence.

Basis of Plea

A Basis of Plea might appeal if the client says 'Well I did hit him (and I realise that I hit him too hard for it to be justified as self-defence) but I did not use a bottle'. It is a means of accepting guilt but on a limited basis.

The risks in submitting a Basis of Plea are that

(a)   the version of events put forward in the Basis are not accepted by the Crown (or the judge); or

(b)   the difference between your client's version of events and that of the prosecution would make a significant difference to sentence;

in which case the judge is likely to decide that a Newton Hearing will be required.

A Newton Hearing is a short non-jury trial; the client accepts his guilt, but not on the facts set out by the prosecution. The judge must decide what those facts are because they will form the basis for sentence.

If the judge decides, as a finding of fact, that the Crown's case is made out then the client will lose their credit for an early guilty plea.

In other words: this is not to be taken lightly. A Basis should be used when you are pretty confident that the Crown cannot dispute your client's version of events – or your client is determined, and understands that they risk losing their credit.

The Basis must be in writing and must set out as much detail as is prudent to persuade the Crown and the judge that your client's version of events is correct. It is tempting to put in additional things which are really mitigation. Sometimes that can be an effective way of getting the client's story across, but beware that an insubstantial Basis will not assist and may just be dismissed as waffle! You are seeking to establish facts which the prosecution can't really dispute; this is a fine judgement based on the evidence.

Goodyear indication

The other useful tool for a client who is dithering about how to plead is the *Goodyear* indication (*R v Goodyear* [2005] 2 Cr App R 20, CA).

This enables the client to ask the judge – 'if I plead guilty today what is the maximum sentence that I will receive?'

You need your client's signed instructions to ask for such an indication and there are things that you are required to explain to him about the limitations of such an indication which are all set out in *Goodyear* itself.

The request must be made on a basis accepted by the Crown – which usually, if done on the day, means the full facts - and in writing. It should, ideally, be done with a bit of notice.

The facts of the case may have to be opened by the Crown, so you must warn the prosecutor of your intention, and the judge will need a bit of time to consider the question. In other words, this is not something to be sprung on a busy judge in the middle of a long list – you will be told that there is no time and to make the application in writing and on notice.

There is no obligation upon a judge to give a *Goodyear* indication, and there are many circumstances where it may be felt to be inappropriate – for example a multi-handed case where some defendants are going to trial, and the trial judge will be better placed to decide just where your client fits once they have heard all the evidence.

However, for a client who might be struggling against strong evidence but who is frightened about the eventual sentence a *Goodyear* indication can provide much-needed clarity.

If the judge says the magic words 'any sentence could be suspended' it may be just what the client needs to hear. It may enable them to think that they can, after all, face accepting the otherwise unattractive thought that they really did steal from their grandmother which results in their first conviction and loss of good name.

You can still ask for a Pre-Sentence Report (PSR) from Probation before sentence and use that and any other mitigation to try to persuade the judge that the suggested sentence should be reduced below the maximum originally indicated.

Preparation for sentence

Whether your client has pleaded guilty or been convicted after trial you will need to warn them about how to prepare for the sentence. If the subject has not come up before, the time when the jury is in retirement is often the time for this. The routine questions are:

1   Can you persuade the court that a PSR would assist the sentencing judge? The answer is usually 'Yes' if:

a   The client is very young and/or of good character.

b   Even if they do have previous convictions they have been out of trouble for a respectable length of time.

c   There is a psychiatric/mental health aspect to the offence. Often there is some aspect of their background or current circumstances that mean a PSR could throw more light on what the realistic alternatives to custody are open to the judge.

d   You want to persuade the judge to keep your client out of custody (which is a real possibility) and Probation can assist with how they performed on a previous Community Order; what orders would realistically rehabilitate or lessen the chances of further offending.

The answer to 'please can we have a PSR' is likely to be 'No' if it is unlikely that Probation could tell the judge anything more than they have already learned during the trial, and/or custody is absolutely inevitable.

If a PSR is ordered, then you must make sure that the client goes straight to the probation office to make their first appointment. In practice this means that you escort them there, tell probation who they are, which court they were convicted in and let them know the date of sentence. Probation will give the client a piece of paper with the appointment date, and strict instructions to turn up OR ELSE!

Sometimes the interview date is posted out, in which case you must impress upon the client that if they do not receive a letter and interview date in the next week then they MUST get in touch with probation to sort it out.

Clients routinely forget to go to PSR appointments, or turn up late, or miss the bus. It is frustrating to prepare for sentence and then have to ask for it to be adjourned because you have a 'Nil PSR'. Probation officers try to be accommodating; they will re-arrange appointments within reason, but they are offering the client a life-line, a potential Get Out of Jail card, and it is not to be taken lightly!

It is sometimes useful to remind clients that PSRs are professional risk assessments, not cosy chats. It is up the client what they say, but there is no harm in reminding them that the question is 'how can this person best be punished?' and not 'was it really the other guy's fault?' That question will have been resolved. Do also remind them that sentence is ultimately for the judge: if you tell them to pack a bag, they should pack a bag whatever curfew they believe they have been 'promised'.

2.   What is the likely sentence? No doubt you will have already gone through this in your initial conference, but it's always worth looking at the Sentencing Guidelines again

3.   Is a Restraining Order likely? If so, is the proposed wording acceptable? What does the defendant think about it? How will it affect their ability to see their children?

51

4.   For sex offenders: notification requirements need to be explained. It is automatic for most sexual offences and means that the defendant will have to notify the police of their address within a very short period. Look carefully at any Sexual Harm Prevention Order proposed and consider if it is compliant with *R v Smith and Others*

5.   Is a compensation order a possibility? If the conviction is an assault and the client can turn up at sentence having saved up some money it may encourage the court to keep them out of custody in order that the victim receives compensation.

6.   Can the defendant provide references from their boss, their college or even their mum? If you are trying to persuade the judge that this is a nice young person who lost their temper or acted completely out of character, then those sort of references can be very helpful.

If the next hearing is going to be for sentence and custody is a real possibility, then tell the client to bring a bag. They will need to pack clothes, medicine, a list of necessary phone numbers and money.

If they, or you, are interested there are websites with a lot of practical information about what (and what not) to take into prison.

Professional clients and prosecution conferences

Whether you are instructed by defence or prosecution the golden rule is to maintain communication, and (like the crocodile sandwich) to make it snappy. Both independent solicitors and the CPS are very busy; they need good, clear communication from you, and promptly.

When prosecuting, your first contact with the case is from your instructions, reading the Digital Case System, and preparing a Bar Standard form or advice about the case. This is sent by you to the CPS and by them to the OIC, or Officer in the Case. They must then reply to your questions. As we will see below, a good advice can be a useful reference point for a later conference.

It can be helpful to start an advice by listing the material you do and don't have, eg 'Many thanks for the helpful bundle containing an unused schedule. Please can I have access to the material disclosed to the defence. I note reference to CCTV but I do not have that as yet. '

Look at the case from every angle:

•   Is the indictment properly worded or does it need re-drafting? Go back to the statute and check the wording. You will be the person standing up in court and explaining to a grumpy judge just how this charge reflects the facts alleged by the witnesses.

- What additional evidence is needed?

- Identify any holes in the case; set out what is needed to fill them.

- How would you approach the case if defending it? That will give you a good idea of what additional evidence is required.

- Are all the witnesses on board? If not, do you need a witness summons? Do any require special measures?

- If there is a video-interview of the complainant, it will need to be edited. Get in early and do it as soon as you can, take control of how the evidence will be presented. Then ask the CPS to send it to the defence for their approval.

- Are there people mentioned in the papers or the unused material who have not given statements but who may be able to help? Often the answer lies deep in the small print of the Occurrence Log in the Prosecutor's Bundle. You must read the whole thing or risk: (a) annoying your OIC – you don't want to do that because you will be depending on him or her to help you at trial; and (b) looking a fool.

- Which exhibits do you want to show the jury? The OIC will bring into court the drugs, the cash, the weapons which have been exhibited. Often it is both interesting – and very illuminating – for a jury to see the real item, not just a photo. It might demonstrate that the defendant's assertion 'this quantity of cocaine was just what I used on a daily basis' to be nonsense. What's more, to have so much cocaine hidden inside their underpants must have been uncomfortable ....'.

- If the defendant is remanded in custody, then note the Custody Time Limits (CTLs). The expiry of CTLs is a huge bug-bear for the CPS because the consequences of someone being held illegally, or released when they should not be, are so serious.

- What legal issues arise: do you need to consider hearsay or bad character applications? Is there likely to be a contest about the admissibility of evidence?

- Case presentation issues: do you need maps, plans, photos or schedules to explain this case to a jury?

- You should be familiar with the unused material on the case; things that are not currently relevant can become relevant in trial. Have you read the schedule(s) and are happy with the disclosure decisions made? Do further reasonable lines of enquiry need to be pursued?

- Anything relevant to the case needs to be served or scheduled. If material is alluded to but you can't find it, follow this up.

Whether prosecuting or defending, if the case is tricky or complicated do not hesitate to ask for a conference. Prosecuting, you want the OIC (who should be the fount of all knowledge and will be the person to go and find answers to your questions), the CPS lawyer and the CPS Caseworker. The conference will either be in chambers or at the local CPS office.

Make sure that everyone is aware of the purpose of the conference so that it doesn't become a chat. List the questions or concerns you have. It is useful to prepare a brief agenda to circulate ahead of time that others can supplement: then the police know to bring an item or get the telephone analyst to come along, and the CPS lawyer has time to consider a suggested change of tack.

The key with the CPS, just as with a defence client or indeed a judge, is clarity.

Do not be afraid to ask questions; you are the person who will be explaining the case to the jury and if you don't understand it, they never will.

If you have drafted a detailed advice, you can work through your headings (Evidence, Unused, Witness Issues, Case Presentation) in your conference, always making it clear that you have read all the papers/responses sent in the interim.

A good relationship with your CPS lawyer and OIC is invaluable; establish a rapport by demonstrating that you know the case and have control of it.

As with your written advice, be clear in conference about what material you have and what is missing. A police officer may believe something has been 'served' when it has been sent to CPS.

Don't keep talking about 'raw data' to a constable whose opening gambit was 'I'm not that tech-savvy'. Use language clearly. Break down what you actually want to happen, if necessary, with promises to email guidance later, and a suggestion that they consult their digital download guru. Conversely, if you have no idea what Holmes or ACESO is, ask. Honesty goes further than bluster and you can't afford not to understand.

Be clear at the start of a conference who is keeping a note. It is often useful if you keep a note alongside the caseworker who may attend so you can compare notes via email later. You each will have picked up on different points. Make it clear who 'owns' any actions.

Be clear in your own mind about your role. You have been instructed as an independent and informed mind to advise CPS and to present the case. You should therefore not be afraid to give advice that may be unpopular. However, even if you are leading the team, you still need to be part of the team: robust advice is still advice and not an order.

To be persuasive, you need to have thought through ways to solve the problems you have identified. Demonstrate that you want to keep the show on the road if you lawfully and properly can and that you are genuinely receptive to lateral thinking, new ideas or fresh information. Make it plain by your actions that you are not frightened of hard work or presenting a difficult case, and then give your advice clearly. It often helps to set it out in writing before a conference so that everyone has time to digest it.

In practice, you will give advice about issues that are often arguable in various ways. You will be trying to help CPS avoid pitfalls and put their best foot forward. You should be familiar with all the ethical and policy codes that apply to your role as a prosecution advocate, but if you are fretting over the interpretation of Farquharson Guidelines, then a wheel has already come off. The earlier you put in the hard yards on a case, flag up the possible pitfalls, and chart a course to a sensible resolution, the easier it will be to bring the prosecution team along with you.

A conference with CPS is a good opportunity for you to demonstrate that you are genuinely a persuasive advocate: one who is familiar with the material, able to adapt their approach when new information is received, and able to make an argument without getting into an argument.

Result sheets

Communication is at the core of what we do. Your brilliant job will lose much in the performance if you forget to tell anyone what you have achieved.

Both CPS and defence solicitors need a Result sheet from you as soon as possible after the hearing; often it's easiest to make sure that this is sent before you leave the court building. At the very latest make sure that it's done that day.

Each CPS area has its own form of Result sheets. Defence solicitors do not, so (unless your chambers has a standard version) either create your own or send an email. Keep a copy where you can find it easily and send a copy to your clerks so that they know what has happened and when the next hearing is. Ensure that a Result sheet includes who was your judge/opponent, any information provided/requests made by your opponent, all orders made by the judge, the Custody Time Limit expiry or bail conditions, and the date and purpose of the next hearing. Highlight any actions you are asking others to complete.

Do not fall into the trap of thinking that because you are fluent and persuasive in court that you do not need to communicate with those who cannot see you because they not there: Ie, your absent client; the instructing solicitor; the CPS lawyer; the CPS caseworker; the OIC.

Try to make sure that everyone who needs to know what is happening is kept up to speed at all times.

That is the sign of a good communicator and communication is what your job is all about, in court or out of it.

DO

- Listen carefully

- Gather as much background information as you can (proof, solicitors notes)

- Be on top of the papers and ready to explain them in simple language

- Sketch out a conference plan with key points to cover

- Always explain credit, trial in absence

- Be alert to trial participation issues like mental health problems

- Know your code of conduct obligations

- Give *advice* – not just options

- Get an endorsement where necessary

DON'T

- Stereotype your client

- Assume technical knowledge on the part of your client (or police officers when prosecuting)

- Be afraid to give robust advice, delivered sensitively

- Forget it's your client's choice whether to plead guilty or not guilty

- Become your client's friend or social worker

Chapter 6

The adversarial system

Andrew Langdon QC

Crown Court trials are not judge-led inquiries searching for the truth. Rather they are a process by which the answer to one important question is sought: has the prosecution made the jury sure, on admissible evidence, of the defendant's guilt?

The process in other words is not inquisitorial, but adversarial. An important 'truth', namely whether guilt has been sufficiently proved, emerges in the contest between the parties.

At its heart is the idea, part of our political and common law heritage, that 'truth is best discovered by powerful statements on both sides of the question' (*ex parte Lloyd* 1882 Mont 70).

What are the practical consequences for you, an advocate in an adversarial, as opposed to an inquisitorial, system?

Most fundamentally, you must immediately appreciate that the court has no role in: (a) investigating; (b) selecting; or (c) presenting the relevant evidence.

Each of these is the responsibility of the parties.

In an adversarial system you, the advocate, will have a critical role in relation to all three:

- First, you will have to decide upon which parts of your side of the case have been under-investigated and work out how best to rectify the default.

- Secondly, you as the advocate need then to select from the evidence available to you, the evidence you actually want to adduce. Often, less is more. Many cases are won by the decision *not* to call a witness.

  This selection process is a responsibility requiring judgment and confidence, which if avoided, amounts to a derogation of your duty to your client.

- Finally, you as the advocate have to decide how best to present the case: the order of witnesses you call; how best to elicit what you need from them; which documents and other exhibits you want to adduce from them; and how best to place them attractively before the court. The responsibility for all this is yours. In an adversarial system, if you don't do this for your client, no-one else will.

So much for the presentation of your own case. But the adversarial system requires you to take on your opponent's case, by objecting to inadmissible evidence, by cross-examining witnesses whose testimony runs contrary to your case and by exposing bad or weak arguments deployed against you, for what they are.

If you do not do these things, a weak or false case against your client may prevail.

No advocate in an adversarial system can assume that a judge will step in to the fray to thwart an undeserved victory. So whilst remaining fair, you need to be fearless in defence of your own case and fearless when scrutinising or exposing the opposition. This does not mean however that you should not make concessions.

On the contrary, concessions are often necessary to maintain credibility and a timely concession can, of itself, amount to attractive advocacy. Indeed, the stronger the advocate you become, the more likely you are to make concessions.

The adversarial system works best when there is an equality of arms between the parties, both in terms of resources and of skill. Most good advocates will tell you that they are at their best when they are against skilful opponents.

- First, there is a natural tendency to raise your game when the quality of the opposition requires it and a corresponding tendency, hard to avoid, of performing less well when the opposition is poor.

- Secondly, your tribunal (judge or jury) will be less impressed by what may be good arguments advanced by you, if they sense that what you are saying is not under scrutiny or informed rebuttal by a capable professional tasked with the role of opposing you. A claim that withstands scrutiny is always more persuasive.

Equality of advocates does not mean equality of resources, especially in relation to the investigation. Your responsibilities are different depending on which side of the case you appear. It is important to note the apparent inequality of the resources which arise from the fact that the prosecution have the police to investigate and collect evidence for them. The defence lack this powerful facility. This inequality is ameliorated somewhat by the duty upon the prosecution to disclose material the police have obtained which helps the defence.

Your role as a prosecution advocate includes doing what you can to ensure that your opponent has been given all that they might choose to deploy against you. In this as in other respects, the adversarial system depends upon trust. The system breaks down if the adversaries mistrust each other. Earning the trust and winning the respect of your opponents will make you a much more effective advocate.

As an advocate in the crown court you must 'prepare and conduct the case in accordance with the overriding objective' that 'criminal cases be dealt with justly', which includes 'acquitting the innocent and convicting the guilty' (Criminal Procedure Rules 2015, r 1.1).

There is no conflict between the overriding objective and your task as an advocate for one side of the case, because, as such, your role is to assist the court in its task of reaching the right conclusion. You do that by testing and challenging your opponent's evidence and submissions, and presenting your own in opposition.

If you fail to do so, because you regard yourself as on the 'wrong side' of the case, you are positively hindering the overriding objective. In an adversarial system, miscarriages of justice are most likely to occur when one side fails to advance its case with the requisite vigour.

Because the system is adversarial you must not confuse your part in delivering the overriding objective with a belief that it is up to you to arrive at the answer and deliver it in triumph. Your role as prosecution advocate is to present the relevant evidence to the court, and to test the defence.

Your role as defence advocate is to persuade the tribunal, within the rules, that your client's case should prevail. But you are not your client's mouthpiece. You need to be detached, even sceptical about what you are told, in order to sift the good points from the bad, and to make judgements about what will work.

In a trial, your advocacy has to take account of both the judge and the jury. Because our system is adversarial, the judge will not know what your instructions are. Neither will they have access to other information which you have, such as unserved evidence, the personal qualities of your client or your witnesses, nor how effectively or otherwise you are being supported by your team. A good judge will keep all that in mind when assessing what you are saying or doing. But judges have responsibilities to manage the trial to ensure it proceeds fairly and expeditiously and that the parties are assisting the jury by narrowing and simplifying what is really in issue between them.

You need to win the trust of your judges. If they trust you, they will intervene less. The better the advocates, the less the judge's voice is heard.

Most jurors instinctively understand that our system is adversarial and so will understand your professional role and give you some leeway. They will not make the mistake of associating you personally with your client's cause.

Nonetheless you are required on occasion to be bold and to take a course which may jar with the jury's present perception of the case. Taking the path of least resistance may sell your case short, and so contribute to the wrong outcome.

Occasionally, when putting your client's case to a witness with low expectations of a helpful reply, you may be surprised to receive an answer which confirms that what your client has told you is, after all, correct. If you avoid the question altogether, for the sake of trying to stay on the right side of the jury's perception of you, the validity of your client's case may never emerge.

In the final chapter of this book consideration is given to your ethical and professional duties. However, it is important to remember that whilst staying within the constraints of the rules and remaining courteous and fair, you have earned the freedom of choosing how to make the best of the hand that you have been dealt.

Your skills will develop, case by case. The style and content of your advocacy will inevitably improve with experience. As with all forms of combat, physical or rhetorical, the best adversaries learn fastest from the experience of coming second to skilful opponents. If you are a really good advocate, you will keep learning those skills from others, and you will be prepared to dispense with outworn methods once your opponents have shown you ways to improve upon them. It's because our system is adversarial, that we can continually develop towards excellence in advocacy.

Part IV

Evidential submissions

Chapter 7

Judicial advocacy v jury advocacy

Ray Tully

These are two very different skills. They share common DNA but they are different. It is important to recognise the differences and reflect them in your advocacy. At root, all advocacy is about the art of persuasion. Judges are different animals from juries and should not be addressed in the same way. Don't confuse one with the other. You'll know pretty soon when you are getting it wrong because either the judge will intervene and remind you they are not a jury – or the jury will take on a rather glazed look as you unnecessarily address them about the intricacies of the law. If either of those situations occur, you'll have got it badly wrong. The best way to avoid that is to be aware of the different skill sets required from the outset.

JUDICIAL ADVOCACY

Let's first consider the core elements of judicial advocacy. The most obvious times at which you will be addressing a judge directly are during pre-trial hearings, legal arguments, sentence hearings and appeal hearings. In truth though, every time you address a judge about anything in a Crown Court you are engaged in advocacy – or at the least you are presented with an opportunity to showcase your advocacy. The fact that someone is a judge should tell you something important. It tells you they have relevant experience. They expect to be addressed as such. That means keeping what you have to say focused and succinct. What do you want the judge to do? It is often a good tactic to tell them in headline form upfront, so they know exactly where you are going with your submissions. Judges do something which juries don't. They talk back to you. It's important to listen to what they say. It will provide you with invaluable information about what they want you to concentrate upon in your submissions. Also, with a judge you can take the opportunity to set out your submissions in writing – whether or not that is formally required. It makes you think about what you're asking for and why the judge should grant it. It provides an opportunity for you to persuade the judge before you even say anything. Judges are less susceptible to the power of argument based purely on emotion so keep what you have to say measured and logical.

JURY ADVOCACY

Juries are a wonder. The chance to be an advocate before a jury is probably what drew you into the profession in the first place. The opportunity for emotional engagement is clearly much greater with a jury than with a judge. The possibility to be more expressive and expansive in your use of language also clearly exists. That does not mean that many of the core skills you've hopefully deployed with the Judge do not also apply before the jury. Keep it measured. Keep it logical. Keep it persuasive. Always remember it's not about you – it's about your client.

Chapter 8

Bad character

Alistair Haggerty

Key references

- *Archbold: Criminal Pleading, Evidence and Practice 2020*, Ch 13

- *Blackstone's Criminal Practice 2020*, F13–F15

- Crown Court Compendium, Ch 12

- Criminal Procedure Rules 2015, SI 2015/1490 (CPR 2015), Part 21

- Criminal Justice Act 2003 (CJA 2003), ss 98, 100, 101

- Police and Criminal Evidence Act 1984 (PACE), s 78

Case law

- *R v Hanson and Others* [2005] EWCA Crim 824

- *R v Lamaletie* [2008] EWCA Crim 314

- *R v Nelson* [2006] EWCA Crim 3412

- *R v Phillips* [2011] EWCA Crim 2935

- *R v Sheikh* [2013] EWCA Crim 907

INTRODUCTION

Evidence of bad character can be very powerful evidence indeed. However, before making an application to adduce bad character, there are two important tactical questions to ask yourself before turning to the law. First, is the evidence actually bad character? Second, do I need to adduce this evidence?

The definition of 'bad character' is contained in the CJA 2003, s 98. It is any evidence of misconduct, other than that which is to do with the alleged facts of the offence with which the defendant is charged or evidence of misconduct in connection with the investigation or prosecution of that offence. Consider both whether the material you want to adduce is 'misconduct' and, if so, whether it is 'to do with the alleged facts of the offence', eg the existence of a restraining order in the case of an alleged breach of the same order.

The second key question is more difficult to answer. Applying to adduce bad character is always superficially appealing. However, the evidence should tangibly strengthen your case in order for it to be worthwhile. A sensible advocate will consider not only whether a judge could be persuaded to permit the application, but whether the admission of the evidence will help persuade a jury of their case. Once the evidence is before the jury it gives them a window into the defendant's history, so adducing minor convictions, or those with more limited relevance, might actually make them more sympathetic towards them once they see that their record is not so bad after all. When defending, the risks of adducing bad character of prosecution witnesses are even more acute, especially if your client has a criminal record himself.

Nevertheless, there are clearly occasions in which adducing bad character, or even putting the bad character of your own client before the jury, can be advantageous. There are seven ways in which the bad character of the defendant can be adduced (often referred to as the 'seven gateways') and each comes with its own tactical considerations. There is also a route through which bad character of non-defendants can be put before the jury.

THE SEVEN GATEWAYS

The gateways are set out in the CJA 2003, s 101(1)(a)–(g).

- *Gateway (a)* concerns bad character evidence which is admissible by agreement. When defending, you may have cases in which you want to adduce your client's previous convictions or misconduct. For example, this might arise in circumstances where your client has suggested an ulterior motive for being falsely accused or identified, on the basis that they have offended in the past. It can also be an effective way of limiting the extent and form of bad character evidence, something which was famously done by George Carman QC in the trial of Jeremy Thorpe. Tread cautiously and establish with your opponent the reasons why the evidence is being agreed. Outline this to the judge so that advance consideration can be given to jury directions.

- *Gateway (b)* is for situations in which the defendant tenders evidence of their own bad character. This is sometimes used to enable the defendant to assert that they do not commit offences of the type of which they are accused. In addition, it can be deployed in cases where your client has old or minor convictions to obtain a modified good character direction from the judge. Putting your client's character before the jury in chief can be disarming and does provide you with a degree of control over how it is presented. If applying to adduce bad character under this provision, set out in oral submissions the ways in which the evidence is relevant and the ways in which it is not. If you are clear that it is not relevant to propensity you should ask the judge to direct the jury accordingly.

- *Gateway (c)* is for important explanatory evidence. The test for admissibility under this provision is a narrow one as the evidence must be of such a nature that, without it, the jury would find it impossible or difficult to properly understand the evidence in the case, and its value for understanding the evidence as a whole is substantial. The Court of Appeal has emphasised that this gateway should only be used to admit evidence which is genuinely important for a proper understanding of the case and should be limited to what the jury needs to know (*R v Sheikh*).

- *Gateway (d)* is the subject of the majority of applications made in advance of the trial. It is for evidence which is relevant to an important matter in issue between the defendant and prosecution. The most obvious examples of such evidence are those which indicate that the defendant has a propensity to commit offences of the type with which they are charged. However, it is not only propensity evidence which is admissible under this gateway. For example, evidence that the defendant has downloaded indecent images of children may be admissible in a case of alleged sexual activity with a child, as it is relevant to the important matter as to whether the defendant has a sexual interest in children. When making, or responding to, an application under this gateway, the important case to consider is that of *R v Hanson and Others*. This is especially useful for opposing applications as it sets out criteria for the judge to bear in mind before admitting the evidence.

- *Gateway (e)* concerns evidence of substantial probative value in relation to an important matter in issue between a defendant and co-defendant. This is therefore relevant to cases in which 'cut-throat' defences are being pursued. Such evidence is not limited to that which indicates that the co-defendant is more likely to be the offender, but can also include that which undermines the co-defendant's credibility. *R v Phillips* outlines the test for the court to consider in relation to gateway (e): does the evidence have substantial probative value in relation to a matter of substantial importance to the case as a whole? Old or tenuous previous convictions, or disputed allegations of misconduct are unlikely to be admitted through this gateway.

The final two gateways arise out of assertions made by the defendant. If he gives a false impression (CJA 2003, s 101(1)(f)) or attacks the character of another person (CJA 2003, s 101(1)(g)), either in interview, through cross-examination by his barrister, or in his own evidence, his bad character may be admitted.

- *Gateway (f)* applies to situations in which your client creates an obvious false impression; the judge will be anxious for this to be corrected. If the false impression is given in their interview, the first step should be to remove it during the editing process if the prosecution agrees. However, even if it arises in evidence, steps can be taken to mitigate the impact. First, you can adduce evidence from your client to ensure that they withdraw the assertion so that the jury are not left with a false impression. Second, if evidence of bad character is adduced by the prosecution, you should ensure that this goes no further than is necessary to correct the false impression.

- *Gateway (g)* codifies the long-established convention that when a defendant attacks the character of another they lose their 'shield' and their own bad character may be put before the jury. Although this can apply to an attack on the character of any person, the Court of Appeal has emphasised that it would be unusual for evidence of the defendant's bad character to be admitted where their attack is on the character of a non-victim or non-witness (*R v Nelson*). The gateway can be invoked by an accusation that someone other than the defendant committed the offence, or an assertion that a prosecution witness is telling lies. There will be some situations in which avoiding an attack on another's character is impossible. An obvious example is in cases of self-defence. Whether bad character is admitted in these circumstances is likely to depend on the nature of what is suggested by the defendant and the fairness of admitting the bad character evidence in all the circumstances (see the case of *R v Lamaletie*).

NON-DEFENDANT BAD CHARACTER

The CJA 2003, s 100 outlines the rules relating to the admission of non-defendant bad character. This is admissible if it is important explanatory evidence, is adduced by agreement between the parties, or has substantial probative value. The test for substantial probative value mirrors that in relation to co-defendants in the CJA 2003, s 101(1)(e). The CJA 2003, s 100 can therefore be used to introduce evidence of the bad character of an alternative suspect, or to undermine the credibility of a witness. However, adducing the bad character of a non-defendant will inevitably amount to an attack on the character of that individual and, if your client has previous convictions, it will be very difficult to argue that the jury should not be told of these.

PREPARING THE APPLICATION

It is always a good idea to think about questions of character at an early stage and long before the trial date. Where possible, advance notice should always be given of the intention to adduce bad character. The rule in relation to bad character of defendants is outlined in CPR 2015, r 21.4, which applies to all gateways, with the exception of evidence adduced by agreement (CJA 2003, s 101(1)(a)). The prosecution is generally required to serve any bad character notice at Stage 1 in Crown Court proceedings.

The requirements for the defence, both in relation to evidence of co-defendant and non-defendant bad character (CPR 2015, r 21.3), are less prescriptive, but the notice should be served as soon as reasonably practicable and not more than 14 days after disclosure of the material on which the notice is based (ie case summary(s) for the offence(s) in the application) Where an application to adduce bad character is opposed, the response must be served within 14 days.

The court has the power to extend the time limit for service for any of the notices upon application. The main consideration in these circumstances is the interests of justice. The judge will be influenced by the need to ensure that the responding side is not taken by surprise and has sufficient opportunity to properly respond.

In addition, there are some situations in which it will not be possible to provide advance notice. For example, the defendant might unexpectedly make an attack on the character of a prosecution witness, or create a false impression, during the course of his evidence. Be alert to this and ready with the correct section at your finger-tips to make an application if necessary.

It should be noted that the CPR 2015 only provide time limits for service of the notice of the intention to adduce bad character. They do not preclude advocates from serving a more detailed application after the time limit has expired. Where the issues concerning bad character are complex, or require detailed argument and consideration of authorities, it is good practice to serve a comprehensive skeleton argument in advance of the trial.

There are three routes through which bad character applications can be opposed.

(a)   The first is to argue that the relevant test set out in the statute is not satisfied. Each of the gateways has their own considerations, which have been expanded upon in recent cases, and it may be that the tests set out are not met.

(b)   Second, the evidence can be excluded under the CJA 2003, s 101(3) although this provision is expressly limited to evidence admissible via gateways (d) or (g). The test in s 101(3) is whether it appears to the court that the admission of the bad character would have such an adverse effect on the fairness of the proceedings that the court ought not to admit it.

(c)   Third, and in relation to all other gateways, it can be argued that the evidence should be excluded under the general discretion in PACE, s 78.

Case law suggests that this discretion is likely to be exercised in cases in which either the bad character evidence is adduced to bolster an otherwise weak prosecution case, or where the evidence is disputed and likely to result in complicated 'satellite' issues (both considered in *Hanson*).

MAKING THE APPLICATION

The application to adduce bad character is generally made during the trial, although it may be heard in advance of the trial date, particularly if it will affect whether it is necessary to call a witness. The gateway under which the application is made also tends to influence the stage in the trial at which the argument is heard. When you are prosecuting and seeking to adduce evidence to demonstrate propensity, it is usual to make the application at the outset of the trial. This enables you to open the bad character to the jury in your opening speech. This can be highly effective in shaping the jury's view of the defendant right from the outset. In situations in which the bad character is relevant to correct a false impression or counter an attack made on the character of another, the judge may wish to see how the evidence emerges during the prosecution case before hearing oral arguments, even where a notice has been served in advance. The issue of bad character can be revisited at any stage during the trial, depending upon the evidence which emerges. An application under gateway (d) may be refused, only for that evidence to later become admissible under gateway (g). It is important to be alert to the potential for applications to be revived and to properly advise your client on the risks.

Written applications to adduce bad character should provide the structure for your oral submissions. The key to making the submissions persuasive is to ensure that they are tailored to the specific facts of the case. It is therefore good practice to have access to the facts and circumstances of the previous convictions of the defendant or witness to whom the application relates. If, for example, a defendant is on trial for an alleged distraction burglary of an elderly victim, the simple fact that they have previous convictions for burglary may be admissible. However, if you have ascertained that these previous offences concerned distraction burglaries on elderly people, and you have served the case summaries to prove it, the application will be more persuasive and the evidence more potent if admitted at trial.

Be realistic when responding to bad character applications. There may be some cases in which the bad character evidence is inevitably going to be admitted. In these situations, it may be better to reach an agreement with prosecution counsel in advance of the trial and reduce the evidence to agreed facts. This will allow for damage limitation by making the evidence more prosaic and protecting your client from being taken by surprise in the witness box. When defending, it is always preferable that the bad character application is determined before your client gives evidence. This at least enables you to prepare your client and question them about the relevant matters before they are cross-examined.

Chapter 9

Hearsay

Alistair Haggerty

Key references

- *Archbold: Criminal Pleading, Evidence and Practice 2020*, Ch 11

- *Blackstone's Criminal Practice 2020*, F16–F18

- Crown Court Compendium, Ch 14

- Criminal Procedure Rules 2015, SI 2015/1490 (CPR 2015), Part 20

- Criminal Justice Act 2003 (CJA 2003), ss 114–121

Case law

- *R v Andrews* [1987] AC 281

- *R v Jurecka* [2017] EWCA Crim 1007

- *R v Musone* [2007] EWCA Crim 1237

- *R v Riat and Others* [2012] EWCA Crim 1509

- *R v Twist* [2011] EWCA Crim 1143

INTRODUCTION

Before drafting the application, you should consider the commentary on hearsay in *Archbold* (Ch 11) and *Blackstone's* (F16–F18), as well as Ch 14 of the Crown Court Compendium which provides guidance on how the judge should approach the various categories of hearsay evidence.

There is a general rule in criminal cases that evidence must be given in person by a witness who speaks from their own recollection or knowledge. This enables the jury to assess the evidence from that witness and for the opposing side to challenge it. Evidence which is given second hand is hearsay. This includes the statements of non-witnesses, evidence of what someone else has told a witness, statements in documents, and audio recordings of things said out of court. Despite there being a general rule that hearsay is inadmissible, there are several exceptions. Sometimes its admission is routine and uncontroversial but, on other occasions, it can be the subject of considerable legal argument.

Upon receiving the case papers, it is important to identify any hearsay issues at an early stage. Each type of evidence comes with its own rules and considerations. These are set out in the CJA 2003, ss 114–121. Hearsay is defined in s 114 as a statement not made in oral evidence in the proceedings *which is tendered as evidence of any matter stated*. The first part of this definition is straightforward but the second part can cause confusion. For example, it is common in cases concerning the supply of drugs for text messages to be adduced as evidence to show that the defendant is a drug dealer. Such text messages do not typically assert that the recipient is a drug dealer but are instead requests for drugs or comments on the quality or price.

The case of *R v Twist* has made clear that where the messages do not contain any statement that the defendant is a dealer, and it was not the intention of the sender to cause someone to believe this, the messages are not hearsay when they are adduced as evidence to show that the defendant is involved in dealing drugs. Therefore, a text message saying, 'you are the best dealer …' would be hearsay, but one saying, 'that wrap of cocaine was way under' would not be.

There are many situations in which evidence does fall within the definition of hearsay and can only be adduced on application. First, ask yourself whether you actually need the evidence. If, for example, it is simply a throwaway line said by a bystander in an affray which was seen first-hand by several witnesses, it may add nothing. In these circumstances, the line can be edited out of an agreed statement read to the jury, or you should steer the witness away from mentioning this in his oral evidence. If, however, you are satisfied that you do need the evidence, the next step should be to consider how to adduce it.

CATEGORIES OF HEARSAY EVIDENCE

There are a number of different routes through which hearsay can be admitted and these depend on the type of evidence. There may be some cases in which the admissibility of hearsay is agreed.

Then there are cases in which a witness is unavailable. Evidence from these witnesses is admissible under the CJA 2003, s 116 in circumstances where the relevant witness is dead, is unfit to be a witness because of his bodily or mental condition, is outside the United Kingdom, cannot be found, or cannot give evidence due to fear. Where the witness is in fear, the court may only admit the evidence if it is in the interests of justice to do so. Where a witness is outside the United Kingdom, or cannot be found, the court must be satisfied that all reasonably practicable steps have been taken to secure the attendance of the witness including investigating video link. Evidence will be needed to substantiate any application under this section, including medical evidence in a case relating to a physical or mental condition. This may need to cover both whether a witness was competent when the statement was made and why they are no longer able to attend.

The next category of hearsay evidence relates to that contained in documents. The test for the admissibility of this type of evidence is contained in the CJA 2003, s 117. In a nutshell, the evidence is admissible if it is contained in a business document, or where it is contained in a document prepared for the purposes of criminal proceedings and where the relevant witness is absent or cannot be expected to have any recollection of the matters dealt with in the document, eg a police officer producing a custody record. Evidence which falls within s 117 is subject to an exclusionary discretion where there are doubts about its reliability.

The CJA 2003, s 118 preserves the exceptions to the general hearsay rule which existed under common law. The most important of these are the rules relating to confessions, admissions by agents, and *res gestae*. With the introduction of digital recordings of 999 calls and increased use of police body cameras, *res gestae* has taken on even greater significance. It typically relates to statements made by a person so emotionally overpowered by an event that the possibility of concoction or distortion can be disregarded. Classic *res gestae* would therefore be where a witness is giving a panicked running commentary of an incident on a call to the police.

When prosecuting, 999 calls can be very useful evidence, especially when they are emotionally impactive or provide compelling evidence of the complainant giving an immediate consistent account. However, they can sometimes make matters more confusing and should not be adduced in all cases. Where the 999 call undermines the prosecution, it will need to be disclosed to the defence and, if they wish to adduce it, the evidence will generally be admitted. It is worth remembering that there is no power to apply to admit anonymous hearsay, such as when a 999 caller refuses to give his name, unless the parties agree it.

The CJA 2003, ss 119 and 120 relate to previous statements made by witnesses. Section 119 enables a previous inconsistent statement to be put to a witness in cross-examination. Section 120 enables a previous consistent statement to be adduced from a witness and includes provision for adducing recent complaint evidence, under s 120(7) and (8). These latter provisions permit a called witness to give evidence of a complaint made to them by another witness. This evidence is frequently adduced in cases concerning alleged sexual offences, where a disclosure has been made to a friend or family member by the complainant. Provided it is consistent, this can be powerful evidence. The complainant must provide evidence of the conversation they had with their friend before the friend's evidence could be admitted under this section.

Evidence which does not fall within any of the aforementioned sections may still be admitted under the CJA 2003, s 114 if the court is satisfied that it is in the interests of justice to do so. Section 114(2) makes clear that before evidence is admitted on this basis, a checklist of nine factors must be considered. These include the probative value of the statement and the circumstances in which it was made, and the importance and reliability of the evidence and the amount of difficulty involved in challenging it.

The nine factors in the CJA 2003, s 114(2) should also be considered in relation to multiple hearsay, which can be admitted via s 121, see *R v Musone*. Owing to the obvious risks related to multiple hearsay, the threshold for admissibility under this section is a very high one.

Some of these provisions contain specific tests for admissibility. However, the admissibility of all hearsay is subject to the exclusionary provisions of PACE, s 78 and the CJA 2003, s 126 which enables the court to exclude evidence which lacks probative value. The case of *R v Riat and Others*, which is essential reading on this subject, suggests that the factors in section 114(2) are of assistance in assessing the value of all hearsay evidence (see also *R v Jurecka*, in which consideration of the CJA 2003, s 114(2) criteria was approved in relation to applications made under s 116).

DRAFTING THE APPLICATION

Some types of hearsay evidence will require a notice to be served, but this does not apply to all types. Applications made under the CJA 2003, ss 114, 116, 117(1)(c) (evidence in a statement prepared for the purposes of criminal proceedings) and 121 require notice to be given in accordance with CPR 2015, r 20.2. Applications made under the other provisions (eg *res gestae* and recent complaint evidence) do not. Where the hearsay application is made by the prosecution, the notice should be served within 14 days of the defendant pleading not guilty in the Crown Court. Where the application is made by the defence, the notice must by served as soon as is reasonably practicable.

Even where a notice is not required, it is advisable to indicate to all parties that you intend to rely on specific hearsay evidence, especially where its admission may be controversial. This can be done by serving a short document, indicating what the evidence is and the provision under which it is admissible. If objection is taken to this evidence being admitted, a skeleton argument should be served outlining, in detail, the basis for its admissibility.

MAKING THE APPLICATION

Written applications to adduce hearsay should be made at the earliest opportunity and in accordance with the CPR 2015. However, the court does have the power to extend the time limit for serving notice and can dispense with the requirement entirely (CPR 2015, r 20.5). This allows for situations in which complying with the CPR 2015 is not possible. For example, a key witness may die shortly before the trial commences, or a previously cooperative witness might suddenly go missing on the day of trial. Where a witness is absent, the judge will require efforts to be made to secure his attendance. If these then prove fruitless, a hearsay application can be made at short notice.

Where the hearsay evidence is fundamental to the case, such as an ABE interview from a deceased complainant, the application may be listed for legal argument in advance of the trial date. In other cases, the application will be heard at the outset of the trial, or at an appropriate stage during the trial.

An effective hearsay application will persuade the judge that the importance of the statement overrides any concerns regarding the inability of the other side to challenge it by questioning the witness in court. You will therefore need to highlight the factors which demonstrate that the evidence is reliable, draw the judge's attention to the other evidence which supports the statement, and, if the witness who made the statement is absent, outline the reasons why. Acknowledge the balancing exercise that the judge will need to carry out and emphasise why that balance is weighted in your favour.

There will be some situations, such as where the witness has died, in which it will generally be easier to persuade the judge that the evidence should be admitted. Where a witness has refused to attend court, but has not stated that he or she is in fear, the application will need to be made under the CJA 2003, s 114, or consideration given as to whether there is material that may amount to *res gestae*. These applications sometimes arise in domestic violence cases and there are examples of such evidence being admitted even where it is the decisive evidence in the case. Nevertheless, the court will be more reluctant to admit it and it is important that any application to adduce evidence in these circumstances sets out in detail all steps which have been taken to get the witness to court.

OPPOSING THE APPLICATION

The rules for opposing a hearsay application are stricter than the rules for making one. If the admissibility of any hearsay is opposed, irrespective of whether a notice is required from the party seeking to adduce it, a notice of objection must be served (CPR 2015, r 20.3). This notice should be served within 14 days of receipt of the notice to adduce hearsay, or within 14 days of the service of the evidence which is objected to. Therefore, where evidence of recent complaint or *res gestae* has been served by the prosecution, the defence will need to submit a written notice in good time if the admissibility of that evidence is opposed.

When defending, it is good practice to identify any potential hearsay as soon as the prosecution papers are served. If you oppose the admissibility of any of the evidence, this should be set out in a notice or, at the very least, in the defence statement. This way, even if no application has been made by the prosecution, your opposition to the evidence is clear.

When drafting the notice of opposition consider carefully the admissibility tests set out in the CJA 2003. The most useful are the nine criteria in s 114(2). The response to the hearsay application should address each of these criteria in turn and outline the reasons why the balance should be weighed in favour of excluding the evidence. Where a witness is absent, highlight any of the inadequacies in the other side's enquiries into the whereabouts of the witness or their attempts to bring that witness to court. The disadvantages in challenging hearsay evidence should also be emphasised.

Opposing *res gestae* can be difficult, especially when the evidence arises from a 999 call made at the time of, or shortly after, the incident. *R v Andrews* sets out a series of steps which should be considered by the court before the evidence is admitted; address these factors in any notice seeking to exclude this material. An application opposing *res gestae* is also more likely to succeed where the prosecution has declined to call the maker of the original statement.

There will occasionally be situations in which hearsay evidence emerges unexpectedly. This typically occurs when a witness mentions something they have been told by someone else. Stop them as soon as possible. The judge might intervene, but may not know the status of the evidence. Counsel should steer the witness back on track. If you are defending, you may not want to draw too much attention to an aside from a prosecution witness. However, if the evidence has caused you concern, it is good practice to ask the judge to specifically direct the jury to disregard it.

Where, despite opposition, hearsay evidence is admitted, the judge will need to direct the jury appropriately. If you unsuccessfully opposed the admission of the evidence, invite the judge to highlight to the jury the points in dispute, any issues regarding the reliability of the evidence, and the fact that the evidence cannot be tested under cross-examination. If you know how the judge will direct the jury you can tailor your submissions in your closing speech.

Chapter 10

Excluding evidence

Ian Fenny

Key references

- *Archbold: Criminal Pleading, Evidence and Practice 2020*

    – Investigatory powers, PACE, confessions and the discretion to exclude evidence, Chapter 15 (see 15-493 particularly)

    – Competence of Witness, 8-52

    – Identification evidence, Chapter 14 (see 14-57 particularly)

- *Blackstone's Criminal Practice 2020*

    – Unlawfully obtained evidence, the exclusionary discretion, F2

    – Identification evidence, F19

- Police and Criminal Evidence Act 1984 (PACE), ss 76, 78, 82

- Youth Justice and Criminal Evidence Act 1999 (YJCEA 1999), ss 53, 54

Case law

- *R v Pearce* 69 Cr App R 334

- *R v Turnbull* [1977] Q.B. 224

INTRODUCTION

The legendary barrister Patrick Back QC once said, 'if a piece of evidence doesn't look right and it doesn't smell right, then it isn't right'. It's an interesting litmus test for the admissibility of evidence. If the opposing party wants the evidence in, and it's against the interests of your case, you must seek to exclude it.

In a perfect world advocates should agree on what is admissible in a trial, and where there is disagreement a civilised discussion ought to provide consensus. The reality of our adversarial system often proves otherwise. Almost all the evidence called by the Crown to prove a case will be prejudicial to the defendant. The core principle will always be 'does its probative value outweigh its prejudicial effect?' If it does, then it's admissible; if it's not, it should be excluded.

Here are the topics most likely to arise in any application to exclude evidence:

- Identification evidence

- Admissions and confessions

- Irrelevant material and collateral issues

- Opinion evidence

- Illegally or improperly obtained evidence

- Wholly self-serving statements

- The competence of a witness

Of course, exceptions apply to most of the above. Bad character and hearsay provisions are dealt with in **Chapters 8** and **9**: without an appropriate application being made and granted, all bad character material and virtually all hearsay is inadmissible.

In the final analysis the trial judge must decide where fairness lies and balance the competing arguments against the principle of the interests of justice. In exercising discretion, the judge must apply balance, logic, reason and good sense to the facts of the case. If that is done, then the Court of Appeal is unlikely to interfere with the ruling.

WHERE TO START?

Prosecuting a case is about building a structure. Defending a case is about knocking it down. Always have that in mind when approaching any aspect of the case, and nowhere is that more applicable than with the exclusion of evidence.

PACE, s 78(1) and (2)

This is the mothership for all defence arguments challenging admissibility. It's worth reciting here:

> 'In any proceedings the court may refuse to allow evidence upon which the prosecution proposes to rely to be given if it appears to the court that, having regard to all the circumstances, including the circumstances in which the evidence was obtained, the admission of the evidence would have such an adverse effect on the fairness of the proceedings that the court ought not to admit it.

Nothing in this section shall prejudice any rule of law requiring a court to exclude evidence.'

PACE, s 78 is not only the foundation of many applications to exclude evidence, but is often a fall-back position when all else fails. It is one of the most important statutory provisions within the criminal law and should always be at the forefront of an advocate's mind.

WHEN AND HOW TO OBJECT TO A PIECE OF EVIDENCE

The simple answer is: as soon as possible. Admissibility is a topic that should be covered pre-trial, but since that isn't always possible, provided objection is taken before it reaches the jury, then it might be said it's never too late. Good practice suggests that defence objections should only be raised during the trial itself when there has been late service of material.

Whilst the arrival of the Defence Statement should reduce the risk of the defence springing inadmissible material upon the Crown, the likelihood of objection 'on the hoof' is perhaps more likely in the prosecutorial context.

When mounting an argument to exclude evidence try to formulate your submissions. A skeleton argument served pre-trial is important for several reasons:

- it will focus your mind upon the issue at an early stage of preparation; and

- it will alert the judge to the issue. A skilfully drafted submission may well influence the argument before it is rehearsed in court.

Where there is an unresolved issue as to admissibility the evidence should not be before the jury unless and until a judge has admitted it. Ensure you make your objection clear to the Crown and ask that it not be included in their opening speech. If this can't be resolved, then raise it with the judge before the case is opened. It's more difficult where objection is taken to defence evidence. When defending you should alert your opponent to the evidence you want to call to give them the opportunity to object. A failure to do so could have disastrous consequences.

What if you've overlooked the point? It happens to every advocate. Don't panic and don't say nothing in the hope no-one will notice, or console yourself with the thought, 'It doesn't matter'. Make the application and apologise.

Never forget that if you get the timing wrong the consequence is likely to be the discharge of the jury and re-trial at a later date.

Never raise the fact or topic of an objection before the jury itself, simply ask for them to retire, then deal with it in their absence. Self-evidently objection must be raised before the evidence is called.

There are circumstances where the judge cannot rule until evidence has been heard. In such circumstances the judge will conduct a Voire Dire. The judge will hear live evidence upon which a determination as to admissibility will be made. Witnesses are examined and cross examined upon oath in the absence of the jury (*Archbold*, 15-497).

If the evidence is admitted, then that witness may be cross-examined upon any inconsistency with evidence given during the Voire Dire.

When arguing the point, it's as well to remember that no jury is involved in determining admissibility. The skills required to persuade a judge are quite distinct. Make your submissions in an ordered and concise manner. If you want to cite authorities make sure they are fairly and suitably summarised and edited. Identify the principle points and focus upon them. Only raise secondary issues if they bolster the primary argument. Always phrase your submissions upon the presumption that the judge has the case at his/her fingertips but always frame it upon the basis that they haven't. Never flog a dead horse or convince yourself that by pursuing a bad argument you will impress the defendant. If it is a sound argument but you face a resistant tribunal, develop as much as you need to cement the basis of an appeal should a conviction follow.

Objections to the admissibility of evidence apply equally to written documents adduced in evidence. Central to this will be the almost inevitable editing of documentary exhibits. Some, such as recorded evidence in chief (Achieving Best Evidence (ABE) interviews), will demand you formulate ideas from the earliest stage. Others, such as transcripts of police interviews, whilst done in advance wherever possible are sometimes done toward the end of the trial, by which time everyone has the best idea of the evidence in its final and developed form.

Where a settled position is essential before a trial begins but the parties are at odds, then the matter must be resolved pre-trial. As pre-recorded cross-examination of young and vulnerable witnesses gains momentum then consideration will also have to be given to editing. It will be interesting to see whether an ill-advised question that prompts a prejudicial answer will found the basis for exclusion.

IDENTIFICATION EVIDENCE

The principles are governed by *R v Turnbull*. Legal textbooks are awash with commentaries upon this seminal case.

The mechanisms and procedures for the formalised aspects of identification are set out in a variety of codes set out under PACE, s 78. Breaches of those Codes will establish a sound basis for exclusion, though it does not follow that a breach will automatically render the evidence inadmissible. It is worth noting that Code D Para 3.12 states that if a witness asserts that they would be able to recognise a suspect, and the defendant denies, being present then an identity parade *must* be held (with certain exclusions). The failure to hold an ID parade may provide fertile ground for an application to exclude the identification evidence.

ADMISSIONS, CONFESSIONS, AND IMPROPERLY OBTAINED MATERIAL

An admission or confession can be made in a number of ways. An admission is broadly speaking a statement against interest. A confession is defined by PACE, s 82(1). It must be voluntary. A defendant making an admission must have the capacity to do so.

The exclusion of such evidence is generally determined by PACE, s 76. Read this section carefully and the surrounding case law, for in virtually all applications to exclude confessions, you will want to rely on s 78 either by itself or alongside s 76. Be aware that *some* applications to exclude confessions will not engage s 76: if there is no question of oppression, and no suggestion that something has been done that may render the confession *unreliable*, and your real complaint is about other unfairness such as eavesdropping, you may want to re-focus your submissions on s 78 and examine the ways in which PACE has been breached.

Illegally and improperly obtained material is not always inadmissible, and the exercise of the s 78 discretion is highly case specific. Nonetheless trends can be identified in the case law and these include the differing attitudes to mistake as opposed to bad faith by the police.

IRRELEVANT MATERIAL AND COLLATERAL ISSUES

A judge has a duty to exclude irrelevant evidence. The test of relevance is case specific and rooted in good sense. Collateral issues (or side issues) are similarly unhelpful and should be excluded to assist a jury focus upon core factors. Unsurprisingly, what constitutes a collateral issue will often be in dispute.

OPINION EVIDENCE

Opinion evidence is inadmissible and should be excluded. The sole exception is the evidence of experts, dealt with under the chapter on witness evidence (**Chapter 13**). Opinion evidence includes any view on the ultimate issue (ie whether or not the defendant could have committed the crime). This includes character evidence and extends not just to obvious opinion, but an observation masking an opinion. 'This defendant has worked in a position of trust in my shop for seven years and I've been satisfied with his work' is an observation; 'It came as a real shock to hear about this case, I can tell you' is a coded opinion that the defendant did not commit the crime.

Unless a police officer is being called as an expert and has complied with all the requirements of the CPR 2015 the fact that they are a police officer does not change the rules about opinion evidence. It can be hard for an officer in the case dealing, by agreement, with the actions of other officers, to know where the line is. 'I can confirm that DC Hawthorn has made no notes of any house to house enquiries, and I note that the alleged offence occurred at 2.30 am' is fine; 'I doubt anyone would have opened their door to us in that area at that time' is straying into opinion.

If you are defending – be careful: if you seem to ask the officer for their opinion, they will give it, it probably won't help you, and some judges will consider that is just bad luck!

WHOLLY SELF-SERVING STATEMENTS

This is a much-overlooked principle, but it remains the law that a statement made by a defendant, with the sole purpose of exculpating themselves, is inadmissible (*see R v Pearce*). Where it slips through the net is when it is a mixed statement containing exculpatory and incriminatory evidence. The prosecution generally wish to rely on defendants' interviews as mixed statements, or as the basis for an adverse inference, or as material for comment in a speech about the poor explanations offered, but be alive to this general principle.

THE COMPETENCE OF A WITNESS

If a witness fails the test of competence, then their evidence should be excluded. The criteria are set out at the YJCEA 1999, s 53.

A witness is competent, unless:

(i)   the witness can't understand the questions to be asked of them; and

(ii)   cannot give answers that could be understood.

Either party may raise the issue, as may the judge. The issue is often determined through a Voire Dire (see above). Expert evidence may be called. (see YJCEA 1999, s 54).

If challenged, it is for the party calling the witness to establish, on the balance of probabilities, that the witness is competent. Again, although in some respects this argument is rarely made in practice, advocates can get into a muddle when they conflate ideas about competence with special measures and other provisions designed to assist vulnerable witnesses.

By way of example, the prosecution must make available for cross-examination someone who provides an ABE interview. If anyone suggests this cannot or should not take place, analyse what is being said: has the witness' bodily or mental condition declined such that a hearsay application is necessary; are special measures required; or is there a real question mark over their competence, and if so, was that question mark there at the time of their recording?

As with all aspects of advocacy, submissions made to judges about the exclusion of evidence require a clear analysis of the facts of your own case as well as a good knowledge of the law.

Chapter 11

Insufficiency of evidence

Ray Tully

Key references

- *Archbold: Criminal Pleading, Evidence and Practice 2020*, 4–362

- Crime and Disorder Act 1998 (CDA 1998), Sch 3, para 2 (2)

- Criminal Procedure Rules 2015, SI 2015/1490 (CPR 2015), r 9.16, Part 38

- Criminal Justice Act 2003 (CJA 2003), s 58

Case law

- *R v Galbraith* [1981] 73 Cr App R 124;

- *R v Sardar* [2016] EWCA Crim 1616

INTRODUCTION

The right to challenge the prosecution case is an important weapon in the armoury of the defence. It should be used sparingly. Where used appropriately it is the forensic equivalent of a tactical nuclear weapon. If used unwisely, it can easily result in significant self-inflicted harm.

There are two circumstances in which you may be considering such an application, either:

- pre-trial, as an application to dismiss; or

- as a half-time submission at the conclusion of the prosecution case.

THE APPLICATION TO DISMISS

In deciding whether to make an application to dismiss, the obvious starting point is ensuring you properly understand the statutory test set out in the CDA 1998, Sch 3, para 2(2) namely;

> 'The judge shall dismiss a charge (and accordingly quash any count relating to it in any indictment preferred against the applicant) which is the subject of any such application if it appears to him that the evidence against the applicant would not be sufficient for him to be properly convicted.'

If you wish to make an application to dismiss, it is necessary to comply with the CPR 2015, r 9.16 which sets out requirements regarding written notice and the correct form of the application.

In general, it is best to keep your written documents in support of the application short, sharp and focused. Don't enter into lengthy argument. This will better reflect your point that there is no scope for debate.

The judge has to assess the application in the light of all the evidence in the case as it stands. They are unlikely to adopt a narrow view of the evidence. Instead considerable persuasion will be required to convince them that there is no prospect of a conviction at such an early stage in the proceedings. The judge is not entitled to act as a substitute for a jury and weigh the evidence. It is not a question of considering whether the case 'looks a bit thin' or thinking that the prosecution is 'unlikely to get home'. In order to succeed you will need to clearly demonstrate that there is absolutely no prospect of the prosecution succeeding at trial. That is a high bar to get over.

There are some kinds of case that lend themselves to such an application. It may for example, be that upon a regulatory charge there is a strict time limit for bringing the charge which has not been complied with and is fatal to the prosecution case. It might be that the case is based upon inherently weak identification evidence which is unsupported by any other form of evidence. In such circumstances an application to dismiss may be entirely justified.

You need to think about the consequences of succeeding. The 'dismissal' of the charge is not necessarily an end to the case. The prosecution is perfectly entitled to go away, lick its wounds and then carry out any necessary repair work to its case (where such is possible) and come back again, with a fresh charge supported by additional evidence. If they do that, all you will have achieved is to identify the weaknesses in the prosecution case pre-trial. You may have succeeded in embarrassing them, but to what end?

Equally the prosecution may be able to amend the charge to side-step the flaw you have identified. If so, again what has actually been achieved apart from helping the prosecution to sharpen up their case?

For these reasons most advocates only ever make an application to dismiss in the clearest of cases when resting upon the most secure of ground.

You will also need to weigh up whether the devastating point you have identified might be better left until half-time in the trial when the opportunities for the prosecution to put it right may no longer be so readily available.

HALF-TIME SUBMISSIONS

If you are making a half-time submission you will inevitably be referring to the well-known test set out in *R v Galbraith*:

'(1)   If there is no evidence that the crime alleged has been committed by the defendant there is no difficulty—the judge will stop the case.

(2)   The difficulty arises where there is some evidence but it is of a tenuous character, for example, because of inherent weakness or vagueness or because it is inconsistent with other evidence. (a) Where the judge concludes that the prosecution evidence, taken at its highest, is such that a jury properly directed could not properly convict on it, it is his duty, on a submission being made, to stop the case. (b) Where however the prosecution evidence is such that its strength or weakness depends on the view to be taken of a witness's reliability, or other matters which are generally speaking within the province of the jury and where on one possible view of the facts there is evidence on which the jury could properly come to the conclusion that the defendant is guilty, then the judge should allow the matter to be tried by the jury' (per Lord Lane CJ at p 127).

Make sure you are fully familiar with the authority and understand whether your application is based on the first or second limb. The chances are that it will be based upon the second limb.

Where the prosecution case is based wholly or mainly on circumstantial evidence the Court of Appeal has further developed the *Galbraith* dicta. In *R v Sardar*, Sir Brian Leveson P [at para 17] referred approvingly to King CJ in the Supreme Court of South Australia when summarising the common law position in *Questions of Law Reserved on Acquittal (No 2 of 1993)* (1993) 61 SASR 1 as follows:

'If there is direct evidence which is capable of proving the charge, there is a case to answer no matter how weak or tenuous might consider such evidence to be (sic). If the case depends upon circumstantial evidence, and that evidence, if accepted, is *capable* of producing in a reasonable mind a conclusion of guilt beyond reasonable doubt and thus is *capable* of causing a reasonable mind to exclude any competing hypotheses as unreasonable, there is a case to answer. There is no case to answer only if the evidence is not capable in law of supporting a conviction. In a circumstantial case, that implies that even if all the evidence for the prosecution was accepted and all inferences most favourable to the prosecution which are reasonably open were drawn, a reasonable mind could not reach a conclusion of guilty beyond reasonable doubt, or to put it another way, could not exclude all hypotheses consistent with innocence, as not reasonably open on the evidence.'

Applications of 'no case' should always be made in the absence of the jury. There are no formal notice requirements as there are with applications to dismiss. Nor are there any relevant provisions of the CPR 2015 that have to be complied with.

It is a wise precaution to forewarn your judge that you intend to make such an application. The judge will wish to consider issues of jury management and will want to consider how your application impacts upon such matters. You should therefore inform the judge at a convenient stage towards the end of the prosecution case that you intend to make a submission. The judge may also want to consider asking you (and the prosecutor) to provide skeleton arguments. Even if the judge does not require a written skeleton argument it may be to your advantage to offer to provide one. It gives you the chance to persuade the judge in advance of the oral argument.

As with applications to dismiss you will need to carefully weigh up the tactical advantages of making the application. These are not always straightforward calculations. Will your submission simply result in the prosecution being permitted to make an application to amend the indictment and so deprive you of a line of argument that might have been better advanced to the jury at the end of the case in your closing speech (when the potential for amendment without causing prejudice has long since passed by)?

If the indictment contains multiple counts where the evidence is strong on some counts and not on others, what are the tactical pros and cons of potentially knocking out some of the counts? Might the weaker count(s) have been better left in play, so that you have the camouflage of having much to say about those counts in your closing speech to help gloss over the paucity of what there is to say about the stronger counts?

If you succeed in the application the judge will usually ask the jury to return to court and direct them to return a not guilty verdict upon the count(s) in question. If there are other counts remaining the judge may choose simply to tell the jury what has happened and the ruling they have reached but leave the mechanics of returning a not guilty verdict upon the particular count(s) until the conclusion of the trial.

If you do not succeed, nothing will be said to the jury about what has taken place in their absence.

PROSECUTION RESPONSES TO APPLICATIONS TO DISMISS/HALF-TIME SUBMISSIONS

The key factor to be aware of is ensuring that the judge properly understands the test to be applied. Judges are human. Sometimes they fall into error and may become tempted to substitute their own views of a case for those of the jury. Where you perceive that risk to be present, you will need to guard against it and remind the court of the proper test to be applied and the high bar that has to be met. There are many examples within the relevant case law in which the Court of Appeal has stated and re-stated the strict limitations placed upon the judge to stop the case before verdict.

If the defence has spotted a good point which had eluded the prosecution, consider whether there are other remedies open to you. Is it too late to plug the evidential gap? Can you apply to amend the indictment to address the issue? If that would cause undue prejudice to the defence because of the way they have approached cross-examination of the prosecution witnesses, can you apply to amend the indictment and concede there would have to be a retrial? Keeping the case alive to fight again another day is at least better than losing it.

In extremis it may be possible to consider an appeal against a terminating ruling under the provisions set out in the CJA 2003, s 58 and CPR 2015, Pt 38. There are strict time limits which apply. If you do not already have instructions in place you will need to apply for an immediate adjournment to seek such instructions. Such a course should never be embarked upon lightly.

Chapter 12

The Youth Justice and Criminal Evidence Act 1999, ss 41–43

Tara Wolfe

Key references

- *Archbold: Criminal Pleading, Evidence and Practice 2020*, 8-238

- *Blackstone's Criminal Practice 2020*, Section F7

- Rook and Ward *Sexual Offences Law and Practice*, 5th Edn (Sweet & Maxwell), Chapter 26

- Criminal Procedure Rules 2015, SI 2015/1490 (CPR 2015)

- Criminal Justice Act 2003 (CJA 2003), s 100

- Criminal Practice Direction V Evidence 22A: Use of Ground Rules Hearings When Dealing with s 41 YJCEA 1999 (Evidence of Complainant's Previous Sexual Behaviour)

- Crown Prosecution Service guidance: Rape and Sexual Offences – Chapter 4: Section 41 Youth Justice and Criminal Evidence Act 1999

Case law

- *R v A (No 2)* [2002] 1 AC 45

- *R v Evans (Chedwyn)* [2016] EWCA Crim 452

- *R v M* [2009] EWCA Crim 618

- *R v T; R v H* [2001] EWCA Crim 1877

INTRODUCTION

The Youth Justice and Criminal Evidence Act 1999 (YJCEA 1999), ss 41–43 aim to achieve the correct balance between protecting a complainant of a sexual offence against unmeritorious questioning about their sexual history and ensuring that the defendant receives a fair trial. It is based upon the premise that consent to sexual activity should be given freely and independently on each occasion. The statutory framework establishes a general prohibition against the introduction of or cross-examination about the sexual behaviour of a complainant unless certain limited exceptions apply. An application by the defence can only succeed if the court is satisfied that one of the exceptions apply and that a refusal of leave may have the result of rendering unsafe a conclusion of the jury on any relevant issue in the case.

This chapter is not intended to rehearse the law, which is set out at length in the practitioner texts; it is intended to provide some pointers as to issues that may arise and how best to deal with them.

This area of the law has seen much coverage in the press in the last few years, with journalists and others sometimes conflating how fit for purpose the law is and how well it is applied in individual cases: there is a real concern amongst judges that they are seen to be upholding this general prohibition scrupulously. Be conscious when making a YJCEA 1999, s 41 application that you are asking the court to adopt an exceptional course and you will be expected to provide good reasons for it do so.

The court will be on the alert for any argument that seems to suggest that anyone who has sex with multiple partners or on a regular basis is 'in general terms' more likely to consent to having sex with A.N. Other, or that there is any connection between sexual behaviour and telling the truth. The YJCEA 1999, s 41 was designed to do away with these twin myths and to ensure that juries looked at the issue of consent as something that was occasion specific.

However, one can readily see that a total prohibition on sexual history may be unfair to a defendant. It may well be appropriate to apply to cross-examine a complainant who tells a police officer, perhaps out of embarrassment, that they would never consent to the particular sexual act alleged in any circumstances, if messages emerge revealing they had previously consensually performed that act with the defendant. Although the admission of this material may affect their credibility with the jury, the primary purpose of admitting the messages may be to rebut the prosecution case or, depending on the facts of the case, bolster the defendant's defence of reasonable belief in consent. What one must never do is to suggest that because someone once consented to a particular act with a particular person, they invariably would do the same again, nor should one ever suggest that someone is less worthy of belief simply because of their sexual history.

At the outset, if the defence advanced amounts to a denial that any alleged sexual activity took place, it is difficult to envisage any situation in which an application under the YJCEA 1999, s 41 would be relevant. For example, in a case involving an allegation of a sexual assault on a bus by a stranger in which the defence argue that any touching was accidental, the sexual behaviour and history of the complainant would be entirely irrelevant. Further, it will be a rare case in which the sexual activity of the complainant with a third party will be admissible under s 41; see *R v Evans (Chedwyn)* for an example.

PROCEDURAL REQUIREMENTS

Strict rules apply to YJCEA 1999, s 41 applications as set out in CPR 2015, Part 22 and the Practice Direction.

First, applications must always be made in writing. This is a mandatory requirement. Always err on the side of caution. If in doubt as to whether or not the evidence you seek to adduce is caught by the exclusionary rule, draft an application to avoid the embarrassment or the time pressure of being required to draft an application at court. This will have the added benefit of focusing the mind and will improve the quality of oral submissions. The CPR 2015, r 22.4(2) sets out what must be covered in the application. This 'checklist' is particularly useful if the material upon which the application is based is disclosed on the day of trial.

Secondly, the application must be made at a hearing in private and in the absence of the complainant. It is not uncommon for the court to forget to clear the public gallery prior to the application being made. If prosecuting (or defending), ensure that the correct measures are taken to protect the privacy of the complainant by reminding the court of this requirement.

Thirdly, time limits do apply to when applications should be made, but the court has the power to vary the time limit or to hear an application out of time. If the application is being made out of time, ensure you start your submissions with an acknowledgement of this fact, state the reason, apologise if necessary and request that the court uses its power to hear your application out of time.

Finally, the court is required to provide reasons for either allowing or refusing an application and, if the application is successful, the extent to which questions can be asked of the complainant. Good practice requires that the proposed questions will have been drafted in the body of the application. If in any doubt as to whether a certain question or line of questioning is permitted do not be afraid of seeking clarification. The potential consequences of embarking on cross-examination and straying into impermissible territory are best avoided.

If prosecuting, even if there is no objection to the questions the defence seek to pose, it is a matter for the court. The issue cannot be agreed between the parties.

THE APPLICATION

The first point to note is that the section prohibits questions about 'any sexual behaviour'. This has been interpreted very widely by the courts and will include for example words said, diary entries and social media posts. If in doubt, assume that it could fall within the definition and draft an application. Second, any question must refer to a 'specific instance(s)' of sexual behaviour and relate to a 'relevant issue in the case'. Articulating to what relevant issue the evidence or question relates is not always an easy task but is imperative for any successful application.

Motive/bias

Evidence that relates to why a complainant may have made a false complaint against the defendant may, in limited circumstances, be admissible under the YJCEA 1999, s 41(3)(a). For example, if the defence seek to argue that a malicious allegation has been made following the defendant's rejection of the complainant's sexual advances, it may be permissible to ask the complainant whether that is the reason underlying the complaint. Where the defence seek to argue that a malicious allegation has been made in response to the defendant ending the relationship following infidelity on the part of the complainant, it may be permissible to ask questions seeking to elicit whether or not the complainant is acting out of spite and the factual background to the causes of that spite. However, if the underlying purpose of adducing evidence of the complainant's sexual behaviour is to impugn their credibility the evidence is not admissible (YJCEA 1999, s 41(4)): judges are vigilant in ensuring that defence advocates do not use speculative suggestions about motive as a cover to get irrelevant matters in the complainant's past before the jury. Equally, it may be that the defence can be put without reference to the sexual behaviour in which case the court will limit the ambit of the question.

Previous sexual behaviour between the defendant and the complainant: YJCEA 1999, s 41(3)(a), (b)

Sexual behaviour between the defendant and the complainant may be so relevant to the issue of consent that to exclude it would undermine the defendant's right to a fair trial, *see R v A (No 2)*. However, such evidence is likely to be relevant to whether the defendant had a reasonable belief in consent (YJCEA 1999, s 41(3)(a)) and therefore an application can be made under that subsection. Where the complainant and defendant have engaged in sexual activity shortly before the alleged assault it may be admissible under YJCEA 1999, s 41(3)(b).

Rebuttal/explanation evidence: YJCEA 1999, s 41(5)

The defence are entitled to apply to adduce evidence of 'sexual behaviour' to rebut a suggestion made by the prosecution. For example, if the prosecution lead evidence that the complainant avoided the defendant after the alleged assault, evidence of a provocative text message sent after the event could be the subject of a YJCEA 1999, s 41(5) application to rebut that suggestion. Similarly, if the prosecution lead evidence that a complainant is a heterosexual male and therefore would never have agreed to engage in sexual activity with the defendant, evidence that the complainant has engaged in consensual homosexual behaviour on a prior occasion may be admissible.

Previous false complaints and statements about sexual behaviour

Evidence that the complainant has made a previous false complaint is relevant both to credit and to the issue of whether or not there was a sexual assault at all. It has been established that such evidence falls outside of the ambit of the YJCEA 1999, s 41, see *R v T; R v H*. It should properly be considered under the CJA 2003, s 100 (evidence of the bad character of a non-defendant).

However, the courts are concerned to avoid abuses of the statutory regime designed to protect complainants. Thus, the defence must establish a proper evidential basis for asserting that a false statement was made by serving material which demonstrates that the complaint was false. Evidence that a previous complaint was not proceeded with will not be adequate. Whilst it may be tempting to rely upon the scepticism of the police or CPS, opinion evidence remains irrelevant and inadmissible. Apart from anything else, attitudes have changed markedly and you may well encounter historic case files that were not progressed due to perceived evidential difficulties or a lack of 'corroboration': such cases would be treated very differently now. The court will not allow the current trial you are involved in to be hijacked into an *exploration* as to whether an old complaint was true or not: you have to have an evidential foundation that demonstrates it was false.

It is for the court to decide whether or not there is a proper evidential basis for the questions that the defence seek to put. Therefore, it is advisable to draft an application under both the YJCEA 199, s 41 and the CJA 2003, s 100. If there is not a sufficient evidential basis for the assertion that a previous allegation was false, by extension the application under s 100 should fail on the basis the evidence does not have substantial probative value in relation to an issue in the case.

Evidential submissions: key points

DO
•   Be aware of time limits to make applications
•   Think carefully about why you want a piece of evidence admitted
•   Know the law, including the pieces of legislation and cases that don't help you

- Generally, raise the point once you spot it (but perhaps hold fire on applications to dismiss until you are confident you are on safe ground)
- Gather further evidence you may need to make your application, eg medical records for some hearsay applications
- Think about the *purpose* of the legislation and the steer in the case law; are you going with the flow of the caselaw, or asking a judge to do something exceptional?
- Be realistic, direct and succinct
- Write a skeleton argument if possible.

DON'T

- Make an application out of time, without acknowledging that fact and explaining why it should still be heard
- Take every point you can, without thinking about whether you should
- Waffle, bluster, or use unnecessarily emotive language
- Ignore the judicial feedback you get as you make your submission

Part V

The Trial: Witnesses

Chapter 13

Witnesses

Mary Cowe and David Scutt

Key references

*   *Archbold: Criminal Pleading, Evidence and Practice 2020*:

    –   8-70a (Rules of evidence and questioning witnesses)

    –   8-146 (Examination-in-chief)

    –   8-215 (Cross-examination)

*   *Blackstone's Criminal Practice 2020*:

    –   F6 (Examination-in-chief)

    –   F7 (Cross-examination)

EXAMINATION-IN-CHIEF

Conducting the examination-in-chief of a witness is an under-rated skill. A good examination-in-chief allows the witness to impart all helpful information in a way that builds confidence in your case.

Preparation is vital: read the witness statement several times and be clear where this witness fits into your overall case. If the statement is cryptic or incomplete, ask the CPS to get a clarification statement. You do not want to be on a voyage of discovery.

Ensure that you only elicit information that is both admissible and relevant. The witness statement or proof that you have may not be the best constructed document, so work out an order of questions that is going to help both the witness and the jury follow the evidence, and prepare to signpost the topics for the witness: 'I'm going to ask you some questions now about New Year's Eve'.

Many witnesses will want to get the whole story out at the start. Approaches differ: many judges prefer that you pause the witness before they move on to the third clause in their sentence. Some advocates will be keen to prevent the very nervous witness clamming up for good and so will risk a little judicial wrath, allowing the initial account to tumble out whilst quickly noting the key points, and then when she stops for breath say, 'let's just recap that slowly'. With a truly garrulous witness, you may need to raise your hand to indicate that a pause has become necessary: apologise for letting them go on without helping them to break matters down, and then re-cap, reminding them that a note is being taken.

You can avoid these dilemmas by explaining in the witness waiting room that evidence will come out much more slowly than in ordinary conversation because the judge will take a note. Explain that you will ask open 'who, what, why, where, when, how' questions: they will get the chance to give the whole story, but it needs to come out fact by fact. Help the witness by asking short, one-fact-at-a-time questions to get the detail from the statement. This approach encourages the witness to get into a rhythm with you.

Further topics to deal with when meeting witnesses pre-trial are explained in the next section on complainants, but remember this meeting is a useful point at which to explain what the actual process of answering questions will be like.

Witnesses may be anxious, tentative or nervous. It is perfectly understandable for a witness to worry about the unknown, worry about public speaking or worry about ruining the case. You are asking them to reconstruct something that happened months ago and was probably upsetting; and to do this under oath, in front of a crowd of strangers, in a nice loud voice. It is intimidating.

Remember that the witness will effectively have been interviewed by a police officer in order to produce the statement. Most people talk about 'going to a girl's house' rather than 'attending the address of a young female'. When you ask the witness questions, use their language – if they want to talk about what Tim did, don't keep calling Tim 'the defendant', when it's clear they are the same person.

Friendly formality is a useful tone to have in mind. Never say anything that could be patronising: if they want to talk about pubs, cars and willies, don't talk about public houses, motor vehicles and penises. You will alienate yourself from the witness and the jury. You can use the witness' words. The rest of your language, your tone and your pace will be enough to indicate to everyone that you are being formal.

The witness will be encouraged to look at the jury at the start of their evidence. Position yourself so that the witness can see your face when you ask your question and you can see the witness answer, but remember that its not a conversation. Remind a witness to look at the jury by turning towards the jury yourself. In chief or in cross examination, you should only look at a jury briefly (always with a neutral expression) to remind the witness of their presence or to check if they can hear.

Some advocates write out all their questions verbatim, some simply jot down some bullet points – this is an individual preference and it will develop, and change, with experience. Having some sort of list will be a comfort and a guide, especially if a witness becomes 'difficult'. If you are 'thrown' by a witness, it will help you get back on track and will help you to keep your thoughts in order. That said, don't be robotic – don't stick to a script come what may. Be prepared to be flexible. Think through how you can sensibly move the witness on from one topic to the next. If there are parts that you foresee being problematic, consider in advance multiple ways to ask the same question.

Don't fear a pause/silence. What seems like an eternity in your own head as you desperately try to think of the next question is probably only a few seconds in reality. Be swan-like on the surface. If you are panicking, don't show it. Take a breath, re-group, carry on. Do not make yourself a hostage to fortune by using 'filler' phrases: 'a few questions if I may' might not be understood or – worse – might be answered with 'I don't have much choice, do I?'.

Ask only essential questions (for example, if identification is not in dispute, you don't need to get a description out of the witness). If you are in any doubt about what may or may not be in issue, speak to your opponent about it.

In a good examination-in-chief, the witness will do most of the talking with short prompts from you. Whether in-chief or in cross-examination, remember to watch the witness and actually listen to the reply you receive. Witnesses often add detail when they are giving evidence. If you are listening properly and that detail is helpful, you can ask piggy-back questions about it and you can amplify it. It's harder than it looks to listen properly and consider if the next question needs to be modified, all whilst maintaining that friendly formality. Keeping the pace measured helps.

If a witness is struggling, be patient. The temptation may be to get it over and done with, but you should take your time. A witness struggling to remember detail may be more compelling from a juror's point of view than a witness who can 'breeze' through the process. A struggling witness may be trying to be as accurate and reliable as possible. You could make a virtue of it in your closing speech.

If a witness strays from the evidence that you want them to deal with, you will see and hear that. You will need to think quickly and carefully about how to coax them back on track. Don't panic. If a witness hasn't answered the question and you need an answer, ask it again. If necessary, you can take the blame for not being as clear as you could have been or find some other appropriate form of words. Be patient, be calm, be kind, take your time. Juries will forgive most witnesses if they falter but they will be less forgiving of the 'professional' who: (a) allows it to happen; and (b) does little or nothing about it.

If what the witness says is inconsistent with other parts of your case, make sure that you have 'trailed' with the jury how it all fits together in your opening. Don't cross-examine your own witness, but draw out what their viewpoint on events was, whether physical or emotional. Be clear about the difference between things the witness actually saw and what they assumed.

If you shut down a witness or airbrush inconvenient bits of evidence the jury will lose their trust in you and in your case. This is true whichever side you are on, but remember that as a prosecutor, you are there to facilitate the truth emerging. If something important in the case is unclear then it is your job to clarify it, not to leave it in a muddle that suits you but doesn't help the jury.

CROSS-EXAMINATION

In cross-examination, you are trying to build a platform of points for an effective closing speech. What are you going to achieve through this witness and how does each question take you towards that purpose? What is an effective questioning sequence? How will your words and tone affect the witness or strike the jury?

Always remember that cross-examination can be 'constructive' as well as 'destructive' (and, if done properly, it can be almost anything between the two). It doesn't *have* to be 'destructive' at all – only when absolutely necessary. You can accentuate the positive aspects of what a witness has to say to suit your case; you can seek to put a different emphasis on the evidence of the witness; you can, where there a number of different witnesses, seek to drive a wedge between them. All of that falls short of actively discrediting a witness – being positively 'destructive'.

When preparing to cross-examine a prosecution witness, read the witness statement and your client's defence statement/proof/interview side by side carefully. Review the unused material and consider how to deploy that which assists you.

There are certain things that you cannot do, such as ask questions simply to insult witnesses or to introduce inadmissible evidence. The one thing you must do is to put your client's case. This means giving a witness the opportunity to comment on key things on which your client relies: the kind of things that featured in the defence statement. Think of this as your duty rather than your right. You do not need to put your draft closing speech to them line by line. Make sure you are asking questions and not making comments.

You can put a case in a variety of ways. 'You're a liar, aren't you' signals to everyone that no new information will now be generated. Prosecuting or defending, avoid Punch and Judy cross-examination. A jury will judge how reasonable your case is in part by how reasonably it is put. Whether the witness agrees with you, and importantly, whether the jury accepts the witness's answer, is likely to depend on how you lead up to that 'case-putting' question.

Are there key points on which a witness may be mistaken? Might the witness accept an error (and thus accept part of your case) if you lead them gently, making it clear from your tone of voice and choice of words that everyone understands why they got the number of knives wrong in a fast-moving incident? You catch more flies with honey than vinegar.

You can often put your case using the formula 'did you/were you' more effectively than via the tag 'isn't that right?'. It's easier to build up an effective sequence of 'did you' questions that take the witness along with your perfectly reasonable suggestions. 'Were you looking forward to your first night out off crutches? Did you go to Steve's house before the club? Was Steve making everyone White Russians? Did you have any? How many? Were you actually quite drunk before you arrived at the club?'

If you need to, you can round off at the end by saying 'You were drinking heavily throughout that night, weren't you?'. The combination of question styles is easier on the ear and the witness will either meet you half-way or look unreasonable.

Closed, leading questions are a vital part of any cross examination, and they should be short. If you are asking one-fact-at-a-time questions, you can test the water as you go along. You will learn when to press on and when to back off.

Be polite, but firm: don't let partial, vague or 'non' answers go, but ask again. Politely ask the witness if they want you to re-phrase the question or ask it again if they are being evasive: make it clear to the jury you are not trying to bamboozle anyone, and you will help if understanding is a problem, but you need an answer. Sometimes asking the question once more will suffice to make the point it hasn't been answered: with some witnesses and some central points, coming back to your question a number of times can be highly effective.

If a witness goes off on a tangent, let them do that initially, and then ask your simple question that hasn't been answered: don't interrupt the witness as this may look rude or as though you don't want the jury to hear the answer. Ask questions as though you are relaxed, in control, and not troubled by any answer.

You should avoid letting (or getting) the witness to repeat their evidence in chief. This is wholly distinct from pressing for a proper answer to your proper questions. Inexperienced cross-examiners (and a worrying number of experienced ones) will 'cross-examine' along the following lines: 'In your evidence today you have said X' (and then asking a question about it).

Don't do this. It amounts to a repetition of examination in chief and, worse still, *you* are doing it for the witness! You are repeating the evidence and you are potentially re-emphasising it and reinforcing it!

Only seek to discredit a witness where you have to. There are many ways of doing so all of which will be case-specific (previous inconsistent statements, bad-character/dishonesty etc). An eye-witness can be seriously undermined by CCTV (where it exists). If the eye-witness has given an account in examination-in-chief which is inconsistent with CCTV you will need to consider whether it is necessary to cross-examine or whether it is better to leave it to your speech. If you cross-examine you risk giving the witness a chance to explain/excuse themselves.

It is a myth that *only* leading questions should be used in cross-examination. You could usefully ask an open question to a witness who has committed themselves to an implausible position. 'Can you help us with what you were doing at Steve's for two hours whilst your friends were drinking?'

Equally, if there are helpful details in a statement that the prosecution didn't adduce, consider eliciting them via open questions. 'You've been asked some questions about the concussion you had suffered before the incident, can you tell us a bit more about how that affected you?'

101

A combination of honeyed 'did you' questions and open questions also work well for prosecutors preparing to cross examine a defendant. This style can build on any admissions made in interview or any undeniable facts. The aim is to bridge the gap between what is beyond dispute and proving the rest of your case. Some defendants will talk themselves half-way there. Be alert to the real possibility a defendant may genuinely not understand you. Keep your questions simple. Expose how unreasonable an evasive or angry defendant is being by continuing to ask short, easily understood, sensible questions.

Testing the evidence of witnesses means asking them questions which may generate doubt about the reliability of their evidence. As we have seen, you want to aim to write a sequence of questions that tests the evidence and ends in you putting your case.

When you defend, you can test a witness' evidence by asking questions concerning the elements of the offence, but you can't state as a fact something that isn't in your instructions. 'You told the jury you were shouting at the man before he attacked you, is that right? How loudly? How close?' tests whether the witness' account leaves self-defence open. But don't accidentally state as a fact 'Mr Reiss only hit you when you hit him first' if your client says he wasn't there! You still need to put his case that he wasn't there.

You must not ask a witness to speculate or put to them other people's evidence. You therefore don't test Mrs O'Leary's identification evidence by telling her that Mrs Singh says it was a confusing scene. Mrs O'Leary can't answer that. However, what you can do is put a flag for the jury: 'You live next door to Mrs Singh I think? Would you say that when you looked out that day, it was a "hideous muddle of bodies"? No? You maintain it was easy to see what was happening?' and move on.

In terms of unused material, make sure that anything that you want in front of the jury is reduced to writing as Agreed Facts before you question any witness.

If you want to rely on something a witness told a third party who created a record (e.g. social services), you will have to ask the witness about that meeting in case they dispute the record made (depending on the witness' vulnerabilities and the extent of the record). Get clarity from the prosecutor about which facts are agreed and which are provisional. Be open with your opponent if you think it's a case to deviate from the usual rules about putting records, and if necessary, justify your position to the judge. Better to have any argument about it without the jury present. Know in advance what you need to put, and what is 'in the bank'.

You need to know what you will do if the witness answers in an unexpected way. This includes the witness unexpectedly agreeing with you! Can you show that they have to agree with you because they have been caught out, or do you just bank it and move on? Don't ask pointless questions just because you have written them down.

Avoid cross-examining witnesses on their statements (or defendants on their interviews) unless there is a meaningful gap between what they said there and what they said in their oral evidence. Judges can take witnesses to any part of their statement, particularly once you've introduced it, if they think you are being selective. Do not lose the confidence of the jury by looking underhand. If a defendant is being more honest now than he was in interview, is that a point worth making or is it counter-productive?

Remember, the ultimate purpose is to build a platform for your speech, not to make a speech. The jury should know what your case is from the questions, but you don't need to make the clever point to the witness: draw the threads together later. Do enough to put your case, generate the material that you need for your speech, and if possible, leave the jury with a question mark over the witness.

Advocates all have different approaches to the issue of risk in cross-examination. Experience will teach you when it is safe to underline a point to take the jury along with you, and when you need to stop talking. You can underline most points in a speech. You can't tell a witness to stop answering the question you wish you hadn't asked! So, when you have built up a good 'speech point', don't ruin it by asking that extra question that allows the witness to generate another excuse or explanation.

Always remember that you are taking the risk on behalf of the client. Only ask questions that have purpose: do not grandstand.

Chapter 14

Complainants

Nick Lee

Key references

- *Archbold: Criminal Pleading, Evidence and Practice 2020*, 8-182 (memory refreshing), 8-197 (hostile witnesses)

- *Blackstone's Criminal Practice 2020*, F6.16 (memory refreshing), F6.48 (hostile witnesses)

- CPS Guidance Speaking to Witnesses at Court: https://www.cps.gov.uk/legal-guidance/speaking-witnesses-court

- Prosecutor's Pledge: https://www.cps.gov.uk/prosecutors-pledge

- Criminal Justice Act 2003 (CJA 2003), ss 120, 139

- Criminal Procedure Act 1865, s 3

INTRODUCTION

The complainant is usually the witness for whom giving evidence will be most stressful – requiring him or her to re-live a traumatic experience in front of strangers, under the gaze of their assailant, and with the defence advocate chipping away at their credibility.

This chapter deals with how to get the best evidence from a complainant when prosecuting. The kind of case envisaged is a theft, a fight in a pub, or domestic violence up to the level of an ABH. Other chapters in this book address vulnerable and child witnesses.

PREPARATION

The complainant may have given several witness statements. You will need to read these carefully. Is a clarification statement needed, or do police need to make further enquiries about additional evidence, such as medical records or text messages? If the complainant's support for prosecution is wavering, consider whether a witness summons should be obtained, or whether it would be counter-productive at this stage. Do the police need to arrange transport to court?

SPEAKING TO WITNESSES AT COURT

As the prosecutor, you will meet witnesses before they give evidence. The CPS Guidance on 'Speaking to Witnesses at Court' (STWAC) sets out your role and obligations. Although this guidance signalled a sea-change in terms of contact with witnesses at court, be aware that it remains absolutely forbidden to discuss the evidence itself with a witness, however briefly or for whatever reason.

This can be a stressful time. If your witnesses arrive at 9.50am for a 10am start, you will need to get a lot of information across to them quickly, while appearing calm. Witness Service volunteers can assist with the mechanics of giving evidence if you have to rush to court to ask for further time.

You should be accompanied by a CPS paralegal when you go to introduce yourself to witnesses. They will have photocopies of the witness statements and expense forms. They should take a note of what is being said.

Do not underestimate how worried most complainants will be about giving evidence, even if they pretend otherwise. They may be desperate for reassurance. You may, unhelpfully, be introduced as 'your barrister'. Gently explain to the witness(s) that you represent the prosecution and that you cannot do your job without witnesses. Their evidence is crucial.

It is good practice to ask complainants (and the other witnesses) what they have already been told about giving evidence by Witness Service. Make sure they understand that:

(i)   They cannot watch the trial until it is their turn to give evidence.

(ii)   They will be brought into court in front of the jury and the judge.

(iii)   They will first have to swear an oath or an affirmation and it is important they answer all questions truthfully. If the answer is 'I don't know', that is the answer. They should not guess.

(iv)   They should say if they do not understand a question.

(v)   (If relevant) There will be special measures in place and what this entails.

(vi)   You will be the first to ask questions; they will be open questions (what, when, where, how and who) designed to elicit a step-by-step account, so the judge and jury can follow and make notes.

(vii)   They should try to keep their voice up and directed at the jury.

(viii) Once you have finished, the defence advocate will begin the cross-examination. This means that the advocate will ask questions to check or test the witness' evidence. They will also make suggestions to the witness

105

based on what the defendant says happened. The witness should answer all the questions truthfully, knowing that if something inappropriate is asked, you will intervene.

(ix)   They do not need to agree with what the defence advocate suggests. If the answer is a firm 'no', that is the answer. If the question asks for a yes or no answer but that does not tell the whole story, it is fine to say 'yes/no, but let me explain'.

(x)   Once they have been released, they are welcome to sit in the public gallery or leave, as they prefer. If they remain, they must not react to the evidence.

It is generally preferable to go over the above points before giving the witnesses copies of their statement(s). Once you do, explain:

(i)   The importance of reading it through carefully before going into court (if they struggle with reading, Witness Service will gladly and discretely help).

(ii)   That the jury will decide the case based on what is said in court and will not read their statement, but the defence and the judge do have it and can ask about it.

(iii)   (Where relevant) That you cannot ask questions about some parts of their statement. You have read the whole statement and understand the background, but the trial will focus on, e.g. what happened on one particular day.

(iv)   They will not have their statement in front of them when giving evidence, but giving evidence is not a memory test, so if their mind goes blank they can ask to refer to their statement.

(v)   If there is anything in their statement which they realise is incorrect when reading it through again, to let one of the Witness Service volunteers know that they need to speak with a CPS paralegal (you may need the OIC to take a further statement).

(vi)   They may be shown exhibits in court. If they haven't seen those exhibits before, ask your opponent and the judge if they can to look at them before giving evidence (it may be best for all concerned to allow the witness this opportunity in a case involving personal or distressing photographs, for example).

(vii)   If there is CCTV footage, they will generally see it in court for the first time, and then only after giving evidence. Their recollection of what happened is what the court really wants to hear.

You should let a complainant (and any other witness) know the general nature of the defence case, e.g. mistaken identity or self-defence. Before disclosing this, you should warn that you are not asking for a response and that you cannot provide details.

If the defence have been given permission to cross-examine on the complainant's bad character or sexual history, you should let the complainant know, without speculating on what questions might be asked.

Likewise, if medical records or other records (such as social services records) have been disclosed, the witness should be informed. Do not speculate on what they might be asked about.

Explain to the witness that you cannot discuss what other witnesses may say, but allow any questions to be asked, even if your answer is just that you are not allowed to discuss that subject. Don't leave your witness(s) worrying about what they are allowed to say.

Communicate all this information in a professional but human way. Check the witnesses' understanding as you go, rather than delivering a high-speed monologue. This should lead to a more confident performance by the witness. A complainant who knows why they are being asked questions in a particular way will be better able to deal with them, whether that means answering slowly in-chief or not being daunted by leading questions in cross-examination.

The record of what the complainant says during their meeting with you should be reviewed for disclosure by you on the spot. If you need time, ask for it. You may simply be able to tell the defence advocate what the witness said (whilst keeping a note for CPS); eg 'I have to say, my memory of the end isn't that good'. It may be something more ambiguous: 'I know what he is going to say, I've been on Facebook'. Don't get into a discussion with the complainant yourself or you risk becoming a witness; instead, task the OIC to obtain a further statement clarifying anything cryptic. Don't leave things hanging.

Don't shy away from other disclosable information, such as if the complainant/witness smells strongly of alcohol. If so, ask the witness (with a CPS member of staff on hand to take a note) if they have been drinking. Let the witness know that you will need to disclose that they smell of alcohol/admit they have been drinking (it may be sensible to let the judge know too). You will need to form your own view on whether you can call them as a reliable witness in their current state.

Be careful not to disclose what each witness has put in their statements to the complainant and ask witnesses not to discuss the case together while waiting to give evidence. You will need to speak separately with any witnesses who have particular concerns or whose statements raise particular issues, at least on those points.

Complainants and other witnesses should be warned that criminal trials rarely proceed smoothly and they may have to wait. Do your best to keep them posted on any delays. Thank the complainant for coming to court and acknowledge it is a difficult thing to do. It may also be helpful to manage expectations more generally in some cases and to remind a complainant – if necessary through the OIC – that giving evidence is an important achievement in itself.

NON-ATTENDING COMPLAINANT

Witnesses who do not show up are a worry; without them you have no case. If they are late, ask the Witness Care Unit or the OIC to contact them. Keep the court updated with your enquiries. It may help for police to attend their address and offer a lift to court, or you may need to consider asking for a witness summons.

If a summons is already in place, consider carefully, in consultation with the CPS, if you are going to apply for it be executed. Considerations include the welfare of the complainant, the public interest in proceeding with a case with an unwilling witness, and the likely quality of the resulting evidence. Make sure you have a proper understanding of the source of the reluctance before taking any significant steps: pressure from defendant, genuine ill-health, conflicting emotions? Ask for time if in doubt; don't start inviting others to make case-ending decisions simply because a witness who has been a bit volatile in the past is not in the building at 10.33 am; there may be many reasons for this. If the witness cannot be found, an adjournment to gather more information will be the first step.

The complainant may have an Independent Domestic Violence Advisor (IDVA) who will be well-placed to inform your decision-making.

EXAMINING ON EXHIBITS

There are generally two aspects to adducing exhibits: provenance and significance. Whenever possible, try to reduce the provenance of exhibits into agreed facts in advance (eg 'The photographs exhibited at page 4 of the jury bundle were taken at 02:13 on Saturday 9 May 2020 by PC Miller').

If the provenance of an exhibit is not agreed, this will need to be adduced from the relevant witness. Keep it simple: 'Who took this photograph? When did you take it? Where did you take it?'. Don't shy away from anything that requires explanation: 'Why did you wait for two days before taking photographs of your injury? Had anything else happened to you in the meantime that could have caused this bruise?'

The significance of the exhibit is usually something the witness will have to explain in his evidence, eg 'I got that black eye when the defendant punched me'. When to put an exhibit to a witness is your decision. Consider the 'flow' of their evidence, including when will be a natural point in the story to pause and look at the photograph, and whether it will distress the witness. The usher will hand a copy to the judge first (in case there is any reason the exhibit should not be adduced), before the witness and jury. If it is an object like a piece of clothing, consider in advance if you want the jury to look at it immediately, or if you will ask for it to be passed around later.

Any exhibits which are adduced during trial (whether CCTV clips, knives, photocopies of VAT returns or the MG15 interview transcript) require a number. So when you adduce the exhibit, ask for it to be 'exhibit 1' and so on.

MEMORY REFRESHING

The statutory provisions are set out at the CJA 2003, s 139. The witness may ask to refresh his memory, or you or the judge might suggest it if the witness is floundering to remember a certain detail.

It is not enough that the witness is not giving you the answer you wanted – it must be because he genuinely cannot remember the detail in question. Asking the judge's permission for your witness to refresh his memory from his statement is your application, not that of the witness. You do not have to wait for the complainant to say, 'I can't remember'.

Before the statement is given to the witness, you must:

(i) Adduce that his statement was made at an earlier point in time when his memory of the event was likely to have been significantly better than it is now ('did you make a statement on the day of the incident? Were events any easier to remember then than they are now?').

(ii) Ask the judge's permission for the witness to refresh his memory from his statement.

If permission is given, the judge will inform the jury that this is normal practice. Once the statement is handed to the witness, you should:

(i) Confirm that is the statement he made on such and such a date.

(ii) Guide him to the specific part of the statement he has been struggling to recall.

(iii) Ask him to read the relevant sentence or paragraph to himself first, and then ask your original question again: 'having read that, can you remember the colour of the second car?' (he may say no, in which case consider whether you can elicit the detail another way, whether he is being hostile, or whether that is a detail your case will just have to do without).

(iv) Ask him to put the statement to one side.

(v) Continue your examination-in-chief.

The judge retains a discretion not to allow a witness to refresh their memory from their written statement. The more controversial or unusual the detail, the more likely permission will be refused, as the judge may feel such a distinctive detail should have stuck in the memory.

You may ask a witness to refresh their memory from notes – such as a police officer's notebook or some other contemporaneous record. The defence must be given a chance to inspect the notes first. The notes themselves do not become evidence in the case unless cross-examination goes beyond the section on which the witness has been asked to refresh their memory, and you make a successful application for the notes to be shown to the jury so they can follow the witness's evidence more easily. Under the CJA 2003, s 120 you would then be entitled to ask the jury to rely on the notes for the truth of their contents.

HOSTILE WITNESSES

The Criminal Procedure Act 1865, s 3 prevents a party from calling into question the credibility of their own witness unless the witness proves to be 'adverse'. In short: you cannot accuse your own witness of lying unless the judge gives you permission to do so.

The judge must conclude that the witness is 'hostile' to the prosecution and no longer 'desirous of telling the truth', rather than simply a poor witness. The judge will make this decision based on the demeanour of the witness, the answers given in response to questioning, or a refusal to answer without a sensible explanation.

There are numerous reasons why a witness might turn 'hostile'. The complainant may be reconciled with their partner and lie to protect them. A witness may have been intimidated before trial, or have their own reasons for not co-operating.

Before applying to treat the witness as hostile, you must first give her the opportunity to refresh her memory from her written statement. If the complainant is still 'not desirous of telling the truth', an application should be made to the judge to treat the witness as hostile. It is exceptional for this stage to be reached. If permission is given, you may cross-examine your own witness about any aspects of the case, and suggest a reason for why they is now lying (eg they now trying to protect the partner who assaulted them).

You are then permitted to suggest in your closing speech that what the complainant said in their witness statement, or during their 999 call, was the truth – not what they said in evidence.

A judge will warn a jury about the need for caution when approaching the testimony of a witness who has fundamentally contradicted themselves. It is a significant step to make this application; do all you can to bring the witness to their original account by means of memory refreshing and traditional questioning.

Hopefully, this situation will not arise because you will have identified the complainant's reluctance when meeting them before she gives evidence, and any concerns they wanted to raise will have been ventilated.

RECALLING A WITNESS

A witness may be recalled by the prosecution if the defendant's evidence raises new matters which were not put to them in cross-examination. Before doing so, you will want the OIC to take a statement from the complainant on the new matters.

The defendant will usually conclude their evidence (including your cross-examination) before the witness is recalled for examination-in-chief and cross-examination on the new matters. The defendant will not usually have a chance to respond – they have forfeited that right by bringing up these issues so late.

Chapter 15

Child and vulnerable witnesses

Ian Fenny

Key references

• Criminal Practice Directions 2015 Division V: Evidence https://www.justice.gov.uk/courts/procedure-rules/criminal/docs/2015/crim-practice-directions-V-evidence-2015.pdf

• The Advocate's Gateway: https://www.theadvocatesgateway.org/

• CPS guidance on ABE interviews and special measures: www.cps.gov.uk/publications/docs/best_evidence_in_criminal_proceedings.pdf

• Inns of Court Training Materials: Advocacy & the Vulnerable (Crime): icca.ac.uk/advocacy-the-vulnerable-crime

• Achieving Best Evidence in Criminal Proceedings: www.cps.gov.uk/publications/docs/best_evidence_in_criminal_proceedings.pdf.

• Youth Justice and Criminal Evidence Act 1999 (YJCEA 1999), ss 16–30, 41–43

• Modern Slavery Act 2015, ss 1, 2

• Criminal Procedure Rules 2015, SI 2015/1490 (CPR 2015)

Case law

• *R v Lubemba (Cokesix)* [2014] EWCA Crim 2064

• *R v PMH* [2018] EWCA Crim 2452

• *R v YGM* [2018] EWCA Crim 2458

A BRIEF HISTORY

Believe it or not it wasn't that long ago that children and vulnerable witnesses were almost entirely disenfranchised from the Criminal Justice System and were in practice unable to give evidence.

The media view was that the paedophile personality of Jimmy Savile changed the landscape. Not true: in fact, by the late 1980s there existed a growing acceptance that the exclusion of children and vulnerable witnesses was an injustice in itself. By the early 1990s there was a sea change. From then on, children and vulnerable witnesses would be spared the ordeal of repeating their allegations live before a jury.

Their evidence-in-chief was to be recorded by way of an ABE (Achieving Best Evidence) interview (YJCEA 1999, s 27). A trained police officer would ask the questions.

Cross examination would be conducted in accordance with special measures applications that allowed for:

(i)   livelink; the witness cross-examined via a video link from another room;

(ii)   cross-examination behind screens, out of sight of the defendant, but in view of the jury; or

(iii) if the witness so chose, cross-examination in the conventional form.

This was a hybrid solution. It had obvious flaws, the principle one being the significant time lapse between the ABE interview and the trial, which was particularly unfortunate where the witness was a child or was vulnerable.

The trial process has waited two decades for the solution now provided by the YJCEA 1999, s 28. Examination-in-chief remains the initial interview conducted by the police – the ABE interview. Cross-examination of qualifying witnesses will now take place well before the trial. The cross-examination (and re-examination) will be digitally recorded and played later at the trial.

THE BACKDROP

It's important to emphasise that the digitisation of the evidence of a qualifying witness is not an easy option or an excuse for minimal preparation.

Subject to appropriate editing, ABE interviews are now admitted as a matter of course. Their framework is set out in 'Achieving Best Evidence in Criminal Proceedings'.

Upon application by the defence, the court has a discretion to exclude the interview, in whole or in part, where it considers it against the interests of justice to admit it (YJCEA 1999, s 27(2), (3)). This is a rare occurrence, and usually only raised if there has been a breach of the guidelines. If the court is satisfied that, irrespective of such a breach, the witness has given a credible and accurate account, then it will be left to the jury to decide if it is reliable or not.

The statutory framework for all special measures is set out in the YJCEA 1999, ss 16–30.

Those eligible are defined in ss 16 and 17 and include:

(a)   all child witnesses (ie those under 18 at the time of the special measures application);

(b)   someone with mental disorder, significantly impaired social functioning or intelligence;

(c)   someone with a physical disability or disorder;

(d)   someone eligible through fear, distress or intimidation.

A child witness enjoys an automatic qualification for special measures.

Applications for witnesses suffering from a disorder, mental or physical, will require evidence in support. The test is 'Does their disability, and/or vulnerability diminish the quality of their evidence? Will the granting of special measures help this?' Where a judge is so satisfied, then the application is invariably granted.

A frightened, distressed or intimidated witness will require some contextual evidence (an additional statement) in support, save where the allegation involves offences of slavery or human trafficking (Modern Slavery Act 2015, ss 1, 2).

Child witnesses and those with other vulnerabilities may require assistance in expressing themselves and understanding what is asked of them. The CPR 2015 provide that assistance from an intermediary can be granted for any young or vulnerable witness.

An intermediary is a communication specialist whose role is to enable the witness and any questioner to understand each other. The Registered Intermediary Procedural Guidance Manual 2019 (which can be accessed through the Advocate's Gateway) sets out how their support can be obtained in practice by prosecutors: police officers should consider obtaining an intermediary assessment of a witness prior to an ABE if there are concerns around understanding or communication.

An intermediary is obtained through a 'matching service' which marries up the particular skills of the intermediary to the particular needs of the witness. It is important for sufficient information to be provided to the matching service (which may include third party records) for an appropriate specialist to be identified. Intermediaries can also be invited to conduct assessments post-ABE. In any case, the intermediary must produce a comprehensive report which will be considered by the judge when deciding whether to grant an application for the intermediary to assist at trial.

There is no statutory framework in relation to the use of intermediaries by defendants, but the judge has the inherent jurisdiction to grant such an application. It is vital that the need for an intermediary for a defendant is flagged at an early stage. A formal application will then be required. It is the court who will authorise payment for the intermediary to either attend throughout trial or when the defendant gives evidence. Building up the required evidence to show that that such an intermediary is needed and then to identify an appropriate non-registered intermediary will all take time.

PREPARATION FOR TRIAL

At the earliest opportunity consideration must be given to the content of the ABE and certainly no later than Stage 2 of the Pre-trial process. Does it require editing? They almost always do. It is a matter of style as to who begins the editing process (prosecution or defence) but the obvious areas to address are

(i)   irrelevant material;

(ii)   repetitive material;

(iii)   inadmissible evidence;

(iv)   evidence where a complainant has spoken of previous sexual experiences or encounters (see YJCEA 1999, ss 41–43); and

(v)   ensuring that evidence of truth and lies is sufficiently covered where the issue of competency may be important.

On rare occasions an ABE is so bad that it is advisable for the prosecution to consider whether it should be abandoned, and the witness called to give live evidence. Such a sensitive decision will be determined by the age, capability and resilience of the witness.

There is then the decision about what form special measures should take during the trial. In a case where a witness's face has never been seen by the defendant and the witness is anxious to remain unknown, a screen will give better protection. Video-link may feel safer (the witness will not be in the same room as the defendant), but the defendant will be able to see the witness's face clearly on the video-link. With screens they will hear but never see the witness.

It's important to note that however much the authorities seek to digitise the Criminal Justice system, a trial remains a resolutely analogue experience. Jurors will assess witnesses however their evidence is presented. Be alive to the danger that evidence presented through the medium of a screen or via a video link may distance the jury from the witness. The younger the witness, or the more obvious their vulnerability and the more traumatic the allegation, the less the risk. The converse applies.

Many prosecutors deal with the possible alienation of the witness from the jury in their opening speech, particularly where a video link is being utilised. In that way, the jury are aware that they are not watching television but a real experience of importance and that they must try not to be distracted by the format in which it is presented.

When prosecuting, always satisfy yourself that special measures have been properly considered and understood. Many who would ordinarily qualify for video link will consider screens if they are aware of any potential disadvantage to them. Special measures are designed to achieve best evidence, and thus always witness specific.

The decision as to which special measure is to be applied can be varied at any stage before the trial (or indeed during the trial itself). A judge will always be open to a request for a change to special measures if you explain the reason.

At the Pre-Trial Preparation hearing (PTPH) the preparatory steps for trial will be considered and timetables set.

When prosecuting ensure the following:

(a)   You are aware of all vulnerabilities and requirements that will affect the witness's ability to give best evidence. Put in place strategies that will minimise the risks identified. Touch base with the Officer in the Case as soon as you can.

(b)   Consider how long each witness will take. Create a list of the order of witnesses, often known as 'a batting order' (an art as much as a science) that avoids a witness being kept waiting or being adjourned part heard overnight.

(c)   Where the YJCEA 1999, s 28 applies (see below) make the application and if opposed argue it.

(d)   Where you have more than one young or vulnerable witness, consider the order in which you call them, bearing in mind the impact each will have on the jury and which witnesses will take more time to settle.

(e)   Where you are relying upon the evidence of one complainant to support the complaint of another ensure you have drafted the appropriate bad character notice.

(f)   Make sure that any expert report upon which you rely deals with important points and dispels any myths that might exist, eg be clear about whether a negative forensic finding means that something could not have happened, or if it is in fact neutral.

(g)   It is good practice to conduct a hearing which sets out the 'ground rules' for questioning witnesses in any case involving a vulnerable witness. It is essential in a case involving an intermediary. Read the toolkit on ground rules hearings.

(h)   Plan when you propose a meeting with the witness. Not too soon, or they will forget you, not so late that it seems rushed and ill considered. Such meetings are dealt with in the complainants' section of this book.

(i)   Consider the state of third party disclosure, eg whether the police/ CPS have contacted agencies such as schools, social services, doctors, counsellors or the Family Court, setting out in detail the issues in the case and the species of material that may undermine the prosecution or assist the defence. This will need to be reviewed after a defence statement is received.

QUESTIONING VULNERABLE WITNESSES

It is critical to understand that the days of child or vulnerable witnesses being exposed to lengthy, rigorous, and combative cross examination are gone. In their place has come targeted, economical and appropriate questions. These are routinely reduced into writing for an intermediary to scrutinise and, if necessary, modify.

Decisions about whether questions need to be reviewed in advance and the ultimate decision about whether any question can be asked is for the trial judge, not the intermediary. You will find that the more you constructively engage with the intermediary to find another way to get to a particular question, the more likely you are to be effective.

Useful general guidance on the appropriate styles to be employed when questioning children or people with vulnerabilities is on the Advocate's Gateway under toolkits but read any intermediary report in your own case carefully: a witness-specific approach is required.

In approaching cross examination of any child or vulnerable witness the following are self-evident:

(a)   Understand the capacity and capability of the witness.

(b)   Phrase any question with that in mind.

(c)   Make sure questions only contain one topic at a time.

(d)   Always sign post the questions to be asked.

(e)   Questions should follow a logical (and if possible) chronological sequence.

(f)   Never ask a leading or tag question.

(g)   Pace your questions appropriately.

(h)   Adopt a calm and neutral tone.

Consider carefully the extent to which you must put your case to the witness, and how this is best done. Always discuss such an approach with the judge.

There is a tension between the judicial desire to prevent vulnerable witnesses being cross-examined about unnecessary points of detail that can be put to other witnesses, and the need to ensure that the core defence case is in some way put to the witness.

The Court of Appeal in *Lubemba* said:

'It is now generally accepted that if justice is to be done to the vulnerable witness and also to the accused, a radical departure from the traditional style of advocacy will be necessary. Advocates must adapt to the witness, not the other way round. They cannot insist upon any supposed right 'to put one's case' or previous inconsistent statements to a vulnerable witness. If there is a right to 'put one's case' (about which we have our doubts) it must be modified for young or vulnerable witnesses. It is perfectly possible to ensure the jury are made aware of the defence case and of significant inconsistencies without intimidation or distressing a witness.'

Judges will doubtless continue to remind advocates of these sentiments, especially those advocates in danger of straying into 'traditional' methods of cross examination which are partly aimed at attracting the jury's attention rather than a response from the witness.

However, judges have also been alerted to the fact that a failure to put a case to a witness can in some cases disadvantage the defence, and in other cases, it can disadvantage the prosecution. What is a jury to do if a witness says she was sexually assaulted and in cross-examination she agrees that sometimes the defendant innocently tickled her, but she is not asked about the assault? It should be possible to find a way to let the witness understand that it is being suggested that the assault did not happen. Prosecutors should be aware that it may cause unfairness to their case if a witness is not allowed to comment on the defence being advanced.

The Court of Appeal in *R v RK* said:

'Although this court has in the past doubted the *right* to put every aspect of the defence case to a vulnerable witness, whatever the circumstances, it has not questioned the general *duty* to ensure the defence case is put fully and fairly and witnesses challenged, where that is possible.'

The case of *R v YGM* provides useful guidance on a staged approach to these issues.

Where a witness is under 18 at the time of the special measures hearing or suffers from a relevant mental disorder or physical disability or a significant impairment of intelligence and social functioning, the enactment of the YJCEA 1999, s 28 means that cross examination will take place before the trial. It will be conducted by live link, recorded, and then played during the trial.

The Criminal Practice Directions 2015, PD 18E (as amended) is essential reading. Early identification of a case as 'a section 28 case', and swift consideration of all aspects of disclosure are needed. The prosecution application will be heard at the PTPH by which time the case will need to be in a good state of preparedness. The ground rules hearing will normally be shortly after the service of the defence statement, and the section 28 hearing itself will be shortly after the ground rules. The section 28 hearing will take precedence over other hearings and once such a hearing has been conducted by the instructed advocate, they are then committed to the subsequent trial.

The same considerations, as outlined above, will apply to the questioning of witnesses in this way in terms of questioning style. The case of *R v PMH* considered the impact of the YJCEA 1999, s 28 on trial preparation and questioning, and the particular care that must be taken in terms of reviewing the risk of cross examination.

An excellent training programme for those involved in questioning vulnerable witnesses can be found at 'Advocacy & the Vulnerable (Crime) icca.ac.uk/advocacy-the-vulnerable-crime' alongside links to other useful material that can make your advocacy more effective.

A general word of caution when defending in such cases: recognise that the default position of a jury will be to have sympathy towards a young child or a vulnerable adult. The jury will understand the real difficulties that such a witness encounters: make sure you do, too.

Chapter 16

Dealing with police witnesses

Susan Cavender and David Scutt

INTRODUCTION

The term 'police witness' covers a wide range of different roles within police forces. Some are police officers (of various ranks), some are civilians. Your starting point is to know how to address the witness properly. 'Officer' will cover police officers, although you may choose to address them more formally by their rank. If you are prosecuting, you should meet your witnesses before they give evidence and take the time to ask them their preferred mode of address; if you are defending take your lead from the prosecutor (who will have called the witness before you cross-examine).

A police witness will deal with a wide variety of topics, some more technical than others. Other chapters of this book deal with your approach to witness handling – much of this guidance will be applicable to police evidence.

PROSECUTING

Do not assume that your police witness is going to be an experienced or confident witness. Some will need help and guidance, just like many other witnesses in the Crown Court.

Most police witnesses will take their allotted place in the running order of the trial but if you are prosecuting you will want the 'officer in the case' (OIC) to be present at court (preferably in court, sitting right behind you, unless there is objection made to that course which you either concede or is upheld by the judge) throughout the trial.

Although a case-worker from the Crown Prosecution Service may well be present in court during the course of the prosecution case, there are many ways in which the OIC will be a valuable resource.

They can, by way of a few examples, be your 'sounding-board', your guide to the evidence overall, your fact-checker, your researcher, your witness manager, and a willing officer will even be your runner and administrative assistant when an extra pair of hands is needed urgently. However well you prepare for a trial, there will always be questions to be asked and, hopefully, the OIC will have the answers -or can get them for you.

At trial the OIC:

- will be responsible for getting exhibits to and from court and looking after them once they are there (you are *not* responsible for guns, knives, drugs etc);

- can deal with any defence questions, informally as the trial progresses and/or formally in their evidence to the jury. Whenever possible it is best to formulate Agreed Facts which the jury will take away with them as a written reminder of the agreed evidence, and also to reduce the number of questions to be dealt with in evidence;

- can deal with any particular part they played in the investigation (eg observations, arrest, interview etc);

- can (and almost invariably will) help with the presentation of the defendant's interview(s) to the jury. The time-honoured approach is for the officer to read the questions and for the prosecutor to read the introduction/summarised portions and the answers given by the defendant (which is not as easy as you might think – sending the agreed edited version the night before they are due to read it out can help officers present it properly);

- can deal with 'sweeping up' questions. These are the sort of questions which explain why something was done or not done as part of the investigation – but be careful that they do not deal with things outside the officer's remit/knowledge unless you have the agreement of the defence;

- can deal with the defendant's good/bad character. If the latter you will, of course, have obtained the consent of the court first. In any case, agree a formula of words with the defence and the officer to prevent inadmissible detail emerging or to prevent an officer giving a begrudging 'I believe so' answer when asked about good character.

Make sure your officer is 'on the same page' as you about their role. Sometimes you may have an officer who (understandably) is keen to point out that they were not the original OIC or tells you this is their first case of this sort. This is useful information, but if they are the OIC now they will have to get up to speed and be familiar with all aspects of the case. Gently check this: are they on top of the evidence, have they read the crime log of enquiries to gain an overview of the investigation, are they aware of what has and has not been disclosed to the defence?

Your officer will know that is their job to investigate all reasonable lines of enquiry and not to gather evidence to secure the conviction of a suspect, but this fair-mindedness should come across in their evidence. If the officer signals that they are inexperienced, ensure they know it is not their job to stick the boot in. They need to be clear, accurate and fair in their evidence. However, it is also not their job to agree with any defence proposition to get out of a tight spot: if they are asked a question and they don't know the answer, make sure that they know it is better to admit that and ask for time to find the answer, rather than make unwarranted concessions.

It can be useful to ask the defence in advance if there are any particular documents the OIC will need in the witness box during their evidence. This will focus your officer's mind and also make them more confident in saying 'that particular document is on the desk behind the prosecutor, may I retrieve it to check' rather than agreeing with a loosely phrased proposition.

DEFENDING

Treat generic police witnesses in the same way as you would any other witness. Follow the basic 'rules' of cross-examination. Ask yourself: 'do I *need* to ask any questions?'.

The OIC can be asked questions about the investigation which are designed to point out where you think there has been a failure to follow lines of enquiry which might undermine the Crown's case or assist the defence. That, of course, is part of their remit but it can be an angle of the investigation that can sometimes be forgotten in the rush to prove the defendant guilty.

Why were there no house-to-house enquiries? How much effort went into tracing the other people seen on the CCTV? Why was there no identity parade requested from witnesses who thought they would recognise the culprit if they saw them again? Check the PACE Codes for these points – and be ready to quote them to the officer.

Cross-examination of the officer in the case can be highly effective but there are risks. You may want to highlight gaps in the evidence or purported 'failures' in the investigation but be careful, feel your way. Some officers will give you straightforward 'yes/no/don't know' answers but others will be more expansive and may successfully explain away the point you want to make.

It's therefore important to make sure you are on firm ground before you embark on this sort of questioning; hopefully these are matters of disclosure raised in your defence statement and you know for sure (for example) that others weren't traced from CCTV, and you can tell from reading the crime log that efforts weren't made. Then, if the officer says he *thinks* some efforts were made, you can ask confidently where this is recorded. This is generally not the time to find out new information: this is time to let the jury know via the officer about the gaps you have already identified.

Even if the officer has given you a helpful answer, there is still a risk from effective re-examination, particularly if the prosecution advocate is in a position to say 'did the suspect mention that possibility in interview? Have you ever been asked to make those enquiries by the defence?'.

Many defence advocates, understandably, want to get 'good points' into the jurors' minds as soon as possible but be aware that this can risk diminishing the point you wish to make:

- the officer may be able to provide an explanation or excuse; or

- your prosecutor may or may not have been alert to the point and ready to deal with it in re-examination and/or in their closing speech. By making the point in cross examination you flag it up and *ensure* that your prosecutor is not only aware of the point but will also have ample opportunity to deal with it in re-examination or their closing speech.

You are not obliged to give the officer in the case an opportunity to explain or excuse anything done or not done.

If you have 'good points', consider saving them for your closing speech when no-one can answer back.

Chapter 17

Expert witnesses

Anjali Gohil

Key references

- *Archbold: Criminal Pleading, Evidence and Practice 2020*, 10–35

- Crown Court Compendium 10–3

- Criminal Procedure Rules 2015, SI 2015/1490 (CPR 2015), Part19

- Criminal Practice Directions 2015, Div V, 19A

INTRODUCTION

By now you will understand that ordinarily, witnesses give evidence as to fact – what they saw, heard, touched, tasted or could smell. Their evidence is confined to that experienced through their five senses. Any opinions that can safely be drawn from their evidence is solely a matter for the jury. Witnesses do not give opinion evidence.

However, expert witnesses fall into a different category. They are also permitted to give evidence of fact (eg what is DNA, what tests were conducted) but additionally they may give evidence of opinion (eg to what extent does the result of tests conducted establish that the DNA matches that of X?).

The key is that the jury will be directed that it is for them to decide whether they accept the opinions offered. A good place to start your thinking about expert evidence is to read the draft directions supplied to judges within the Crown Court Compendium – this will assist you in understanding how expert evidence may be used by a jury.

STEP 1: IS EXPERT EVIDENCE ADMISSIBLE?

The first issue is whether the evidence is *relevant to a matter in issue* in the proceedings. That is straightforward if, for example, DNA is discovered at the scene of a burglary, it matches with DNA retrieved from the defendant who denies that they were there. However, be aware of the need for expert evidence to go to a matter in issue – for example, if presence is accepted by the defendant but the issue is whether they participated in any theft, then DNA evidence may have no relevance at all.

The second issue is whether expert evidence is *needed to provide information likely to be outside the court's own knowledge or experience*. Reference to the court includes the jury as well as the judge.

A good example of the operation of this principle in practice lies in the area of CCTV evidence. There is often a temptation to instruct experts to view CCTV and to provide opinion upon the suggestion that person X is the defendant. Indeed, police officers, having viewed a piece of footage may offer their opinion as to what the CCTV shows within their witness statements.

It is important to be clear whether the officer is being presented simply as a witness like any other who is capable of making an identification, perhaps because of their familiarity with the defendant, or whether it is being suggested that because of the officer's training or manipulation of the footage, he is being presented as an expert. If the officer is in reality doing no more than supplying his own opinion of what a jury can see for themselves, their evidence is not outside the knowledge or experience of the court and is therefore inadmissible (*Archbold*, 14–33).

In some cases, you may wish to instruct an analyst who can enhance CCTV imagery and may also be able to comment upon the effect of lighting, height of camera, obstructions, how colours may or may not appear depending upon the quality of cameras used, particularly if stills from one camera are used to identify a person captured by another camera. Such technical information is likely to be outside the knowledge of the court.

Of course, an expert must have the necessary *competence* to be described as such and this is worth examining when you receive an expert report. Ask yourself:

- What are their qualifications?

- What is the extent of their experience?

- Has their work and methodology been peer reviewed?

This is particularly relevant where cutting edge technologies or new scientific methods/diagnoses have been deployed or where subjective evaluations, based on experience, are being provided. It is essential that you understand what is really in dispute in your case so that you can instruct the right kind of expert: does the issue need to be addressed by, for example, a forensic expert, a statistican, a pharmacologist? A complex topic may require more than one expert. Any expert chosen must be competent to give evidence on the specific topic under consideration.

STEP 2: HOW DO I CHOOSE AN EXPERT?

Research is key. Make full use of the internet and expert witness databases in order to shortlist suitable candidates. One practical tip is to ensure that the person instructed not only has the requisite academic or practical experience but is also able to communicate his or her views clearly, persuasively and with authority. That is where your colleagues come in, particularly those more senior – they will have years of experience instructing and cross-examining experts and will be able to provide a steer in the direction of experts who are well respected and perform well in court.

STEP 3: OBTAINING AND CONSIDERING A REPORT

First, identify precisely the issues you would like your expert to consider. This should be contained within an advice setting out the following:

(a)   summary of the allegations and evidence;

(b)   the issue(s) you wish your expert to consider;

(c)   instructions to your instructing solicitor to provide a copy of all relevant exhibits, case papers, data etc to the expert;

(d)   In many cases, a catch-all request for the expert to identify and comment upon any other relevant issue within their expertise – assuming that you don't have any concerns about an expert advising prematurely on any point; and

(e)   a request to advise upon the need to instruct any different type of expert.

It is worth bearing in mind when drafting an advice that this may be disclosable to the other side in the event your expert is relied upon: when you are defending, you may not want notes from the police station or other legally privileged material recited in your report.

If you are prosecuting a case and you are instructed after an expert report has been obtained, and you have concerns about its completeness, it is never too late to set out in writing the other issues that require consideration.

Once in receipt of an expert report it is crucial that you understand what has been considered, the methodology used, the conclusions reached and the reasoning behind those conclusions. To that end, read, read and re-read the report until you are familiar with it.

Where an expert report refers to other research, read it and become familiar with learning on the topic. It is also extremely useful to research best practice guidelines if they exist – whether UK or international.

Thereafter, it is worth drafting a list of questions which arise by reference to highlighted passages. Clarification may be needed, other questions may arise from the material, or you might be concerned about something which has not been explicitly considered. In that situation it is often extremely useful to have a conference with your expert.

An advocate should not be afraid to ask questions of their own expert in order better to develop an understanding of the evidence they will give or indeed the topic at hand.

Use the discussion at conference to consider and enlarge upon the type of questions you might want to ask when cross-examining the opposing expert.

There may be passages in the expert report produced by the opposing side which appear to be stated as matters of fact but which, upon closer examination, you realise are a series of assumptions which require closer scrutiny. Your expert will be in a position to guide you through this when you have your conference with them. It is then your task to craft clear questions which undermine the series of assumptions and – you hope – the conclusions they have reached.

In addition to understanding the subject matter of the report, make sure you are aware of the formal requirements for expert reports found in the CPR 2015. Are you happy that your expert has complied with not just the letter but the spirit of those rules? A conference with your expert is a good time to consider the impact they will have on the jury: will everyone be impressed by someone who is independent, fair-minded and rigorous, or do you have any concerns about how they express themselves or deal with questions?

Once you are confident in your understanding of your own and/or opposing expert views it will be necessary to communicate your advice to the client and to take instructions on whether the report should be relied upon. Be clear, concise and thorough in advising of the pros and cons of relying upon the report – it is often worth setting out your own views in writing for your instructing solicitor.

When you are prosecuting, all of the material generated in this process (notes of any conference which contain further opinons from the expert, the expert report itself) will become unused material if not relied upon by the prosecution.

When you are defending, although you are obliged to tell the prosecution the identity of any expert instructed, you are not obliged to disclose a report upon which you do not intend to rely. You cannot mislead the court in your conduct of the case, but you can use the knowledge in an expert report which you have not served as a basis for cross-examination in order to test the conclusions of the prosecution expert.

STEP 4: PRE-TRIAL

If relying upon expert evidence the first step is to serve your report upon the other side. They will be entitled to peruse all working notes made and materials considered by your expert (except legally privileged material).

Once in receipt of expert reports on both sides, arrange for the experts to discuss the issues upon which they have been instructed and to reach agreement if possible on as many areas as they can.

The result of this discussion can then be reduced into a document summarising the areas of agreement and disagreement, and reasons for dispute, signed by both experts and supplied to the court in accordance with the timetable set by the court.

This document will allow the court to manage the evidence by narrowing the issues and enable the parties to focus upon areas of disagreement, thereby providing the jury with clarity as to the factual matters which they must determine.

Does there need to be a 'voir dire'? The phrase (to see/to speak) denotes a short trial within a trial to enable the court to determine disputed preliminary facts in the absence of the jury, such as a challenge as to the competence of a proposed expert. This should be raised with the court as soon as the issue arises so that consideration as to whether a pre-trial legal argument should be listed.

It is worth considering with the court whether the experts should be interposed at a sensible point during trial in order that they can give their evidence one after the other. It is crucial that both experts are in court to hear the evidence of the other so that they can comment upon it. Again, advocates should be alive to the practicalities.

STEP 5: CROSS-EXAMINING AN EXPERT

Preparation is key. An advocate who is familiar with the experts' jargon but has thought through how to ask clear, concise questions in order to elicit relevant information stands out. Avoid waffle.

Master your papers – have copies of any articles, research, academic papers and best practice guidelines to hand, in addition to the experts' reports themselves. Familiarise yourself with them, and have your own copy marked up/highlighted.

Be clear in your own mind about the points you wish to be able to make in your closing speech and prepare to ask a series of questions which will establish the foundation for your points – set about this task in a clear, persuasive and logical way.

For example, if the evidence in dispute relates to DNA evidence and you want to establish there is doubt as to whether that evidence demonstrates strong support for the contention that X committed a burglary, you may wish to take the expert through a series of questions establishing the difference between primary and secondary transfer. Give easy to understand examples along the way:

1   DNA is contained in sweat?

2   If I touch this glass I may transmit my DNA to this glass?

3   Is that called primary transfer?

4   If I shake hands with you and you then touch this glass, can my DNA be transferred to this glass?

5   Have I deposited my DNA on to your hand by shaking your hand?

6   If you then touch this glass, might that deposit my DNA on to the glass?

7   Is that called secondary transfer?

8   Does that mean that my DNA can then appear on this glass without my ever having touched it?

9   In the circumstances of this case, is it correct that your evidence is confined to the fact that DNA matching that of X was recovered from Y?

10   But you cannot help us with how that DNA came to be there?

Be alert to the fact that once you ask the question, the judge will let the expert answer! You would want to be absolutely sure that the expert had not formally considered secondary transfer/the level of DNA before asking the question above or you may risk strengthening the prosecution case.

Make use of your own expert when preparing for your cross-examination of the opposing expert and be ready to listen to them as they sit in court – they may well wish to inform you of relevant points during the course of the opposing expert's evidence. You will learn how to read notes passed to you as you are in full flow!

The next point bears repetition: listen with care to the evidence-in-chief. Be clear about what the witness has and has not said.

Distinguish between the safe inferences that may be drawn from those that are unsafe. To continue the DNA example:

1   From your evidence would it be safe to conclude that the defendant's DNA was recovered from the scene of the burglary?

2   Is it fair to say you cannot definitively state how the DNA came to be there?

3   Could it be the product of secondary transfer? (Give an example of the scenario provided by your client – 'my client had shaken hands with someone who lives in the burgled house only a few minutes earlier – could that be enough for secondary transfer to have occurred?)

4   Would it explain the DNA found on the door handle?'

5   Or it could have been left there when X visited the premises on a previous occasion? (If this is in accordance with your instructions.)

Chapter 18

Defendants and defence witnesses

Ray Tully

Key references

- Crown Court Compendium at 17-5

- Criminal Practice Directions 2015 VI (Trial) 26P

- Criminal Justice and Public Order Act 1994, s 35

- Criminal Procedure and Investigation Act 1996, s 6C

CONSIDERATIONS WHEN DEFENDING

The choice

It may now seem difficult to believe, but until the passing of the Criminal Law Act 1898 a defendant was generally not permitted to give evidence in their own defence. For nearly a century after the passing of that Act, defendants could choose whether or not to do so with impunity. Indeed judges were required to direct the jury not to hold that fact against the defendant if they did not give evidence. Things changed markedly with the passing of the Criminal Justice and Public Order Act 1994, s 35. It is important that you familiarise yourself with all the practical implications that flow from this important piece of legislation.

A defendant still has the right to choose whether or not to give evidence (the so called 'right to silence'). The exercise of that right comes at a price. You need to understand this and be able to explain it clearly to your client. If the defendant does not give evidence the judge is required to consider giving an 'adverse inference' direction when summing up the case. The standard terms of that direction are set out in the Crown Court Compendium at 17-5.

You will need to consider the options, discuss them, advise upon them and keep a written record which may well involve getting signed instructions from your client.

The first thing to do is to work out your own view. What do you think is the correct course and why? That is obviously fact specific and will depend upon issues in the particular case. What is the strength/weakness of the case? How do you think your client will stand up to cross-examination? How do you think they will come across to the jury? In the large majority of cases the decision ends up being in favour of calling the defendant.

Considerations when not calling your client

Where the decision is not to give evidence, practical considerations arise. You will need to keep a short written record of the advice you gave and obtain signed written instructions from your client. You should also retain a copy of any signed instructions.

Signed instructions should look something like this;

R v Smith

1   I have been fully advised by my barrister and solicitor about whether I should give evidence in my case.

2   I understand the advice I have been given.

3   I have been able to ask any questions that I have.

4   I understand it is my choice whether or not to give evidence.

5   I do not wish to give evidence at my trial.

6   My reasons for making this decision are [briefly specify].

7   I realise that I cannot change my mind later in the trial.

8   I understand the judge will give the jury an 'adverse inference' direction.

9   No pressure of any kind has been applied to me in making this decision.

Signed

Dated

Where the decision reached is not to call the client you will also need to warn the judge of that fact in advance – initially in the absence of the jury. That is because the statute requires the judge to go through a set procedure with you before the jury. This involves asking you a set question in the presence of the jury. The exact wording of the question is set out in the Criminal Practice Direction VI (Trial) 26P.

'Have you advised your client that the stage has now been reached at which he may give evidence and, if he chooses not to do so or, having been sworn, without good cause refuses to answer any question, the jury may draw such inferences as appear proper from his failure to do so ?'

When not calling your client it may be possible to avoid the judge giving an adverse inference direction during summing up. That depends upon whether you can demonstrate that 'the physical or mental condition of the accused makes it undesirable' to give evidence. To do that you will need to have laid a proper evidential foundation. That will normally involve the serving of medical evidence in advance.

Considerations when calling the defendant

If you are calling the defendant you will need to decide upon a structure for your questions. Whilst you should never coach the defendant (in the sense of suggesting answers to particular questions) you should ensure they are properly prepared for the form and structure of the questions you will be asking.

You need to explain that you are not permitted to ask leading questions and explain exactly what that means and how it impacts upon the style of questions you will be asking them – which might otherwise seem unnatural.

Remember to check whether they wish to take the oath or affirm so they are not bamboozled by the first thing they get asked. If it's the oath make sure you know which religious text is appropriate and warn the usher in advance. Remember also to explain they will be giving evidence from the witness box.

There are many different structures you can adopt depending upon the particular case. It may be that the case lends itself to a strictly chronological approach. It may make sense to start part way through the chronology and return later on in the cross-examination to sweep up earlier, less consequential, matters. It may be that the case is more suited to an approach based upon specific topics or themes. You may wish to use the defendant's police interview as a peg upon which to hang your questions, as the jury will most likely have a typed copy of that and will recently have heard the account provided (assuming it was a 'comment' interview).

There is no 'one size fits all' approach to the art of the examination-in-chief of a defendant. Think about what makes most sense upon the facts of the case. Plot it out in advance. Explain the approach you intend to take and the reasons for it to your client. Make sure they know what is coming down the track once they are in the witness box.

Some advocates like to tackle the main issues in the case directly in headline form at the start of cross-examination before then moving on to the details. Others prefer to build towards that as a suitable place to finish. Many like to start with a few easy opening questions to help settle their client. Typically such questions can cover a bit of background information relating to family circumstances, employment etc. Don't labour it. Remember the jury have been waiting for this moment. They want to know what your client has to say about the important matters in the case. Be careful that you don't end up inadvertently bringing in your client's character to this preamble: if you stray into areas like how hard-working or family-orientated she is, the prosecution may want to tell the jury that she has spent the last few years in prison.

In some cases (particularly where the evidence appears very strong) it can be a useful tactic to take on a semi-detached inquisitorial approach. It allows you to put some much-needed distance between you and the client to help preserve your credibility and hence ability to still persuade the jury when it comes to making your closing speech. It can also be useful in stealing the thunder of the prosecution. If you have asked all the tough questions in an upfront and uncompromising fashion it can help to wrong foot prosecution counsel and blunt the force of their questions. If you are going to take such an approach it is as well to warn your client about that in advance and ensure they understand why you intend to do so.

Think about what you have learned about your client and use that knowledge in how you question them. Some are naturally quiet characters. She may come across as withdrawn or, worse still, 'cold'. Think about how you may be able to breathe some life into her ability to communicate with the jury. Encourage the client to look at the jury and address them directly in their answers. Use the tone and pace of your questions to invigorate your exchanges. Some defendants have the reverse problem. They may wish to take over and 'have their say'. You will need to carefully rein them in to maintain focus and shape in their evidence. Don't be afraid to give your own client an early 'yellow card' if that is what is needed to ensure the jury hear their best evidence. That after all is why you are there. You are there to direct – but when doing so, don't take over the stage. Make sure the spotlight remains where it ought to be.

Defence witnesses

The experience of most practitioners is that there is usually little to be gained from calling defence witnesses – and certainly not in significant numbers. The risk-for-reward factor is high. The principle witnesses of fact ought to have been called as part of the prosecution case. Think long and hard before calling defence witnesses. They may offer easy meat for the canny prosecutor who will be able to exploit any perceived allegiance to the defendant as well as the differences that may arise between the account of the witness and that of the defendant.

There are two important exceptions. The first is defence expert witnesses. Such witnesses are likely to have been called earlier in the case and 'interposed' when the relevant prosecution witness was giving evidence. That is the conventional approach so that the jury has the benefit of hearing such witnesses 'back to back'. The other exception relates to character evidence. If calling such witnesses the general rule of thumb is that 'less is more'. Concentrate on quality not quantity. Mere repetition is unhelpful.

CONSIDERATIONS WHEN PROSECUTING

The defendant

It has often been said that cross-examination should not be done crossly. It's not a bad maxim.

The cross-examination of the defendant is one of the great set piece moments of any criminal trial. It's box-office. The jury will be eagerly anticipating the spectacle. Consider your task carefully and how you wish to set about it.

It has been said that there are essentially four basic techniques involved in cross-examination (confrontation, insinuation, undermining and probing). Whatever the actual number of potential techniques, it is obvious that there are several different ways to approach the task.

You may choose to take a 'salami slicing' approach, involving a painstaking dissection of the defendant's case. That can often start by seeking to examine the extent of common ground in the case. What are the things that everyone agrees about? That can be helpful in framing the case for the jury before allowing you to home in on the areas of dispute. You may choose instead upon a 'no holds barred' all out frontal attack. The point is that you need to think about it in advance and be able to adapt your style to the particular circumstances of the case. The same approach will not work in every case.

You have the great advantage of being allowed to ask leading questions, so use it. You will most likely have been taught the basic technique involved in asking closed questions. You'll have been told to stick to one subject at a time. These are all useful tools in helping you to steer the exchanges with the defendant.

It is often said that you should never ask the 'why' question. It's an open question and risks handing over control to the witness. There is much wisdom in the general maxim: however in the hands of a skilled prosecutor the 'why' question can be a devastating tool. If you have closed off every avenue open to the defendant it can be the killer question that exposes the fundamental weakness of their position. It also has the potential to backfire massively so only use it when you've fully calibrated the risks involved.

You need to learn where the line is. It may well be necessary to press home an advantage but don't bully, belittle or ridicule a defendant. Don't make it personal either. If you do any of these things you may end up creating sympathy for the defendant. The jury may become more interested in putting you in your place than finding the defendant guilty.

If the defendant comes across sympathetically to the jury then ensure your advocacy matches the mood of the court. Adopt a 'more in sorrow than in anger' approach. A jury can still convict a defendant they feel sorry for, so long as a finding of guilt is the logical conclusion they feel driven towards. Your task is to drive them there. A light touch is more likely to achieve that outcome.

Other defence witnesses

You should be on notice about the identity of any defence witnesses by virtue of the obligation placed upon the defendant by the Criminal Procedure and Investigation Act 1996, s 6C.

You will of course have to challenge anything important that emerges in evidence from a defence witness. Where that is so, largely the same rules apply as with the defendant.

Think hard about whether it is truly necessary to ask any questions. If you don't need to ask any questions then don't do so. It can be a powerful way of communicating to the jury that the witness is of little or no consequence to the real issues in the case.

That is doubly so with character witnesses. There is usually little profit to be gained by cross-examination of such witnesses.

Witness handling: key points

DO
• Remember special measures
• Read witness statements and expert reports carefully before writing your questions
• Think about what you want to get out of any witness and plan how you will achieve that
• Think about your tone, pace, body language and choice of words
• Meet your own witnesses in advance and ask to meet any expert on the other side
• Know the rules, eg call admissible evidence, know how to refresh memory properly
• Ask simple, clear questions at a measured pace in readily understandable language
• Listen carefully to the answers the witness gives
• Adapt your questions to the witness using the Advocate's Gateway toolkits
• Plan how you will deal with difficult topics in advance
• Put your case, but lead up to those final questions

- Stay calm and move on if you ask a silly question (we all do)

- Start thinking about whether you will call the defendant long before trial and get an appropriate endorsement if necessary

- Be courteous in your manner to all witnesses, whatever you have to suggest to them

- Remember all witnesses are likely to be nervous about giving evidence

- Remember that a jury will have particular sympathy towards children and vulnerable witnesses

DONT

- Ask leading questions-in-chief

- Get into punch and judy cross-examination

- Call inadmissible evidence

- Speak too quickly, use confusing or patronising language, or appear to rush or bully the witness

- Spend too much time talking yourself

- Comment or give a speech during questioning

- Assume that a police officer or expert will have previously given evidence before a jury

- Call a defendant without having a proper discussion with them about the pros and cons of their giving evidence

Part VI

The Trial: Written advocacy

Chapter 19

Jury bundles as a way to persuade

Anna Vigars QC

INTRODUCTION

There is a long list of jobs to be done as you prepare to prosecute a trial. You will have got beyond reading the papers and considering what the weaknesses are in your case. You will have advised on those weaknesses, extra evidence will have been gathered where that is available, and a trial date will be approaching.

Some preparation for a trial is necessarily done on the evening before the trial. That is inevitable. However, the index to the jury bundle really does need to be done several weeks before then. It may be that you will also have to end up producing the jury bundle itself and copying it for everyone, but you will certainly need to produce an index to it well in advance of trial.

Do that in time to provide it to your opponent for their comments before it needs to go to your instructing solicitors for printing. There is no point in turning up at court with 20 copies of the bundle only to find that your opponent objects to, and insists upon the removal of, page 3. If there is any dispute over the content of the jury bundle then work creatively, produce what can be produced and leave yourself some flexibility. It is worth, for example, producing one copy of the bundle with everything in it, including the disputed section. But don't number it yet. Get the issue resolved and then number the master copy and copy it from that. That sounds basic but it is extraordinary how often these things become tangled when you're in a rush and the judge is waiting to begin the trial!

While dealing with the basics of jury bundles, it is worth also considering these things;

(a)   Jury boxes are small, so do not try to put 12 A3 files in there because nobody will be able to work comfortably from them.

(b)   Not everyone will be familiar with handling documents; if you have one bundle between two people you double the chances of each pair of people being on the right page and being able to keep up.

(c)   Try not to produce a bundle which is a mixture of landscape and portrait pages because it is difficult to work with; better to have two smaller bundles, one in each orientation, than a muddle of both.

(d)   Check that you have the best copy of each document before you produce any bundle. It is really frustrating to put thought and effort into producing a bundle only for the jury to have squint at it.

(e)   Make sure that you have sufficient copies of the bundle in court: include the judge, your opponent, the jury, the defendant, and the witness box. Also include your officer in charge (OIC) if you work in a court centre where that officer routinely sits in during the trial. Do not include, however nicely they may ask for it, the press bench.

(f)   Make it look smart; first or second impressions count so make sure that some effort is put into proper presentation, to reflect the overall care that the prosecution has taken with its case. It is the prosecution bundle, not a police bundle. Think carefully about whether you want the crest of your local constabulary on a booklet of photographs, or whether it is appropriate to have words like 'Serious and Organised Crime Division' on such a document.

WHAT IS THE PURPOSE OF A JURY BUNDLE?

Why should you think about it more carefully than simply gathering together a handful of the key documents? Preparation of a jury bundle is integral to your preparation of the case: this bundle can help you to take control of the trial, it can influence the way in which the jury works through the evidence, and steer them towards particular conclusions. For this reason, you will need to carefully select those documents which tell the story you want to tell.

You have lived with the case and thought about it for much longer than the jury will have done. Consider their position on the first day of the trial. For many of them it will be the first time they walk into a courtroom, and they won't know quite how a trial will unfold. Some of them will be frustrated to be taken out of their usual lives, some of them will be fascinated, and some of them will be nervous. One of your jobs is to provide them with reassurance that they will be taken through the trial in a comprehensible fashion so that they are given all that they need to understand it and to make a decision at the end of it. Landing a file full of ill-considered and badly presented documents on them in the opening minutes is not going to achieve that aim.

A jury bundle should not make an appearance in the jury box until you have established a rapport with the jury and you have had an opportunity to tell them about the trial. There are practical reasons for this; as soon as you hand documents to people, they will get their heads down into those documents and they will stop looking at you and concentrating on exactly what you are saying. So, hang on to the bundle. Tell the jury the story first and, only when that is understood should you then hand them the bundle of documents and take them through that. That way you will be able to tie it all into what you have been telling them and demonstrate to them how what you are saying is supported by the evidence. They are far more likely to understand the significance of complex evidence from a witness (eg, how cell site evidence marries up with ANPR) if the dots have already been joined in your opening.

What structure you want to use for your bundle matters and needs some thought. That depends on how you will present your case. Obviously jury bundles can be presented in a number of different ways;

- chronologically depending on the order of creation of the documents;

- by type of document; all the maps together, all the photographs together etc; or

- by witness, with all the documents which each witness will use to give evidence being collected together in one section.

Much of this decision turns on the type of case that you are presenting and what documents you have to hand. If one set of photographs is going to be referred to by three or four witnesses, for example, then you will want to have all those photographs together so that the jury become very familiar with them rather than having them interspersed through various other documents which might fit in chronologically.

While thinking about photographs, it is worth reflecting on this; crime scene investigators are blessed with digital cameras and can capture endless images of the same scene; you may have hundreds of photographs. You are responsible for making a selection and ensuring that you have the right photographs to present the case properly. That means that you need to understand what the photographs are showing you, which way the viewer is looking, how one photograph relates to another. If necessary, ask those questions in conference before you choose what should go into the bundle.

When using photographs, it is often useful also to have a plan in the bundle. Get the jury involved in doing some work themselves in terms of where the photographs fit onto the plan for example; draw them into the case as you present it.

Be ruthless about the material that goes to the jury. If you are not sure about the worth of a document then don't put it in the jury bundle. Add it later if it proves useful to witnesses as they give their evidence. You cannot predict everything and sometimes it may be that a particular document takes on a prominence which you had not foreseen. Better that than getting to the end of the trial and realising that there are great swathes of the jury bundle which you haven't even used.

Similarly, be ruthless with presentational material which others may think is useful. Sometimes, in a longer case, the police will get an analyst working on the data who produces endless charts of association between different defendants and their telephone numbers. It's worth remembering two things; first that a lot of work will have gone into what you are being shown; and secondly that the person who has done the work does not necessarily understand the case in the way that you do. It is your choice whether or not a particular chart goes before the jury and not everything that an analyst produces will be helpful to you. But a clear, well thought-out chart can often have an impact that the same evidence painstakingly given over hours from the witness box would not have. If you have the luxury of an analyst's help, think creatively about what you want to show and how it can be shown.

There is nothing to stop you drawing material into a schedule or putting it on a chart. If you are good at that sort of work, then use this skill to produce a document which will help the jury. However, if you are going to do that, be very clear that you are simply recording the data on the chart. You should not be analysing it because that leads you into the position of a witness rather than an advocate.

It is obvious that you should check material before it goes to the jury. It's perhaps less obvious that you should double check it and interrogate each schedule really carefully. What you want to avoid is the chilling moment when a juror spots a problem with a schedule and points it out to everyone in a note to the judge. So, make sure, for example, that all the duration times for telephone calls are in the same units; some companies provide data to the police marked in hours, minutes and seconds, and some produce it in minutes, seconds, and tenths of seconds. Check that quantities for drugs are being provided in the same units across the document. Check that times are all BST or GMT rather than a heady combination of the two which could lead to all kinds of wholly unsound conclusions.

A jury bundle should operate throughout the trial as an aid to the case, something that supports the jury's understanding and the ability for a witness to give evidence clearly. For that reason, it is worth taking a little time as you come to the end of your speech to introduce the jury properly to the contents of the bundle. Go through it with them. Explain how it fits together and where these documents fit into the case that you have just opened to them. Point out to them the important pages, if you think that there are any particularly important ones. Reassure them that they will come back to it repeatedly so that they will become familiar with it. Tell them that the bundles belong to them and that nobody will check over them to see what notes have been made but that they will be destroyed securely at the end of the trial so that they feel able to use them as proper working documents.

And then use the bundle yourself as you call evidence and as you cross-examine. If you have thought carefully about what should be in there, then you will be able to deploy it effectively by introducing the jury carefully to its contents, taking witnesses to the relevant pages and putting the documents which are most difficult for the defendant to deal with fairly and properly in front of them. By that stage, the jury will also know the document properly, understand your case, and be keen to hear the defendant explain themselves.

AGREED FACTS

Agreed facts lend themselves particularly well to some kinds of cases; for example, the situation in which the defendant is facing an allegation of possession with intent to supply drugs. The defendant accepts being caught in possession of the substance in question, that it was found in the condition in which the police say it was, that it weighs what they say it weighs, and that it has properly been analysed as containing that particular percentage of the specific drug. So, the whole of the prosecution case could be summarised onto one side of A4.

Be a little cautious before you take that step, though. Agreed facts have the distinct advantage of capturing material which is complex, or which easily escapes the memory. But they are dull. Whatever the significance of the fact being read by you, it will not have the impact of hearing that evidence given by a witness. For that reason alone, it is sometimes sensible to agree facts rather than to have them called if you are defending a case. When you prosecute you might want to consider, for example, calling the police officer who found the drugs rather than reducing all of that to agreed facts. Check, if you decide to do that, that the police officer has refreshed his memory from his notes before he gets anywhere near the witness box. You don't want to regret taking the decision to call him!

Sometimes with an expert witness you will want to agree facts because you can appropriately summarise what is said by that witness and you can strip away some of the jargon in their report. If a defendant agrees that it is indeed his DNA which was found on the complainant's knickers but his defence is consent, then you do not need to call a scientist to talk about the way in which DNA works, how it is tested, and what degrees of uncertainty it includes. None of that is relevant to issues of consent.

Sometimes, however, even when an expert witness is agreed, it is useful to have that witness in court to present the evidence. If, for example, you are seeking to present a set of findings relating to DNA or blood found in various different places, it is often more effective to extract the list of it from the scientist's statement and then to get that scientist to come and speak to it than it is to read it out yourself. Don't rush into this. It is expensive to get scientists to attend court and shouldn't be done unless it will genuinely make a proper difference to the quality of the presentation of the trial. In any case with complex expert material involved, it is worth having a conference first with your expert so that you can ensure that you thoroughly understand the material and make an assessment of them and how they might appear as a witness.

Once you have decided to use agreed facts, put some proper thought into them so that you have a document which does justice to the evidence which you are trying to capture. You will want to circulate some agreed facts before the trial begins so that your opponent can understand your approach and you can work out what is contentious. Often agreed facts can flush out proper areas of dispute before a trial begins because, if something is not as straightforward as it appears to you then your opponent may refuse to agree the draft Agreed Facts. As with a jury bundle, think in advance about how you will draft agreed facts so that they properly build up your case; put them into a sensible chronological or topical order.

There are some cases which can be built around a schedule of agreed facts or events. Think about a drugs conspiracy involving three defendants. One perhaps in London, pulling the strings, arranging the transport of drugs; another who is the courier and who drives down the M4 to Bristol; and a third one who is in charge of the Bristol end of the operation. There are three alleged trips to Bristol which feature as evidence of the conspiracy at work.

In presenting this case you have a mass of material; telephone schedules, drugs found on street dealers, drugs found back in London on the day of the arrests, ANPR [Automatic Number Plate Recognition] schedules showing the movement of defendant two's car down the M4, CCTV footage of defendants two and three meeting in a car park in the centre of Bristol, and so on. There is a strong case there but only when you impose some order on it all. Perhaps one place to begin is with a master schedule of events that captures each event on a timeline. You will have other schedules which descend to the detail of these but your master schedule should capture the whole of the picture so that it runs through the case that you are presenting like a solid, trustworthy, dependable spine along the back of your case. It will become the first document that the jury turns to and it is a key way to take control of the case, set the agenda, and make clear the cohesion of the case that you are presenting.

Agreed facts have their place in a trial but they need to be used with proper judgement and with an awareness that your skill is so much more than simply getting through the evidence. They are a useful tool to simplify or draw together evidence but balance their use against the need to breathe life into your case and to make it vivid for the jury.

Chapter 20

The successful skeleton argument

Alistair Haggerty

INTRODUCTION

Effective written advocacy can be just as persuasive as the perfectly pitched and elegantly phrased oral submission. When done well, it will ensure that the judge is on your side long before the hearing begins and will provide you with an ideal framework on which to base your advocacy in court. Most written advocacy is presented in the form of a skeleton argument. Sometimes a skeleton argument will be specifically requested by the judge, on other occasions it will be at the behest of the advocate. Whatever the circumstances, drafting a skeleton argument is almost always advantageous.

With the introduction of the digital system there is far greater scope for bringing written arguments to the attention of the judge, even at short notice. This has increased both the prevalence and value of skeleton arguments. Drafting a skeleton argument and uploading it onto the digital system is more likely to result in a favourable outcome, as opposed to presenting arguments orally without any prior notice. The judge will also be conscious of the interests of justice and may take a dim view of the advocate who catches his opponent off guard by not providing advance written notice of his argument. Not submitting a skeleton argument, especially in situations in which a more complicated argument is being pursued, or where it is likely to have significant implications for the trial, may result in the judge adjourning proceedings for skeletons to be served. For obvious reasons, having a trial derailed in such circumstances is best avoided.

The type of legal arguments which arise during the trial, and which benefit from skeleton arguments, include but are not limited to:

(i)   Applications for joinder and severance of counts or defendants.

(ii)   Applications to exclude evidence.

(iii)   Submissions of no case to answer.

(iv)   Arguments in relation to how the judge should direct the jury.

(v)   Abuse of process arguments, albeit these are almost always made in advance of the trial.

(vi)   Some issues concerning bad character which arise during the trial, although straightforward applications can usually be made orally.

(vii)   Hearsay applications which are made mid-trial.

RULES FOR SKELETON ARGUMENTS

The style adopted for skeleton arguments is, like most advocacy, personal. Nevertheless, there are some useful rules to follow when drafting one and using it as a basis for judicial advocacy.

First, as the name suggests, a skeleton argument should be relatively short. It provides the bones of your argument and should allow room for your oral submissions to apply the flesh. There are a number of good reasons for keeping it short. You want to ensure that the judge reads and reflects on everything that you have written. If it is long and verbose there is a risk that he or she will lose interest, especially if it needs to be considered in the middle of a trial and the judge has other matters to consider in a short space of time. You also want to ensure that you have something to say when it comes to the hearing. It is far more effective to elaborate on the points outlined in the skeleton than to simply read what you have drafted. There are some situations in which a more detailed skeleton argument will be necessary but, as a rule of thumb, aim for it to be no longer than two pages.

Secondly, adopt a logical and easy to follow structure.

(a)   It is often helpful to set out a short summary of your argument in the first paragraph. For example, if you are applying to exclude evidence, state this at the outset and briefly summarise the basis for the application.

(b)   The next step should be to summarise the facts of the case very briefly, with an emphasis on those facts which are most germane to the argument.

(c)   Then outline the relevant points of law. Do not assume that the judge will know everything about the law, especially if the argument involves a more esoteric point. Your judge may not have a background as a specialist criminal practitioner and will appreciate having the opportunity to consider the points of law in advance of hearing the oral arguments.

(d)   Include the full case name and reference of any case referred to in the skeleton (and be sure to provide the judge and your opponent with a copy). It is also good practice to refer the judge to the relevant passages of *Archbold* or *Blackstone's*.

(e)   The final step is the argument itself. Apply the facts to the law in order to explain why your argument is right. Have separate paragraphs for each distinct point and present them in a logical order.

(f)   For completeness, it can be helpful to have a final concluding paragraph briefly summing up your argument.

Thirdly, use sub-headings and numbered paragraphs. This makes the argument easier to follow by clearly indicating the distinct points raised and signposting a change of topic. It also makes the document far more useful when advancing oral submissions. This will ensure that you do not lose the flow of your argument, or your place, whilst on your feet and will also enable you to specifically refer the judge to parts of the document.

Fourthly, use clear, plain and precise language. Although style is a matter of personal preference, a skeleton argument should not read like an academic essay. In written advocacy, florid language and overly long sentences are more likely to dilute rather than enhance the intended impact of the argument. Latin should also be avoided.

SERVING A SKELETON ARGUMENT IN RESPONSE

Where your opponent has submitted a skeleton argument, the judge will sometimes require a skeleton in response. Even when not actually requested, it is good practice to draft one. When deployed successfully, a skeleton is a means of seizing control of the argument and gaining the understanding of the judge. Responding in kind enables you to take back the initiative.

It is customary to respond to points in the order in which they are set out by opposing counsel. However, your skeleton may carry more weight if it starts by setting out your arguments first, explaining how and why your view of the case is preferable before – of course - responding to all of the arguments raised by your opponent. You will also need to identify the cases which support your arguments, and which may well be different from those cited by your opponent, in your skeleton response.

Whether you are drafting the initial skeleton, or preparing one in response, each paragraph of your argument should be drafted with the intention of setting out clearly why you are right. If your argument is a response you should also, politely and respectfully, make it clear why your opponent is wrong.

SKELETON ARGUMENTS AND ORAL ADVOCACY

The skeleton argument should be used like a roadmap, directing the judge from the beginning to the end of the argument and ensuring that nobody gets lost along the way. Occasionally refer the judge directly to the numbered paragraphs in the skeleton to ensure that he can follow the flow of the argument. It is also important to not be a slave to your skeleton argument. You will need to be flexible; ensure that you respond to the points raised by your opponent.

By the time the judge hears submissions, he or she will have had the benefit of reading both documents, so, if you served the first skeleton, you must be prepared to make submissions in response and be prepared for judicial interventions which may divert you from the structure of your skeleton argument. Use your skeleton argument as a way of keeping your submissions on track.

The successful skeleton argument will ensure that the hearing runs more smoothly and expeditiously. It may avert the need for the judge to hear any submissions at all. It should always ensure that the arguments of both sides are distilled down to their most relevant points thereby making the judge's life easier and ensuring that the trial runs smoothly.

Part VII

The Trial: Speeches

Chapter 21

Speeches

Christopher Quinlan QC and Ramin Pakrooh

Key references

- *Archbold: Criminal Pleading, Evidence and Practice 2020,* 4-419–4-424a, 4-427–4-428, 4-342–343, 4-343a–343b, 4-384

- Criminal Procedure Rules 2015, SI 2015/1490 (CPR 2015), r 25.9(2)(c)

- Criminal Practice Directions, VI, 25A: Trial

- Criminal Procedure and Investigations Act 1996, s 6E(4)

Case law

- *R v Lashley (Angela)* [2005] EWCA Crim 2016

- *Bryant and Oxley* [1979] QB 108

PROSECUTION OPENING SPEECHES
(Christopher Quinlan QC)

It is a privilege to open the prosecution case to a jury. It is also an advantage. Probably, after the judge's necessary directions, yours is the next voice the jury hear. The jury is new; the jurors will want help and the court is yours. Those judicial words, 'yes, Mr/Ms X' are the firing of the starter's pistol and you have a head start.

Purpose

The primary purpose of the prosecution opening is to tell the jury what the case is about. If you were a juror, that's what you would want to know: who did what, when and how. So, tell them.

You are not there as a public announcer. You are there to prosecute the case, about which you should make no apology. You will be fair, but you will also want to tell the jury what you say the defendant did and why you say he is guilty. Do not start by saying you 'appear to prosecute …'; you are there to prosecute the case rather than to give the impression of doing so.

Start with a nutshell. Its length will depend on the complexity of the case and the issues. However, you ought to be able to summarise the core essentials in no more than a few succinct paragraphs. Those paragraphs should encapsulate the basic tale and the issues. After that nutshell, the jury should understand the essence of the case. It should also capture the jury's interest. Not every case is exciting, but it is important, and they have a crucial role to play in it.

The following 91 words formed the nutshell of the presecution opening in a four-month case:

> The defendant is charged with thirty-one offences committed against four women over the course of twenty-six months. From February 2015 to his arrests in April 2017 he imprisoned, assaulted, sexually violated and raped four women. Each of those young women was aged in her early or mid-twenties. Each was in a relationship with him. He filmed a good deal of what he did. We anticipate he will assert in relation to those charges that any act of sexual activity was consensual and he never assaulted or held them against their will.

Tell them why you are opening the case. It will help settle them and make them feel part of the trial. Do not patronise them but make them feel part of what is happening, rather than spectators. It comes naturally early in the opening; after the nutshell is perfect. You will find the appropriate words, but this may help:

> Let me now tell you a little more about the case. The purpose of so doing is to inform you of what the case is about; tell you something of the evidence I anticipate you shall hear during the trial; introduce to you by name, some of the witnesses from whom you shall hear. You will then (I hope) be in a better position to understand the evidence as it unfolds, who witnesses are when they are called and how and where they fit into the overall picture.

Tell the jury at that stage the limitations of what you are doing. It is not evidence and is a summary. You can do it in simple sentences.

> Words of caution. What I say is not evidence. Also, it is but a summary; it is an introduction to this case.

Content

The content will accord with the law. The standard textbooks, for example *Archbold*, 4-342-343, help with that. Open only with that which can be proved by admissible evidence. The Criminal Practice Direction VI (Trial) 25A: Identification for the jury of the issues in the case (CPD 25A) provides:

'CrimPR 3.11(a) requires the court, with the active assistance of the parties, to establish what are the disputed issues in order to manage the trial. To that end, prosecution opening speeches are invaluable. They set out for the jury the principal issues in the trial, and the evidence which is to be introduced in support of the prosecution case. They should clarify, not obfuscate. The purpose of the prosecution opening is to help the jury understand what the case concerns, not necessarily to present a detailed account of all the prosecution evidence due to be introduced.'

You should open the core facts upon which the prosecution relies. The opening should include the following: a factual narrative; an introduction of the main witnesses from whom they will hear; reference to special measures (if appropriate); the charges; and, if appropriate, a general running order of the evidence as you hope to present it. Most cases lend themselves to a chronological opening which will aid understanding for those coming to it fresh. It will enable you to build the case, introducing witnesses, relevant people and events as you go.

Using paper materials, such as a jury bundle, is a good opportunity to get the jury working with you. If they do, the relationship is formed and will stand you in good stead as the trial develops. You may already have advised them that *'we will work together'*. If you have not, this is the perfect time to do so. Make them part of what you are doing; they are much more likely to be receptive to your case if from an early stage they are working with you.

Introduce the jury bundle after the nutshell and the purpose of the opening. In an assault case it may contain copies of the indictment, a map or plan, photographs of the scene and injuries and perhaps a schedule of the scientific findings. Tell them they will have in due course (if appropriate) a copy of the defendant's record of interviews and agreed facts, explaining the status thereof. Tell them it is theirs, to use throughout the trial, to mark as they wish, and will remain private to them. You can open the case by reference to those materials.

Watch the jury; and the judge. That seems obvious, but it is not. You will be looking at them, but that is different. When you take them to documents, do so at a pace which allows them to keep up with you; pause if they appear not be to be able to find something. Not all are familiar with working with papers or with files; tell them so. You will not do it in a way which embarrasses, but one which draws them in, so they all feel part of what you are doing.

Be courteous. Do not express personal opinions. Expressions such as 'I think' or 'I believe' have no place in the opening, and indeed in any speech or comment made to the jury, even if the speaker is in silk! Formulate it in this way, for example: 'the prosecution submits ...' or 'I submit ...'. You should avoid unnecessarily emotional or emotive language. The topic may be emotive, such as rape or other sexual crime. Address that fact and remind the jury their job is one for cool minds, assessing evidence objectively and dispassionately and therefore fairly.

Do not open the case too high. Avoid making yourself a hostage to fortune. This is the first stage and you are likely to have the right to make a closing speech as well. This is an introduction so treat it as such. Thereafter the evidence will tell the tale – hopefully one which accords with your opening.

Open only what you can prove by admissible evidence. Open what you are confident you will prove by evidence you can call. You must not open as a fact any matter you cannot prove. Do not open every fact, only those which are central to the case you seek to prove or are important or necessary to or help understand the narrative. Introduce relationships as you do witnesses. For example: 'the complainant in this case is Sybil Claxton, married to Ray; you will hear from both of them.'

You will have witness statements and exhibits so a good idea of what the evidence is predicted to be. However, where there is dispute and where you are dependent upon human witnesses, you cannot always be confident how that evidence will withstand the rigours of a trial. Worse, you may have some idea that aspects of the case are weaker than others. Open such areas carefully, perhaps generally, giving yourself room to move with the evidence. You may wish not to pin your case to a particular mast. You may not even wish to enter the boat yard so far as an aspect of the evidence is concerned.

Remember, you know every detail of the case (or should do). The jury do not. Take the opening at a steady pace, explaining carefully the important details. In a complicated case reassure them that they will soon become familiar with the detail, the names and the places. However, do not underestimate or patronise them; some may be cleverer (even) than you.

Adress actual or potential weaknesses in your case. Do not be defensive nor defeatist about them but recognise them as points the jury will have to deal with. You might couch them in these terms: 'one of the issues the defence may raise ...' or 'you will no doubt wish to consider ...'. You can then advance your own rebuttal to the point and the jury will see you have been candid with them. They are more likely to be receptive to you.

In *Lashley* the Court of Appeal was not minded to criticise prosecuting counsel who referred to the law of theft in his opening. The court, however, observed:

'... he was reflecting a habit which has become ingrained in the system. It is a bad habit, and it should be broken. The presumption should be that an opening address by counsel for the Crown should not address the law, save in cases of real complication and difficulty where counsel believes and the trial judge agrees that the jury may be assisted by a brief and well-focussed submission.'

There is every (good) reason why prosecuting counsel will wish to open the charge faced by the defendant – invariably by reference to the indictment. It is unlikely you will need or want to deal with the law in any detail or that it will assist the jury or your case to do so. In *Lashley* the defendant was charged with theft. We all know what theft is and the jury do not need to be taken through the Theft Act.

Use the indictment but not at the start. The jury do not want to know about the law. It is a charge sheet and jurors are unlikely to be familiar with its format. You can better explain what the case is about with your factual nutshell. The indictment can often be best introduced towards the end of the opening. It can and should be done briefly and concisely, using it to illustrate what issue/s they have to decide. Preface it with the correct observation that the law is for the judge and in due course they will have his/her legal directions which they must follow. You simply wish to identify the charge(s) and explain how it/they fits into the evidence you have opened.

For example, in a rape case, you might deal with the indictment briefly as follows:

> Rape can be committed in a number of different ways. The prosecution must prove so that you are sure each of the following: (1) D intentionally penetrated X's (in this case) vagina with his penis; (2) That X did not consent to that penetration; and (3) D did not reasonably believe that X was consenting at the time. A person consents if they agree by choice and has the freedom and capacity to make that choice. In this case there is no issue whether D and X had sexual intercourse at the time in question, D says she was consenting; X denies it. That is the issue you must decide.

In that example, you have summarised the law, explained how it fits with the evidence you have already reviewed and identified the issue the jury has to decide.

In a case with a number of charges, however, the indictment can help tell the story and build the case around the charges. That is especially useful in a fraud or sexual case where there are multiple charges and/or complainants. In such cases, you can usefully open the facts of a particular count and then take the jury to the indictment and the count or counts which reflects that allegation point by point.

In *Lashley* the Court of Appeal acknowledged that counsel 'perhaps, and we emphasise perhaps …' assisted the jury by mentioning the burden and standard of proof in the opening. It is convention to do so, but by no means obligatory. If done, it need not be laboured. Why would you wish to convey the impression that you face some insurmountable hurdle or underline just how hard it might be to establish guilt?

It can be done in a few simple sentences, perhaps towards the end:

> The Prosecution bring the allegations and so must prove them. You will not convict the defendant [of any count] unless you are sure of his guilt. How do you reach that standard? On evidence which is presented to you.

You may wish to mention the use of special measures to facilitate the giving of evidence by any witness you are calling. They need be told no more than the fact a witness is, for example, giving evidence from behind a screen; that such is commonplace in criminal trials; is done to try to put the witness at ease, away from the public gaze; and that it must not be held against the defendant. If the judge has already dealt with such in their introductory directions, there is unlikely to be any need to repeat it.

You should not open evidence the admissibility of which you know is in dispute. If you need or want for good reason to open it, then you will have asked for a judicial ruling before you begin the opening.

If admissible, either by ruling or agreement, you may wish to open evidence of bad character and hearsay. You should do so without reference to the statutory framework which makes such evidence admissible. Open its status if it is important to your narrative and the presentation of your case. For example:

(a)   the complainant has since died (unrelated to the assault);

(b)   and his evidence cannot therefore be cross-examined, as would ordinarily be the case;

(c)   they will therefore hear his witness statement read; but

(d)   in due course the judge will direct them how they must approach that (hearsay) evidence.

Rulings on the admissibility of evidence of bad character relied upon by the Crown are often left until a convenient moment during the prosecution case. Therefore, you are unlikely to be referring to it during the opening. However, if admissibility is established, either by ruling or agreement, you may want to refer to it. You will no doubt wish to do so by reference to the reason(s) it is being adduced. For example, in a burglary where the defendant's blood was found at the point of entry, for which they advance an innocent explanation, you may, after telling the jury that, then share with them that when considering that account they will no doubt wish to consider whether the defendant's 15 convictions for burglary make it more likely it was left there because this was the burglar.

While each case is different, you might find this general structure useful, the example here being an assault case:

• Nutshell

• Relevant background – the events in question

• The assault

• Immediate aftermath – attendance of emergency services and arrest

• Hospital treatment

• Scene of crime and scientific evidence

• Defendant's police interview

• Indictment and defence, thereby identifying the issue/s – for example self-defence

• Bad character

• Peroration, including burden and standard of proof and (if appropriate) order of evidence

---

DO

• Start with a nutshell.

• Be clear, concise, ordered and accurate.

• Open what you are confident you can prove by available and admissible evidence.

• Use the indictment and other materials to get the jury working with you and to develop rapport.

• Keep any reference to the law succinct and limited to the necessary or appropriate.

DON'T

• Introduce yourself as someone who '*appears to prosecute*'.

• Express personal opinions.

• Start with the indictment.

• Start with the burden and standard of proof.

• Open evidence the admissibility of which is in dispute.

• Open any fact you cannot prove by available and admissible evidence.

• Address the law in any detail and only when necessary or appropriate.

• Ask for the judge's leave to call your first witness: you do not need it.

DEFENCE OPENING SPEECHES (*Christopher Quinlan QC*)

You will find help in the textbooks on the content, for example *Archbold*, 4-343a-343b, 4-384

The CPD provides:

'CrimPR 25.9(2)(c) provides for a defendant, or his or her advocate, to set out the issues in the defendant's own terms (subject to superintendence by the court), immediately after the prosecution opening. Any such identification of issues at this stage is not to be treated as a substitute for or extension of the summary of the defence case which can be given later, under CrimPR 25.9(2)(g). Its purpose is to provide the jury with focus as to the issues that they are likely to be called upon to decide, so that jurors will be alert to those issues from the outset and can evaluate the prosecution evidence that they hear accordingly. For that purpose, the defendant is not confined to what is included in the defence statement (though any divergence from the defence statement will expose the defendant to adverse comment or inference), and for the defendant to take the opportunity at this stage to identify the issues may assist even if all he or she wishes to announce is that the prosecution is being put to proof.'

A defendant is not entitled to identify issues at this stage by addressing the jury unless the court invites him or her to do so, which is very rare. Such an opportunity may be requested. Reasons not to offer or to refuse a request for one include:

'... (i) that the case is such that the issues are apparent; (ii) that the prosecutor has given a fair, accurate and comprehensive account of the issues in opening, rendering repetition superfluous; and (iii) where the defendant is not represented, that there is a risk of the defendant, at this early stage, inflicting injustice on him or herself by making assertions to the jury to such an extent, or in such a manner, as is unfairly detrimental to his or her subsequent standing.'

There remains the right of the defendant to open ('*summarise*') his case where they intend to call in evidence at least one witness of fact in addition to themselves. That is different from, and in addition to, any identification of the issues immediately after the prosecution opening. The reality is that you are unlikely to do both unless a long time has passed between the two opportunities. The right at this later stage goes beyond the identification of issues; it includes the right to criticise the prosecution evidence.

If invited, there would have to be very good reason to refuse. Ordinarily, it is a good opportunity to enter the arena and set out the defendant's case. It will not be as extensive as the prosecution's opening. It is your chance to be cooperative, helpful and reasonable. You can immediately make clear to the jury that there are two sides to this case and that the defendant's case is, at the very least, reasonable or arguable. You can ensure it is placed before them accurately and in the terms you wish.

You can also seek to mitigate any hostile reaction to your client in particular types of case, inviting the jury to focus on the issues they have to decide. For example, in a murder case where the partial defence of diminished responsibility is raised the jury can be told:

(1)   the defendant accepts he killed X, but at the time of doing so;

(2)   he was suffering from a mental illness, supported by (two) consultant forensic psychiatrics from whom they jury will hear; and so

(3)   the central issue for them will be to decide whether his responsibility for the killing is sufficiently diminished or reduced that the appropriate verdict is one of manslaughter and not murder.

In a short or straightforward case, a judge is unlikely to invite you to identify the issues. There would be little or no point in doing so. For the same reason, you would not seek to open the defence case.

If the invitation is extended, defence counsel is not obliged to accept it. If declined, the judge can tell the jury and direct that they are provided with copies of the defence statement in accordance with the Criminal Procedure and Investigations Act 1996, s 6E(4) (CPD 25.A.6).

The right to open the defence case should not be overlooked or dismissed without thought. There are risks but also advantages of opening the defence case, just as there are in identifying the issues. You may choose to open the defence case where it has been a long time since the jury heard the prosecution opening or since you identified the issues. You may also wish to open the case if you will not be making your closing speech for some time. You may wish to make some defence points at this stage and/or to give context for the defendant's account.

If your client has a particular medical or other condition and/or mannerism which may affect the way they present and/or will give their evidence, you can address it at this stage. You will have raised it with the judge first. You are both warning and preparing the jury to concentrate on the evidence, without being distracted or influenced or otherwise by the irrelevant.

The fact you have greater licence at the later stage, may make the risks greater. You might wish to highlight any good defence points as they have emerged during the prosecution case. But, this is a question of judgement. If you will soon be making your defence closing speech, why would you wish to make such points now? If made in the closing speech, the prosecution has no opportunity to respond.

You may wish, and there may be good reason, not to commit yourself to the calling of witnesses. Nor will you identify weaknesses in the prosecution case, especially when they might be addressed and repaired. You will not need or (probably) want to go into the evidential detail of the defendant's evidence. This is an introduction; let the evidence speak and then you can deal with it in closing.

It is a right rarely exercised. There is good reason for that. Just as it is advantage to open first, so it is to close last. You will want to avoid repetition and protect your best points until they are most effectively deployed. That may very well be when you speak last.

DO

- Be clear, concise, ordered and accurate.
- Identify the core issues of the defence case.

DON'T

- Express personal opinions.
- Refuse a judicial request to (at least) identify the issues unless there is very good reason.
- Overlook the right to open the defence case.
- Do it unless you are going to improve the defence case.
- Go into the evidential detail of the defence case.
- Identify witnesses you will call unless sure they are available and prepared to give evidence.

PROSECUTION CLOSING SPEECHES
(Christopher Quinlan QC)

Entitlement

Archbold is helpful on the entitlement of the prosecutor to make a closing speech (4-420–4-424a). The entitlement is summarised in the CPR 2015, r 25.9(2)(c) which provides that the prosecution may make 'final representations', where:

1 the defendant has a legal representative;

2 the defendant has called at least one witness, other than the defendant themselves, to give evidence in person about the facts of the case; or

3 the court so permits.

Where the defendant is represented by an advocate but has called no evidence, the prosecuting advocate may well wish to make a speech to address, for example, inference from silence. In a multi-handed trial, there is an entitlement to make a speech if:

1   one defendant is represented by an advocate; and/or

2   none (all represented by advocates) gives evidence, but one calls evidence relevant to one or more of the others.

The mere fact a defendant has put documents in evidence and not otherwise called or given evidence does not entitle the prosecution to a closing speech.

Timing

Traditionally, the time to exercise the right was after the defence case has closed and before the defence closing speech. With the advent of the split summing-up, it may now be after the judge's legal directions. If you speak after the legal directions, they can provide a very useful structure around which to build your closing submission, particularly if the jury have them in writing.

For example, in an assault case where the issue is self-defence, you can marshal the evidence relevant to each limb of the defence and address it accordingly. If they have it in writing, you can take the jury to the document and tell them what you are doing and why. Bring the law and the evidence together, to help them reach their factual conclusions. Once more, you have them working with you. Similar use can be made of a written route to verdict. Take them through it, organising the evidence to the questions they have to answer.

Purpose

As the court in *Bryant and Oxley* remarked, reflecting the statutory derivation, it is the 'right to sum up the prosecution's evidence, or in modern parlance, to make a closing speech at the close of that evidence'. It is also to persuade the jury to the verdict you seek.

Content

Words are important. They are the part of the advocate's arsenal. Deploy them with care and precision. Think about the construction of the most important sentences at the start and at the end. Just as when you opened the case, try now to encapsulate it in memorable or striking terms. Try to return to the nutshell with which you started. Build on that at this stage; weave in now the points you made in evidence, including when cross-examining the defendant.

Be courteous and helpful, not didactic. As with the opening, the expression of personal opinions has no place in the closing speech. If the speech is of any length, tell the jury the framework or chapter headings. State that you not telling them what to do; rather seeking to make submissions and/or a number of points designed to help them when they retire to deliberate. They are free, you might say, to ignore them if they find them of no use.

The closing speech is more freestyle, less formulaic than the opening. You will know how the evidence has played out and how the issues have been examined. There should be structure, but it can be less rigid, more driven by and shaped to match the case than the opening. It is your last chance to address the jury; make it count.

Freestyle it may be, but you need order and structure. You need the jury to follow the points you are making. You are still engaged in the art of persuasion. Remain alive to the audience, maintain as much eye contact as you can, without being challenging. Do not be oversensitive to reactions. Madness will follow if you try reading the jury's body language (though if one or more is asleep it may be time for a break).

However, you are still constrained by the law. There are things you cannot say, some obvious, others less so. Once more the leading textbooks, including *Archbold*, assist (4-425). Exercise caution in commenting upon the defence's failure to call a particular witness and you must not comment upon any failure to call the defendant's spouse or civil partner. Do not refer to the consequences of conviction. Ensure that challenges to and comments upon the evidence accord with your cross-examination; you'll not be calling anyone a liar unless that was properly put. Any comment on a failure to provide an account in interview must concur with the judge's directions.

You should be able to write the bones of your closing speech before you start the trial. You know your case, what you are seeking to prove and how you hope to get there. Writing the structure of the closing speech before you start the trial will help you with many of aspects of it, from the opening to examining witnesses and cross-examining the defendant. It will help identify strong as well as weak points in your case.

You need to be flexible, to deal with points which have emerged unforeseen during the trial. You need to be nimble too, as you may have little time between close of the evidence and closing speech: part advocate, part mental gymnast. Sometimes the first line of a prosecuting advocate's closing speech comes from something the defendant said (and then regrets) in evidence.

The extent to which you rehearse or repeat the evidence will vary from case to case. It will depend (obviously) on its length, its nature, and the issues. In a case where the complainant's evidence was, in whole or in part, pre-recorded, it may lack the immediacy of a witness giving evidence in court. In such circumstances, do not be shy of reminding the jury of the precise words used to describe the incident(s). There is wisdom in the observation that sometimes you can tell the truth of what a person says not just from what they say, but how they say it.

Many cases will lend themselves to a theme which you develop through the case and the threads of which you bring together in the closing speech. That will include matters you put to the defendant during cross examination. when you cross-examined him. It will include matters you would have put to the defendant had he given evidence.

You are free to comment on the defendant's failure to give evidence, if the judge is giving such a direction. It is not the fact he did not give evidence which is important. It is the inference(s) you invite the jury to draw from it. Therefore, explore with the jury why the defendant exercised his right not to give evidence. Do not get embroiled in the law; deal with what matters and helps make your point.

Juries can be taken by surprise by the exchange between the judge and his advocate when the defendant announces that he is not giving evidence. Only the lawyers know it is coming and it is over in less than a minute. Remind them of the core of it, if you wish. It also makes it less a legal nicety and more a matter of common sense: why didn't he give evidence?

An understandable way to make this point is by reference to the questions you would have asked the defendant:

> As you know the defendant exercised his right not to give evidence. He is perfectly entitled to do so. However, you know – from what the judge told him in your presence - that he knows you may hold that decision against him; you may draw an inference adverse to him. What inference do we say it is fair to draw? That he has no answer to these important questions that you would have wanted him asked.

Once more you are being fair but drawing the jury in to work with you. You then set out the core topics upon which you would have asked the defandant questions; and ask, 'why if there were answers to those questions would the defendant not *share* them with you the jury?' The use of the word *share* is deliberate. It is reasonable; and suggests that the defendant has got no answer or not one he is prepared to divulge because it points to his guilt.

You must address the weak points of your case and the good defence arguments. You know they are coming, and it is nonsensical to avoid them. If you have an answer for them, you should provide it. Even if you do not have a complete answer, now is the time to acknowledge the points, draw the sting or confess and avoid if you can. For example, when commenting on the defendant's good character – 'you will take that into account but as the judge has told you/will tell you, that is not a defence. How could it be – no one would ever be convicted of crime if it was?'

In a sexual case where the complainant has not made an immediate disclosure or remained in a relationship with the defendant after the alleged assault: repeat the explanation(s) the complainant gave; emphasise the need to assess the individual and of the dangers of stereotypes; and while acknowledging they are matter(s) the jury may wish to consider, they do not undermine the truth of what the witness said.

Eloquence is the stock in trade of the successful advocate. As is preparation. There remains a place for the rhetorical flourish, and a memorable phrase has value. Do not underestimate the power of cold hard logic. In the appropriate case the 'I have ten points each of which points unanswerably to the defendant's guilt' approach works as well with a jury as it does a judge. Of course, eloquence and logic are not mutually exclusive.

Bring the threads of your case together at the end. Finish, as best you are able, on a high, linking the end to the start and to the theme you have had running through the case. No matter how good it is, you will not be permitted to give the jury a copy.

If you are fortunate, you will see many good, and a few great, advocates. The best make it look effortless. Learn from them but be yourself. Like most things in life, a good or great speech is the product of hard work. It requires thought, planning and a command of the evidence. Think about what you want to say and *how* you will say it. If you can 'lend variety to sameness and charm to the commonplace' you will be doing well. To take the audience with you, you need to know where you are going and how you will get there. If you can make it interesting on the way, the jury are sure to be grateful.

> '... if by a speech which is finely wrought and well delivered he can arouse the interest and secure the minds of his audience then he will secure a pleasure and satisfaction for himself which can be found in no other occupation.' [The Art of the Advocate, Richard du Cann QC, p 181]. He was right.

DO

- Be concise, structured and clear.

- Prepare the structure in advance of the trial.

- Be flexible.

- Address defence arguments.

- End on a high.

DON'T

- Express personal opinions.

- Hide from the defence points.

DEFENCE CLOSING SPEECHES (*Ramin Pakrooh*)

Introduction

Every defence advocate needs to be able to do two things well. First, you need to be able to find and plot a course over difficult waters, often through the narrowest of straits. Secondly, you need to be able to manually navigate your ship along the course you have plotted whilst recognising and adapting to contingencies if and when they arise. The defence closing speech calls heavily on both of those skills. It is one of the most important aspects of your role *as an advocate* because it relies so heavily on your advocacy itself. Here, your tribunal of fact consists of lay people. Here, you can speak more freely than at any other stage in the criminal trial precisely because you *can* comment on the evidence and on those through whom the evidence was given. Your client, through you, can finally say what she may have been trying, in substance, to say throughout the proceedings (whether she appreciates that or not).

We can simply never know if a closing speech in fact affected the outcome of a trial but we can be almost certain that a good speech has the potential to do so. Although a closing speech can be a thing of beauty, it certainly does not need to be so. Rather, first and foremost and before any such aesthetic considerations, it needs to be *effective*.

It is vital at the outset of looking at closing speeches to understand that they are not simply a last gasp attempt to turn the tide, a sideshow to distract a jury from overwhelming evidence or a mere bolt-on to whatever may have gone before. Rather, they represent the culmination and fruition of all the groundwork that the trial advocate has laid from their first touch of the case. An integrated and holistic approach should be taken in all preparatory hearings and conferences, in the defence statement and any other written document, in all dealings with the evidence, and in every interaction with judge, witness, defendant, and jury. Such should all be conducted *with purpose* and the closing speech is the coming together and final articulation of that singular purpose.

It follows therefore that right from the moment of first instruction, even as soon as the evidence and papers are being preliminarily examined, the defence advocate should already be asking themselves 'what is my speech to be in this?'.

How does a speech work?

Although making a speech is undoubtedly, in large part, an intellectual process, it does not solely operate in that way. Whilst all manner of points will be made as a matter of logic, with the intention that they should be persuasive, there are other important things taking place at the same time without which it can fail to achieve its purpose.

(i)   You are an ambassador for the defendant. Your demeanour, your conduct, your judgement and your treatment of everyone in the case can all contribute to achieving receptivity in your jury to the substance of your arguments. Your speech is your most direct contact with your client's tribunal of fact and you are aiming to appeal to hearts and minds. A defendant's case should be put with conviction, credibility and in its best light. Your credibility as an advocate can be the very thing that keeps a jury's minds open to the merits of your case.

(ii)   A serious case can place a jury under very significant pressure. In your speech, if you speak about difficult aspects of the case robustly but with appropriate language and with humanity, you can model to the jury how they can similarly remain appropriate without having to accept the prosecution case as put, and give them the language with which to express that in their deliberations. You thereby make it easier for them to reach the verdict you invite by relieving them of the awkwardness they might otherwise have had in grasping the nettle when dealing with and discussing difficult facts and situations.

(iii)   A speech can liberate a jury from any adverse feelings they may have for the defendant, or for the way the defendant may have conducted himself at any stage either at the time of the events or during the proceedings. Similarly, it can liberate a jury from a sense of guilt they may feel in apprehension that a not guilty verdict would amount to a rejection of a complainant's account. You can acknowledge those feelings, and then go on to separate the verdict from those feelings.

Getting over the fear of your position

It is natural for many defence advocates to be uncomfortable on some level with the speech that they must make. They may, for example, have decided in themselves that the evidence against their client is strong, their position indefensible and they may anticipate a hostile jury and an uphill struggle. That sort of thinking can cause fear and trepidation in the advocate. It can result in shying away from the weak points of a case, attempting to engage on safer ground and can make for an apologetic and unconvincing speech. A defence advocate should bear in mind:

(i)   Most juries will *want* to hear from the defence advocate. They heard the prosecution open the case. They heard the prosecution's closing speech. They know all that but still want to hear what YOU have to add to that picture.

(ii) A jury might wince when they first hear the indictment, or may feel squeamish when the case is first opened. However, during the course of the trial, if you (and others) comfortably use the language that you intend should become the lexicon of the facts; eg 'the wound', 'the lawful violence', 'the killing' etc a jury will tend to become accustomed to discussion of the facts, the issues and the parameters of the case. You will then be able to use this language in your speech with a jury who is familiar with it and no longer reacting to it as they did at first. They can then be equally comfortable in their deliberations when it comes to discussing these same issues. So, having laid the groundwork throughout the trial, use your speech as an opportunity to show a jury *how* to discuss the issues in the case and how to frame, phrase and approach their doubts about it.

(iii) At the outset, take good care in the drafting of your defence statement. Begin thinking at that stage of how the defence can be properly put at trial – whether it is on a wide or narrow footing and then build on this blueprint throughout the trial. All manner of failures and disgraceful conduct can still fall short of the offence indicted. Know your defence well, its parameters and components. Acknowledge the aspects of the evidence that are problematic, but then go on to demonstrate the considerations that apply beyond those that are merely preliminary.

(iv) Never underestimate the value and importance to the defence of the burden and standard of proof in a criminal trial. All trials take place under its mandate and all defence speeches are rooted in it.

Dealing with divisive topics

Some cases have the potential to divide juries. These might be cases involving social and political topics upon which people have strong opinions which are not easy to shift or change in the context of jury deliberations. Examples might be cases concerning race, gender, immigration, wealth, etc.

Recognise that potential in the facts of your case and think very carefully about how you choose to cast your closing speech. If you cast your speech in such a way as to draw out the controversy, and raise the case to a matter of principle or belief, you may well end up taking a chance on the lottery of people's beliefs and politics or splitting your jurors and triggering a hung jury.

It can often be the better course to refrain from framing your speech in such a way as to emphasise those fixed positions. You could instead attempt to ground your speech in the particular facts of your case and keep it framed within the effect on the individuals in your case. This could allow your jury, notwithstanding their different underlying views and beliefs, to find common ground in their view of the particular justice of your case, whilst they might never be able to agree were the matter refocused from specifics to general principles.

167

Good practice

An advocate will develop their own style of speech preparation and delivery. Some will write it out almost word for word and then deliver it. If that achieves results, and fits that advocate, then they should do that. You might it helpful, however, to try some of these methods until you find your own tried and tested workflow and method.

Gathering your material

The following are some practical steps an advocate can take to help marshal their material into a speech:

1   Collect your points freely as you go along during the trial in a space dedicated to your speech. This may be starting at the back page of your notebook, or in an electronic document, created for that purpose alone, and which remains open throughout your work on the case.

2   Do not place the bar too high at this stage. Allow ideas and even less focused thoughts in at this stage. This will become the 'ingredients' section that you will later sift through and draw upon when you begin to pull the threads together and create your first draft.

3   If you feel strongly about something during a trial, it is worth writing it down and seeing how you feel about it when you get to the end of the evidence. It may have passed and become innocuous or irrelevant. It may have become compounded by other instances of a similar nature which can be woven into a sub-topic for your speech, eg prosecutorial double standards, witnesses exaggerating for effect, persistently recurring misconception in case etc. Write down that response from a witness that you are simply dying to comment on. If it strikes you during the trial that something is being distorted or overemphasised, or overlooked, make a note of it here and punish the error in your speech.

4   Even if you find yourself saying the same thing in different ways, do not edit it just yet. Let your notes build up and then review at the end of the evidence when you prepare your speech. You may find you said it best on a particular occasion and that you like your own phrase in a particular entry which you would have been hard pressed to think of a second time.

5   Many an advocate will have the valuable resource of a reliable sounding board – a person upon whom they can draw as their everyman. You might have racked your brains for days and been stuck for a good example of a phenomenom you are trying to describe to a jury. You might ask your sounding board a question like 'Can you give me a good example of a

situation where people might lie about something purely to cover their own shame or embarassment, but which does no harm to the person to whom they have told the lie?'. Sometimes, that one good example can be particularly effective and fresh, when it did not come from you.

Writing your speech notes

Simply reading a speech out can, even in the hands of the best advocates, present the risk of a jury disengaging. They will know the difference. There is no harm in looking down from time to time – to read a quote accurately, to refer them accurately to some material in a jury bundle etc but there is no substitute, at this stage, for making a connection with as many of your jury as you can and really speaking to them as individuals. To help you do this, you need notes that do not require you to just read them out and that allow you to establish eye contact and rapport with your jury.

1   On your desk, during your speech, should be an aide-memoire but not a script. You should be able to look down, see your own 'reminder' and be able to tell the jury what you want to tell them about that point. If you have prepared your notes carefully and are thoroughly familiar with your notes, you may find that a glance down to a sub-heading is sufficient to trigger your speech in that area.

2   If there is a tricky area of your speech and precision of words is vital, either as to meaning (eg where you want to be strictly accurate about how something fits in with the law or the evidence) or as to impact (say where you want the jury to use *your phrase* as the way of describing something), then write it down precisely and follow your words for that portion. The act of looking down at that point, and the accompanying change in pace of your speaking, will only serve to underline the importance of those particular words.

3   If you want to take the jury to a part of the evidence, have your references to that written down neatly and accurately as a favour to yourself. If it's a page number in a jury bundle, a simple 'JB35' will be sufficient. If it's a quote from a witness's oral testimony, write it down and quote it accurately but above all things, make it easy for yourself by being clear.

4   Have a thematic overall structure to your speech, eg:

Speech

1   Intro – Burden and Standard.

2   Comment – Difficult case for number of reasons

3   Indictment – pros have to prove XYZ. Nature of defence – issues in case.

169

4   Witness 1 and 2 – problems with their evidence.

5   Helpful prosecution evidence: Read sections from s 9 witnesses 4 and 5, as highlighted.

6   Defendant – his evidence – bear in mind ABC, make allowances for EFG.

7   No Comment in interview – bear in mind what D knew at time, environment, etc.

8   3 things in case that just don't add up – witnesses have plainly concealed GHI behaviour.

9   Prosecution can perhaps show A and B but have no evidence to support C. Serious problem in case.

10   End – Burden and Standard of Proof.

5   In a short case, you might have your entire speech notes on a double page spread, in a dozen or so paragraphs, each with a bold sub-heading and a few bullet points beneath.

6   In a longer case, you may have your speech spread over a dozen or more pages, each headed by the sub-topic and the page populated by concise bullet points/references.

7   Above all, you should find your notes easy to read at a glance, crystal clear in structure and they should be VERY familiar to you – so that a quick look down sets you off on that particular sub-topic. On your feet, in front of a jury, is no time to be squinting and trying to decipher messy handwriting, or trying to pick out a phrase that is lost within a sea of uniform-looking 12 point text.

Delivery

A closing speech must be delivered in your voice. It must be you talking. It is not the same you that might be chatting informally about something in another context, but it still has to be natural to you. It can take some years to find that professional voice. In the early stages of your career, if in doubt, err on the side of speaking more rather than less formally.

It is strongly recommended that you physically practise uttering parts of your speech out loud. This might be at home the night before you deliver it. Listen to yourself saying the words. Form the sentences. Become accustomed to saying the things you intend to say. Experiment with different approaches to the same point. A number of things will result:

(i)   It is a form of pressure testing your own arguments. If one of your arguments has a flaw, or a response that is likely to cross a juror's thoughts, it should become clear to you too as you listen to your arguments said out loud. You will find out, very soon, if one of your arguments is double edged and it is far better to hear it for yourself in preparation and then adjust or abandon, than for a previously unforeseen riposte to dawn on you mid-speech.

(ii)   Speech has its own type of memory. A phrase, or group of phrases you have used time and time again will tend to come naturally off your tongue and are capable of adjustment and amendment as you go in a way that *new speech* and *new ideas* are sometimes not. You need to make your own mouth and your own speech centres familiar with the material you will be uttering under pressure in the near future to allow you to do so with fluidity and authority.

(iii)   A thought or an idea can seem acceptable as just that but can fail to carry over into the spoken word. You sometimes need to hear it said out loud to be able to judge whether it works or not, what its impact may be and whether it might, said out loud, sound crass, offensive, far-fetched, pompous or just plain weak.

The utility of the closing speech

The utility of the closing speech is not limited to the outcome of the trial. The outcome may well be an important *goal* to set oneself, but it is not the only *benefit* of a good closing speech. Amongst other benefits of the defence closing speech are:

(i)   A good closing speech can increase public confidence in the criminal justice system. A jury who came to court expecting the defence advocate to deploy aggression, deceit and pedantry may be heartened to find the situation otherwise. A speech in which reality is embraced, no sleight of hand takes place, evidence is robustly but appropriately scrutinised, the weaknesses and failings of human nature are acknowledged and the better side of people is appealed to, may well work wonders for public attitudes to justice. Twelve people at a time, you have an opportunity to play your part in demonstrating that the true fabric of the criminal justice system is formed by the conduct and character of those who act within it.

(ii)   Nobody wants to be convicted, but more than that, nobody wants to be convicted without having had the chance to speak out in defence of their position. A good closing speech can be a critical moment in a defendant's abiding sense that their trial was fair. It shows your client that you were properly representing their position and for many will have been the one and only time in the whole process that they felt that things were going in their favour. Right after your closing speech, unclouded by outcome,

171

can be a good time to ask your client if they are content with how things have been put on their behalf.

The universal underlying theme

We often feel confident in a view that we hold, but were we to ask ourselves about the foundation for that view, we would frequently have difficulty in clearly pointing to the supporting evidence. This challenge – of avoiding prejudgment – can be a powerful theme common to all defence closing speeches. If that question is asked, and its challenge placed over the indictment as an overlay, then a speech begins to emerge naturally. The call to a jury, having taken their oaths or affirmations to 'give a true verdict according to the evidence' must be to hold them to just that standard.

You are asking them to think and judge for themselves, individually as jurors, before doing so collectively as a jury. You are reminding them not to accept things at face value, to look beyond the obvious, to ask 'how do we know this?' and 'if that is right, what then of it?'. You are asking them to look through their own eyes and not through the eyes of others. If *that* is your theme, you can always get behind it and if *that* is what you are inviting the jury to do, *you can say it and mean it every time.*

Chapter 22

Hard things to say

Anna Vigars QC

Also known as 'What to do in those situations which nothing seems to have prepared you for'. Being an advocate can be hugely exhilarating. You won't be heading for a life in the Crown Court if you don't find people endlessly fascinating. But they do also have this drawback; people aren't terribly predictable, neither other people, nor you. And so, there will be times when the unpredictable hits you. How do you deal with those moments?

First, some general rules and then some more specific thoughts.

GENERAL RULES

1   Do your homework, be prepared. You will have heard this at other points in this book but it really can't be emphasised enough; read your papers, know what your case is, *really* know it, stack your brain full of the information about the case. That way you are much more capable of being lighter on your feet and swifter of thought when the unexpected happens. It goes further than just reading your papers again and again: being prepared involves thinking about your case from all angles, so that you really understand what you are saying and from where the attacks might come.

2   Accept that you are human. It would be lovely if every advocate were capable of going to court and never asking a stupid question or misunderstanding an answer. Just because something goes wrong does not mean that you are bad at the job.

3   Think before you open your mouth; sometimes your first instinct will be right, very often even a first instinct is improved with a bit of thought. You will always be forgiven for taking a moment to consider something inside your head before you allow it to see the light of day. Often the judge and your opponent will also be pondering the right direction; sometimes there is no correct answer, just a range of choices to be considered.

SOME SPECIFIC SITUATIONS

What if your client doesn't like you?

You aren't there to become your client's friend. Hopefully the client will have other people there in that role (although they may not always be helpfulif they sit and snigger in the public gallery – in which case be bold about getting your client to get them under control or get rid of them). Obviously, you will hope to gain your client's confidence and trust, but that doesn't necessarily mean they will like you. Be professional, set things out clearly, be patient, be prepared to go over things again.

Set the boundaries for this relationship with a difficult client; what you can and cannot achieve, what you are responsible for and what is outside your role. Set out what your objectives are, let your client understand that you really are on their side, that your objective is getting the best possible outcome for him or her.

Sometimes clients want to do something that you might think unwise. Remember that they are seeing a different picture from the evidential one that you see, and it is your role to advise, not to decide for the client, whose view may be clouded by emotion or unhelpful stubbornness, but it helps to appreciate that they will look at the case in a different light from you. Clients are entitled to make decisions which you don't think are in their best interests but also entitled to your advice, and your help to understand that advice.

Make sure that you take instructions in writing where necessary. You should not do a trial without a written proof of evidence, even if you have to take it yourself. Get the client to agree that proof and to sign it off. Explain that even though you are drafting a defence statement it is their document and they are the one who will be asked questions about it should it be wrong or incomplete. Where you are taking important tactical decisions, get instructions in writing in advance setting out what you have advised, what the risks are, that the client understands, and is content to take the course you're setting out on.

When a juror is nodding off

If it is happening during the evidence it is annoying, if it is happening during your own speech it's very unflattering, but from time to time jurors do drop off. They do so particularly while watching long video-recorded interviews. Sometimes it is worth acknowledging in an opening speech: 'You may find that it is difficult to concentrate on and that your attention wanders. If you do find that then do let everyone know and I'm sure that Her Honour will let us all have a short break'.

However much you try and head it off, sometimes it happens. Keep enough of an eye on the jury to check that they are all awake. Some judges get so wrapped up in taking notes of evidence that they aren't great at checking the jury is being attentive. Get the jury out of court on some pretext; 'Your Honour, there's a matter I need to raise in the absence of the jury' will do the trick. Once they are out of court simply explain what you saw, which juror it was, and then the judge will have the jury back in, often not saying anything to them but trusting the break has done the trick. If it happens again and again then the judge may ask the usher to speak discreetly to the juror to see if there is a problem, but more frequent breaks usually work.

When the jury looks bored

A Crown Court trial isn't supposed to match US television drama for excitement so don't feel responsible for laying on entertainment. Very rare use of humour can be attractive, but it can fall flat and leave you feeling diminished so don't try it simply in a desperate bid to liven things up. A jury cannot escape from your speech so make sure that it is well-thought through and concise.

Again, it is about preparation. Sometimes in a short case you won't get much thinking time before you get to your speech so think about it ahead of time. Sometimes a jury looks bored because that is the way their faces settle at rest, sometimes they look bored because you are being tedious and making points which they got when you first mentioned them. Be ruthless and know when to stop talking. It isn't as much fun for people to listen to you as it is for you to talk.

Most jurors take their task seriously and understand that the decision that they are being asked to make is an important one, even if only for those immediately involved, so, even if they are looking bored, that doesn't mean that they are not paying attention.

When the judge falls asleep

Try not to get to this stage! If you suspect the typing has ceased because sleep is imminent then create a diversion; ask for the jury to leave court – the chances are that if the judge is nodding off at least one of the jury may be doing the same. Once the jury are out address a slumbering judge directly 'I'm going to take the witness to the plan/photographs/exhibit, does Your Honour have a copy of that?'. If your judge really has dropped off, then make a careful note of the point in the evidence at which you noticed the judge sleeping. You will need it to assist with notes when the judge wakes up and need to catch up.

When you ask a stupid question

It happens! It will happen to you.

Think through to the end of a question before you let the first words out. Don't let excitement at getting somewhere with a witness make you speed up and rob you of thinking time. If you have to put or elicit something which is complex or technical or highly emotional consider writing yourself a series of questions so that you can get through it safely.

At some point you will ask a stupid question or one containing a double-entendre so clanging that it still makes you wince at 3am on a Thursday morning ten years later. Let the laughter die down. Take a deep breath. Reformulate the question properly. Ask it and then move on.

Where you say something you didn't mean or a question rambles off into the distance without a hope of being understood by the witness, apologise, say that being understood is your responsibility, and think it through before you try again. You are wise to acknowledge that being understood is your responsibility for two reasons; partly because it is, and everyone in court knows that, so you will just appear straightforward; and partly because it is a way of reclaiming the authority when everyone is laughing at your expense. It emphasises to everyone that you are the person asking the questions, you are the one in control.

Sometimes a smug witness will think that they can run rings around you. You confirm that impression if you get flustered. However you are feeling inside, take a deep breath, slow down. Make the witness wait for the question. Concentrate ferociously on what you are doing in that moment. Pose the question in your head first.

When an opponent is dismissive

Don't let someone get under your skin. Of course, life can be easier if you can persuade someone of the strength of your argument in the robing room. If that doesn't happen you have a simple retort; 'Let's see what the judge says'. And if you have prepared your argument well and thought it through properly then you will be on solid ground in court and any dismissive advocacy from your opponent is likely to be pretty unattractive to your judge. However dismissive your opponent, they are not the one who decides the outcome.

Just occasionally an opponent will be dismissive because you really are arguing something foolish; absorb that with good grace and put it behind you.

Be prepared, be calm, and never forget you are human!

Part VIII

Sentencing

Chapter 23

Opening for sentence

Anna Vigars QC

Key references

- *Banks on Sentence 2020*

- *Thomas' Sentencing Referencer 2020*

- The Sentencing Council website: www.sentencingcouncil.org.uk

---

Case law

- *R v Goodyear* [2005] EWCA Crim 888

- *R v Perkins, Bennett, Hall* [2013] EWCA Crim 323

GOODYEAR HEARINGS

In order that a defendant might know the top of the range of sentences that the judge has in mind, she may instruct her advocate to ask. That should not be done without clear instructions and the judge is also entitled to understand from counsel the precise basis upon which a defendant is to be sentenced. In those circumstances, prosecution counsel might well be called upon to outline the facts of the case and, perhaps, to assist with where in the guidelines the offence falls. Experience suggests that judicial unwillingness to be tied into providing indications and the fact of the guidelines themselves means that the *Goodyear* procedure is less used than was the case a few years ago. Nonetheless it is important that you are sufficiently prepared to be able to help the judge. It is no use opening the case briefly at this stage, without consideration, because, once a judge indicates the highest sentence that would be passed, the defendant is entitled to act in reliance on that: you cannot unpick it by suddenly remembering something else which should have been taken into consideration.

PURPOSE OF OPENING A CASE FOR SENTENCE

Before you do any piece of advocacy, ask yourself why you are doing it. What is the reason for opening your mouth? Understanding that dictates how you approach the task. Here the reasons include these:

(a)   the judge and the defence understand the way in which the prosecution puts the case;

(b)   the public understands the way the case is put;

(c)   the voice of the complainant can be heard where they have chosen that; and

(d)   the relevant sentencing guidance and powers are put before the judge.

It is emphatically not your job to press the court for any particular sentence, especially not the highest sentence possible. Sometimes it is tempting to colour the opening with the worst excesses of the defendant's behaviour while keeping those mitigating features quieter. That is not your role. As prosecutor you are there to be a fair and impartial presenter of facts. The role of the defence advocate is to mitigate, to advocate on behalf of the defendant, to press for a lower sentence; your role is not to mirror that.

Begin by reading the papers carefully. Where one incident is recounted by more than one witness work out how their stories marry together. Do not be tempted to open a case from the police summary of facts. Ever. That document is a tempting convenience but it is a mistake to use it for two reasons; it is often written at an early stage in the case before all of the evidence has been secured and understood, so it may not be accurate, and it is also often an aspirational document in that it is written by someone very much hoping that the evidence bears out what they say. Sometimes close and objective scrutiny of the evidence, rather than the summary, results in a different interpretation.

If an incident was captured on CCTV then watch that so that you can talk the judge through it. Identify the key parts of the CCTV and know which defendant is which, or when the knife is produced, or which car brings the defendant to the scene so that you can be a useful guide. You may have been provided with ten minutes of CCTV when only ninety seconds are relevant. You are not obliged to play it all!

Take account of conflicts between what is alleged and what is accepted. If there are irreconcilable differences draw them to the judge's attention at the beginning of the hearing so that the judge can work out the basis upon which to proceed. It may be that those differences need to be dealt with by the calling of evidence. That is for the judge to decide after you have set out the differences. If the judge decides that the disputed areas will make no difference to sentence, then the defendant will be sentenced on the basis on which they have pleaded.

An opening for sentence is different from an opening for trial. You are not seeking to persuade but to provide information. You can assert as accepted fact the information on the prosecution papers rather than hedging it around as you might when opening the case for trial. You need to think carefully about whether you will take the judge to particular exhibits and if so, why, how will you do that, and what do you want the judge to see from those documents when you go there.

Once you have dealt with the facts of the offence, you need to turn to the defendant's antecedent record and to use your judgement. What offences are relevant to the decision that the judge is making? If you are prosecuting an offence of burglary then it matters little that the defendant was caught driving whilst disqualified ten years earlier, but his string of offences of dishonesty, which began with theft from shops nine years ago and which has included three non-dwelling burglaries and an offence of theft from an employer along the way, are all relevant. Conversely, if you are prosecuting the same burglar but his driving offence was only a week before the burglary and so he was on bail for that when he committed this offence, then the driving offence *is* relevant.

Check the last few offences; did any of them result in a suspended sentence which is still live, or a sentence of imprisonment for which the licence is still running, or a conditional discharge? Are any of those sentences triggered by the commission of the offence which you are now prosecuting? It is no help at all to a judge to say that you don't know the answer to that question and it is rude to have to say that you don't know when the answer, bluntly, is that you hadn't thought about it and so you hadn't checked. You might also want to find out if any records exist of the facts of previous offences where they are of the same kind as this one. One distraction burglary of an elderly person in their own home is more serious when it is the latest in a line of similar offences all targeting vulnerable people. It is your responsibility to do what you can to establish whether that is what you are dealing with by getting in touch with the officer in charge (OIC) ahead of the hearing rather than coming across it as you open the case.

You will also want to turn to any victim personal statement (VPS) that you have been sent. Again, you need to have read this document through ahead of time and to have checked what the author of the statement is expecting to happen. Some people want to read out their own statement, others want you to read it and others want the judge to read it to themselves only (in all cases, obviously, the defence will need to see it ahead of time). Check the VPS before reading it: does it comply with the rules? Concentrate on the parts relevant to sentence, and ignore parts which sometimes creep in unwanted. The court needs to know about the impact of the offending upon the victim, not where they went on holiday last year – unless directly relevant. Before uploading or distributing the VPS, it is good practice to bracket anything which should not be there and which you do not intend to read out: particularly if it includes a witness expressing their desire for the judge to lock the defendant up and throw away the key.

As you prepare a case for sentence you must check the Sentencing Guidelines Council website to see if there is a guideline which applies to this offence. The guidelines divide into two groups; those which are specific to a particular type of offence, and those which cover broad sentencing principles such as the Imposition of Community and Custodial Sentences definitive guideline. Generally, you will be more concerned with the application of the specific guideline but you may wish to draw the judge's attention to the relevant and more general guidelines in particular cases. Look at the guideline carefully and ensure that you are working from the correct section of it. Do not, for example, assist a judge with the sentencing bracket for possession with intent to supply a Class A drug when the defendant whom you are prosecuting was offering cannabis for sale, or the robbery guidelines for street robberies when the victim of the offence was a shopkeeper at work.

Consider carefully which of the aggravating and mitigating features apply in your particular case. It is not your job to find as many aggravating features to the case as you possibly can while dismissing any potential sources of mitigation. Look at the drop-down lists in the online versions of the guidelines and be rigorous in your application of the guidelines to the facts in your case.

Sentencing is a fiendishly difficult area of criminal law because every government thinks that it is sensible to tweak powers to sentence and then tucks interesting twists and turns away into various dark corners of statutes that do not necessarily, by their title, give away their content. The Court of Appeal, in considering cases in which sentencing has gone wrong, will often lament the fact that the very experienced judge was clearly not given 'the help to which he was entitled by counsel'. If it doesn't seem fair to you that counsel, from the outset of a career, is expected to be able to guide the judge (who first appeared in a Crown Court at about the time you were discovering the delights of play-doh) through the arcane delights of sentencing law, then concentrate on learning those arcane delights rather than railing against the injustice of it all. The latter will get you nowhere and the former, assisting with getting the sentence right, is actually part of your job.

Of course, it is always a relief when you are not asked by a judge 'What are my powers in respect of x or y' but you should always be in a position to answer those questions. And, while you are still a pupil or a trainee, it is worth knowing that those who are able to answer those kinds of questions are often the people about whom pupil supervisors or Heads of Chambers or partners receive emails of praise from judges. So, look up carefully what power a judge has to deal with the community order imposed by the magistrates' court a week before the assault with which you are dealing, or with the offence of driving without insurance which has arrived in the Crown Court on the back of a count of dangerous driving which is denied. Judges often struggle with what points to impose for driving offences and which offences require mandatory retests before licences can be renewed because that is not their usual fare. Be alert to those situations.

You need to understand what the effect of imposing a custodial sentence is today if the defendant was sentenced to nine months' imprisonment only six weeks ago by a different court. The ideal place for looking those sorts of things up is not the back of a busy Crown Court on a Friday morning. Sometimes it has to be done there, but that sort of heavy lifting is often better done when you have a bit of thinking time the day before.

Chapter 24

Effective mitigation

Andrew Langdon QC

By a significant majority, defendants appearing in the Crown Court plead guilty. Therefore, most pleas of mitigation are made on behalf of those whose voice is only directly heard by the judge upon their arraignment. It is up to you to make good the deficit, to advance as effectively as you can what may be said for them. You are speaking for them, about what they did and about who they are. Your aim is to achieve the most lenient outcome they can realistically expect.

If convicted after a trial during which their defence has been rejected by the jury, you can and should be considerably briefer, in part because they have had their say and in part because the judge knows all about the offence and is likely to be unmoved by late expressions of remorse.

When sentencing following a guilty plea, the judge will have received information from a variety of sources. She may have read prosecution statements or summaries written by a policeman or a lawyer with varying degrees of accuracy and fairness. She might have read parts of your client's interview. She should have read a pre-sentence report, if one has been prepared. That report may have helped your client but equally it may have made matters worse. Immediately before you address the judge, the facts will have been opened by the prosecution, noted any relevant previous convictions and read any victim impact statements. The content of the prosecution opening has the capacity to change the judge's view of seriousness, one way or the other. Finally, the judge will have the prosecution submission as to which category the sentence should be placed in, according to the sentencing guidelines. As a result of all of that, in almost every case the judge will have an idea of the sentence she should pass before she hears a word from you. She will already have in mind such mitigation as there is on the face of the papers, and factored it into her thinking.

In most cases, when it is your turn to mitigate, the judge is waiting to see if you have anything to say that might make a difference to what she has in mind. You may be able to tell her hem something she does not know, or you may persuade her them that there is another way of characterising what is already known.

What is the most effective way of mitigating? Sometimes you may have an abundance of material. More often you will have little. An inexperienced advocate may sometimes feel that there may be nothing left to say, or nothing

184

that will make any difference. Sometimes saying very little may indeed be the most effective approach, but it is a mistake to believe that you cannot make a difference. In fact, a skilful advocate can make a very considerable difference to the sentence that the judge eventually passes.

A familiar scenario is this: a defence advocate rising to their feet when it seems as if the task ahead is hopeless. There seems to be nothing that can be said in favour of the defendant, still less to soften the crime they have committed, and yet, in the hands of a skilful advocate, little by little, the atmosphere changes. Salient mitigation begins to emerge. It starts to take the edge off the way the prosecution has sought to characterise the offence. It presents another aspect of the offender that permits some empathy. The judge begins to think that after all, she need not pass the heavy sentence that was first in mind. Properly organised and delivered, mitigation carefully advanced will cut the length of a sentence or, on occasion, spare your client a custodial term altogether.

Some advocates make the mistake of thinking that a plea in mitigation is somehow a lesser form of advocacy than trial advocacy. This is not just wrong, it is irresponsible. The adversarial system requires you to try to put the other side of the coin; to say what can be said to mitigate. Contrary to how you will sometimes feel, there is in fact no such case where nothing can be said that will make any difference. There is always a risk that a judge will pass a sentence that is more severe than it should have been if you do not play your part in alerting her to something of which she was unaware, or inviting her to look at the case from a wider perspective. Remember that a court when passing sentence *'must'* have regard not only to punishment but, amongst other factors, also to 'the reform and rehabilitation' of your client; see the Criminal Justice Act 2003, s 142(1)(c).

The circumstances of an offence and an offender are infinitely variable and so it is not possible to provide a blue-print of how to approach mitigation. In any event, you must work out what is the style and method most effective when deployed by you. All advocacy is personal and perhaps never more so than in a plea in mitigation. You have a relatively free hand in how you approach the task.

The course you take in any individual case will be shaped not just by the offence and the client but also by the identity of the judge, the thoroughness and fairness of the prosecution, the nature and attitude of any victim and their loved ones. You will want to avoid timeworn and hackneyed phrases that betray a lack of thought about the case you now conduct. Work out a structure, a plan as to how to approach your task. Once you have it, you must be ready to change tack swiftly when you realise that you need to do so in the face of a development; something your opponent has said (or not said) in opening, or, some unexpected intimation from the judge.

Though the variety is infinite, there are some things you should always consider.

First, on what factual basis is your client to be sentenced? If there is a dispute which may make a material difference to sentence, you will need a signed basis of plea, and your client will need to give evidence so that the judge can resolve the dispute in a *Newton* hearing. Most of the time, if you can, you will want to avoid such a hearing. It will rarely improve the defendant's position, and if the judge concludes the defendant has lied to her, any expression of remorse will sound hollow and you will have lost credit for plea.

Assuming there is no dispute as to the essential facts, you may nonetheless want to say something about the way the prosecution has opened the case or characterised the offence or your client. Can you make inroads there? By using the right phrase, or by pointing to some evidence which your opponent has overlooked or mis-described, you may be able to gently deflate a prosecution that has pitched the case too high.

What additional material if any, do you want to place before the court? Do you have character witnesses, or letters? They can, in the right case, make a big impact, but as ever you must be selective. They can backfire if they reveal that your client has not sufficiently grasped the perilousness of his position. In general terms however, you should not underestimate the potential impact upon a judge reading or hearing from those who really know your client and have good things to say about them. A character witness who is not from the immediate family – a step removed, so that they may be more objective - will usually make the best impact. Most judges will not welcome emotional imploring from family members, but occasionally a letter from a close relative, if balanced and reasonable, will make a judge think again.

Ask yourself, if there is anything that you know about your client that a judge will not know that may incline her to be more sympathetic. You must be careful how to pitch this, because if a judge is unlikely to accept what your client has told you, you must weigh into the balance whether it is wise to risk calling them to give evidence on the topic.

Your knowledge of the particular judge may help you decide how best to present your mitigation. If you do not know your judge's ways, there is every reason to ask others of her/his reputation. Judges are human, and they are different from each other. One judge may be known as guideline-bound; another may have a reputation of being prepared to risk a more lenient sentence where it might yield dividends in terms of the longer-term prospects of reoffending.

The Sentencing Guidelines inevitably import a certain mechanistic framework to sentencing, but it is lazy advocacy merely to refer to the guidelines. You must know where in the guidelines you want the judge to end up; or, you may have good reasons to suggest they are departed from, in the interests of justice. Whatever your submission, you will need to be ready to provide the reasons for your contention by a brief reference to the guidelines. Do it in as pithy and succinct way as you can. A plea which becomes mired in unadulterated guideline terminology will die on its feet.

Never forget that you are there to make a difference which usually means trying to alter the provisional view the judge may have. It is not your job to make sentence easier for the judge, unless of course she intimates she is with your primary submission – in which case, take the hint and stop!

A good plea of mitigation demands a significant amount of work. Once you have read all you need to read and listened to your client, it requires a good deal of hard thought in preparation. Your pleas need not be long: if you have done the work they will be focused and short.

How best to prepare? Ask yourself:

- What is the best sentence I can realistically expect to achieve for my client?

- What is the judge's provisional view on sentence going to be?

- To what extent should I acknowledge what is against me, without making it sound that I know I have no chance?

- What is my best point?

- How best do I capture it succinctly, to make an impact?

- How can I make the judge feel comfortable about passing the sentence I want her to pass?

- If present, what must the public or the press hear me say that they may not know, which means that the sentence the judge passes (if more lenient that they were expecting) can be better understood by them?

Having prepared and planned your approach, get into the courtroom itself, and absorb the atmosphere. Is the judge short of time? If so, how can you legitimately make the most of that for your client? Do you want to point to particular aspects of the evidence, or will it be more effective to focus the submission elsewhere, such as the attitude of your client to their own offending?

You need to be realistic. The judge has a public duty to discharge, and the guidelines set some perimeters. You need the judge to think that you are bringing something useful to the exercise. A mere recitation of the obvious will merely demonstrate that the mitigation cupboard is bare.

Finally, as with all that you do as an advocate, your reputation matters. Judges will work out if you are an advocate who thinks hard about what you want to say, and who makes realistic submissions that help to reach the right sentence. In a nutshell, they learn whether you are worth listening to. The better you become at pleas in mitigation, the more they will be inclined to listen, and the more effective you will become for your clients. What is more, as an advocate who is thoughtful in the selection of subject matter, and realistic in terms of what is sought, you will improve the quality of justice delivered when sentence is passed.

Chapter 25

Hospital orders

Mary Cowe

Key references

- The Department of Health Reference Guide to the Mental Health Act 1983

- Criminal Procedure (Insanity) Act 1964, s 4, 5

- Mental Health Act 1983 (MHA 1983), ss 33–55

Case law

- *R v Edwards* [2018] EWCA Crim 595

OVERVIEW

You will encounter hospital orders in two main scenarios in the Crown Court.

The first are disposals under the Criminal Procedure (Insanity) Act 1964, chiefly when a defendant who was not fit to plead and stand trial is found by a jury to have 'done the act'. Consequent on such a finding, the Criminal Procedure (Insanity) Act 1964, s 5 provides that the court can *only* make either:

(a)   a hospital order (with or without a restriction order);

(b)   a supervision order; or

(c)   an order for his absolute discharge.

The above provisions also apply to those unusual cases where a special verdict has been returned that although the defendant did the act, on the balance of probabilities the jury have concluded he is 'not guilty by reason of insanity'. The reason that rather clinical term 'disposal' is used is because findings that a defendant did the act are not convictions and these orders are not sentences.

188

Often, the fact that the prosecution proceeded with a case which falls under the Criminal Procedure (Insanity) Act 1964, s 5 will mean that the defendant's behaviour is sufficiently serious and his mental health sufficiently poor that a hospital order will generally be foreseeable. However, there will be cases where a defendant is unfit for some other reason, such as having severe learning difficulties, where hospital treatment is not necessary or appropriate and a supervision order or discharge should be sought.

The second, and more common scenario is where a defendant has been convicted on a guilty plea or after a conventional criminal trial but is thought to require clinical assistance and some form of hospital order is being considered.

HOSPITAL ORDERS ON CONVICTION

The possibility that a hospital order may be an appropriate sentence is something that you should consider at an early stage; you may ask a psychiatrist to prepare a report concerning disposal alone, or it may be something that features in a more wide-ranging report dealing with fitness/intent/trial adaptations. Disposal reports will also deal with issues such as whether the defendant needs to be remanded or transferred to hospital for assessment.

You need to have a good understanding of the MHA 1983, ss 35–55 so that you can make informed submissions to the court.

The orders a judge will consider at sentence will be:

– Imprisonment.

– Hospital Order without restriction under the MHA 1983, s 37.

This will be made where the court is satisfied, on the evidence of two registered medical practitioners, that the offender is suffering from mental disorder of a nature or degree which makes it appropriate for him to be detained in a hospital and appropriate medical treatment is available, and 'the court is of the opinion, having regard to all the circumstances including the nature of the offence and the character and antecedents of the offender, and to the other available methods of dealing with him, that the most suitable method of disposing of the case is by means of an order under this section'.

The order is not made for a set period and ends when the defendant is discharged, which can be done by clinicians alone.

– Hospital order with restriction under the MHA 1983, ss 37 and 41.

This order is made when the criteria for a s 37 order have been met, at least one of the registered doctors has given oral evidence, and 'it appears to the court, having regard to the nature of the offence, the antecedents of

189

the offender and the risk of his committing further offences if set at large, that it is necessary for the protection of the public from serious harm' to make such an order.

The order is not made for a set period and ends when the defendant is released with permission of the Secretary of State (this constitutes the 'restriction' element) – in practice discharge by a Mental Health Review Tribunal (MHRT) which is satisfied that the grounds for detention are no longer met.

– A hospital and limitation order under the MHA 1983, s 45A.

The criteria for a s 37 order need to be met and one of the clinicians must have given oral evidence. Sometimes called a 'hybrid order', this is where a term of imprisonment is passed as part of the order, but the defendant is initially taken to hospital. If during the currency of the order the clinicians recommend to the Secretary of State/MHRT that treatment is no longer required, this renders the defendant liable to spend the rest of the order in prison.

There are further requirements in the Act concerning the availability of a bed which are of practical importance, but the above sets out the central choices for the judge. The case of *R v Edwards* sets out how the judge should navigate these choices and is essential reading.

In summary, in a case where a hospital order may be appropriate a judge should consider all the options above and remember the importance of the penal element in a sentence (which would be reflected by a MHA 1983, s 45A sentence). The judge should then assess the offender's culpability. If the judge decides a hospital order of some kind is appropriate, he should consider the MHA 1983, s 45A first. If he goes on to impose either a s 37 or s 37/41 order, he must explain why a penal element is not appropriate.

There is much of interest in this case including a discussion of whether the licence regime under the MHA 1983, s 45A or the conditions that may be attached to a section 37/41 order may better protect the public: as is often the case, it is 'fact specific'.

The court notes in one paragraph of *Edwards* that the fact that the offence would not have happened but for the client's mental illness does not necessarily mean he has no culpability, and in another warns against regarding all failure to take medication as culpable omissions. The court in *Edwards* (just as in courts across the land) tries to balance what can sometimes be competing aims: an offender whose culpability appears to be very low may present a high risk of future offending, and it can be difficult to decide on whether the emphasis should be on public protection or personal mitigation.

Do not abandon your defendant with the words 'it's a matter for the learned judge and the psychiatrists' because you are in hospital order territory.

Now more than ever your defendant needs you to make the legal points on his behalf:

- Have the prosecution put the offence in the right category?

- Is the assessment of risk based on something concrete?

- Is further assessment needed?

- Is there a proper factual link between: (i) the socially undesirable aspects of your client's life that have been ventilated; and (ii) his culpability for this offence?

It is generally advisable to have one expert at court in case they are needed for sentence. It is sensible to speak to the expert, whether they are your expert or the prosecution expert, before they give evidence. If you are speaking to the prosecution expert, your opponent should be there. Make sure you understand why their conclusions are as they are: be curious not combative. Inform yourself beforehand of the different after-care and staged discharge plans available to patients/defendants on different orders: the Department of Health Reference Guide is a good way to do this. Consider asking more around what a particular order would mean for the defendant, why it is necessary, and the basis for this conclusion – the clinician's own experience (which is not be taken lightly), or a paper reviewing the outcomes?

As we can see in *Edwards*, the regime that exists for defendants suffering from mental disorder tries to do several (sometimes incompatible) things at once:

- respect their personal agency;

- acknowledge its limitations at times when they are floridly unwell;

- intervene to reduce risk therapeutically; and

- incapacitate defendants so that they are not free to commit further offences.

We must acknowledge that some sort of system is needed for offenders who are unwell, the extremely difficult task that judges face, and the significant help that experts can provide.

Nonetheless, risk assessment is not an exact science and culpability is not a clinical concept: one cannot look inside a defendant's brain and see guilty neurons.

We all know what these labels mean, but sometimes you may have to probe behind an assertion that someone's behaviour was culpable to assess if the expert means that the defendant was able to act in a different way if they chose, or whether this is a more general assertion that the defendant's behaviour is deserving of punishment.

Ideas from medicine, public policy and sometimes personal morality crop up in these sentencing exercises: you will need to interrogate them to see how they fit into the statutory criteria and if they produce a just result. Your skills as an advocate are still important in a 'hospital order' case.

So do not let your relief that such a case has moved out of the conventional criminal sphere into a more therapeutic zone blind you to your responsibilities. Any of the orders above will represent to your client a deprivation of liberty and the start of treatment that may or may not be welcome. Your client will need to know that you are actively trying to get the shortest s 45A order or to really test the need for a restriction order: you cannot assume that 'not prison' is the end of your task. Not only must the offence be correctly analysed, but everything relevant to personal mitigation must be before the court. This will require you to be active for your client; to have the imagination to ask about whether key workers or others can give references and matters of that sort.

Some defendants will have been convicted having been assessed as 'just fit'. It is particularly important when representing someone who cannot give you full instructions that you think about your submissions on sentence from every angle. In addition to understanding the MHA regime and the case law, you must retain sight of your role as an advocate.

If your client was unfit, you still need to explain what is going to happen, to answer his concerns, and, as much as possible, to engage him in the process. If your client was fit to plead, all this still applies, plus he is in a position to give you instructions. You will need to consider carefully how to obtain those instructions and to what matters they should be targeted. You cannot delegate your responsibility to talk to the client to your client's clinician.

You will still need to discuss with your client the reports that will be before the court from a legal perspective. It may well be helpful for you to take your cue from a report upon sensitive areas, but your client must be involved in the preparation for his own sentencing exercise.

Your client may not agree with something a psychiatrist has summarised about his forensic history or he may explain why he felt inhibited about talking to someone about a personal issue. You will use your own professional judgment about how far to take those points, and of course it may be that someone who has a mental health condition might lack insight into its severity, but do not assume that a client is less honest or less able to formulate a sincere opinion simply because he has have a mental health condition.

You are there to represent your client, and you need to have a relationship of trust. You will lose this trust if a client believes you are trying to dis-empower him from having a say in his own future. As has been said elsewhere in this book, one important aim of representing someone is to ensure that he was able to participate in what was taking place and that he feels his corner was fought. This is perhaps particularly important to defendants suffering from mental illness who are often at risk of feeling isolated or stereotyped.

Chapter 26

Ancillary orders

Tara Wolfe

Key references

- *Archbold: Criminal Pleading, Evidence and Practice 2020*, 5A-805, 19-357b, 19-358b, 20-275,

- *Blackstone's Criminal Practice 2020*, D.25.16, E21.22, E21.23, E21.33

- *Thomas' Sentencing Referencer 2020*

- Criminal Procedure Rules 2015, SI 2015/1490 (CPR 2015)

Case law

- *DPP v Bulmer* [2015] EWHC 2323 (Admin)

- *R v Franklin (Philip)* [2018] EWCA Crim 1080

- *R v McLellan; Bingley* [2017] EWCA Crim 1464

- *R v Parsons (Hayden Graeme); R v Stuart James Morgan* [2017] EWCA Crim 2163

- *R v Pickens* [2006] EWCA Crim 2194

- *R v Smith* [2011] EWCA Crim 1772

INTRODUCTION

This chapter deals with the most frequently encountered behaviour orders: Sexual Harm Prevention Orders (SHPOs), Restraining Orders (ROs) and Criminal Behaviour Orders (CBOs). It is usual for such orders to be debated, negotiated and often agreed in principle prior to any application being made in court. Your skills as an advocate start here. Ensure that you have considered the terms of any proposed order in light of the legal principles and, if defending, sought your lay client's instructions. Thorough preparation is key to obtaining the outcome you seek. If defending, if you intend to oppose the conditions of the proposed order, it is advisable to draft an alternative for the prosecution and the court to consider.

GENERAL PRINCIPLES

It is a fundamental principle of justice that any defendant who is intended to be the subject of an order is given proper notice of what is sought, the evidential basis for the order, and the opportunity to make considered representations. In the case of SHPOs it is a requirement that proposed orders are be drafted and served at least two business days prior to the application being considered but in all cases it is good practice to ensure that draft applications are uploaded as soon as it becomes apparent that such an order may be appropriate. When defending, it may be important to oppose consideration of a proposed order as a result of late service. However, if the order is uncontroversial, reasonable and proportionate and your client agrees to its imposition, do not oppose it for the sake of argument. Some points are there to be taken, but best left.

SEXUAL HARM PREVENTION ORDERS

SHPOs may be made if the defendant is convicted or found not guilty by reason of insanity of a relevant sexual offence or has been found to have done the act. Conditions in the Sexual Offences Act 2003, Sch 3 which relate to the way in which the defendant was dealt with or the age of the victim are to be disregarded for the purposes of the imposition of a SHPO.

A SHPO may be imposed if the court is satisfied that it is necessary for the purpose of protecting the public or any particular members of the public from sexual harm. The order must be tailored to reflect the particular circumstances of the case under consideration, see *R v Smith*. As with any behaviour order, the terms must be proportionate, not oppressive, enforceable, clear and realistic. In short, the conditions should reflect the potential harm as evidenced by the behaviour leading to the conviction.

There are three common areas for dispute: the age of the children in contact restrictions; restrictions in respect of internet use; and, the length of the order:

(i)   Whilst the Sexual Offences Act 2003 defines a child as a person under 18 for the purposes of the SHPO regime, if the offence concerned the distribution of images of a female children under the age of 10, it would be disproportionate to seek a term restricting the defendant's access to all children under the age of 18; see *R v Franklin*.

(ii)   Access to the internet is integral to functioning in society, and any restrictions upon its use must be justified. Do not seek, and do oppose if defending, a term which seeks to restrict internet use when there has been no suggestion of illegitimate use of internet access; such terms should not immediately follow convictions for child sex offences.

(iii) A SHPO is for a minimum of five years or until further order. Both the content and the length of each prohibition must be proportionate and necessary. A SHPO should not be imposed indefinitely as a default position and only rarely should an order exceed the notification period; see *R v McLellan; Bingley*.

The judgment in *R v Parsons* provides a useful template. If seeking to defend or oppose a prohibition, apply the law to the prohibition under consideration in oral submissions reminding the court of the purpose of the statutory regime.

RESTRAINING ORDERS

Restraining orders are most commonly applied for in cases of domestic violence but should be considered in any case in which the victim fears violence or conduct which amounts to harassment. They can be imposed on conviction or acquittal. An order may only be made if considered necessary for the purpose of protecting the victim of the offence or any other person in the order from conduct which amounts to harassment or will cause fear of violence. Such conduct must be proved to the civil standard.

There must be an evidential basis for the imposition of any order. Post-conviction this is unlikely to be controversial. However, different considerations apply if the defendant has been acquitted as a result of no evidence being offered. A complainant's statement may make compelling reading but, unless its contents are not disputed, untested it cannot amount to a proper evidential foundation for the imposition of a restraining order. A restraining order has serious implications for the defendant. It is incumbent on counsel to ensure that the proper procedure as set down in the CPR 2015, Part 31 is followed and the necessity test applied. Acknowledge that the court may have justifiable concerns and bring the court back to the rules and legal principles. As with all successful advocacy, the law is your friend.

When prosecuting it is imperative that the views of the victim are obtained. A restraining order will impact on their future as well as that of the defendant. It is inappropriate for a restraining order to be imposed in order to protect a victim from themselves even if they are at risk of severe violence at the hands of the defendant. The law is not there to prevent people from acting against their best interests. If defending, request that the police seek the victim's views in order to substantiate any claim made by your lay client.

CRIMINAL BEHAVIOUR ORDERS

A CBO may be imposed by the court if two conditions are satisfied: first, if the court is satisfied beyond all reasonable doubt that the defendant has engaged in behaviour that caused or was likely to cause harassment, alarm or distress to any person; and, secondly, if the court considers that making the order will help in preventing the defendant from engaging in such behaviour. There is no necessity test. An order may be made for a period not less than one year and not more than three years.

The second condition is an exercise of judgement and evaluation by the court and is more likely to be an area of dispute. If defending there are some important points to note: the order should not prohibit conduct which is itself a criminal offence; any prohibition must be sufficiently clear to enable the prohibition to be complied with and enforced; and any restriction must be helpful in addressing the offending behaviour.

If the order contains a requirement, it is important not to set up your client to fail. An alcoholic who is required to attend courses to deal with their alcoholism may struggle to comply. Arguably, it would be preferable for such a condition to be attached to a suspended sentence or community penalty, the breach of which would not amount to an offence in itself. Similarly, an order which seeks to address compulsive or addictive behaviour should be challenged. It cannot be correct to criminalise behaviour which, albeit distressing to others, the individual has little control over.

Chapter 27

Confiscation under the Proceeds of Crime Act 2002

Charles Thomas

Key references

- *Archbold: Criminal Pleading, Evidence and Practice 2020*, 5B

- *Blackstone's Criminal Practice 2020*, E19

- Crown Court Compendium Part II: S7-2

- Proceeds of Crime Act 2002 (POCA)

- Powers of Criminal Courts (Sentencing) Act 2000, s 143

Case law

- *R v Ahmad; R v Fields* [2014] UKSC 36

- *R v May* [2008] UKHL 28

- *R v Newton (Robert John)* [1983] Crim LR 198

- *R v Waya* [2012] UKSC 51

INTRODUCTION

It is notorious that confiscation hearings nearly always settle. Many advocates will say that they have never done a contested hearing. There are many reasons for this. Some advocates, who chose to practise criminal law for its human interest, don't feel comfortable picking their way through balance sheets. A lot of judges feel the same way. There are pressures on both sides to reach sensible settlements.

On the prosecution side the application will largely be driven by the Financial Investigation Officer (FIO). They are often very pragmatic. Their resources aren't infinite. Therefore, sometimes the approach is that it is better to pick the low hanging fruit and move on to the next case rather than spend time and resources in respect of possible assets that may be difficult to recover. It is worth bearing in mind that the money recovered from confiscation proceedings (assuming there is no compensation to be paid first) is split as follows: Home Office 50%, Police and CPS 18.75% each, HMCTS 12.5%. People have targets to meet.

On the defence side there is always the concern that a contested hearing may end badly. The Proceeds of Crime Act 2002 (POCA) has been described as draconian. The assumptions that can be made under POCA, s 10 if the defendant is deemed to have a 'criminal lifestyle', (see POCA, s 75), the 'tainted gifts' provisions (see POCA, s 9(1)(b)), and the burden placed on the defendant to prove that the available amount is not the same as the benefit figure, (see POCA, s 7(2)), can mean that a defendant will be facing a substantial sum to pay, real difficulties in finding the money, and a lengthy sentence in default. Agreements that avoid this are often in their best interests.

POCA can apply to a wide variety of offences. Offences under the Theft and Fraud Acts are obvious ones. Equally, offences involving drug supply and the money laundering offences associated with them frequently lead to proceedings under the Act. In more recent years, the Modern Slavery Act and other exploitation offences, relating to prostitution for example, have also led to confiscation orders.

The rationale behind POCA is that those convicted of crime should not be allowed to retain the financial and material benefits of their crime. The Act came into force on 24 March 2003, meaning that it will now be a very rare case that requires reference to its predecessors such as the Drug Trafficking Act 1994.

ISSUES AT THE PLEA AND TRIAL STAGE

'Criminal Lifestyle' is one of the most important concepts under POCA. Whether a defendant has a criminal lifestyle is the first matter that the court must determine at any hearing. POCA, s 75 sets out the test. Conviction for certain offences, eg drug trafficking offences and money laundering offences, automatically qualify (see POCA, Sch 2). Alternatively, the defendant needs to have been convicted of one offence committed over a period of six months or more, four separate offences, or to have been convicted on two other different occasions within the previous six years, with the total benefit exceeding £5,000. It is important to bear these criteria in mind if drafting an indictment or considering what pleas should be offered or accepted. When prosecuting it is also worth bearing in mind that the sort of evidence that the FIU will be gathering for later POCA proceedings might be very useful evidence at the trial itself. For example, evidence of unexplained cash being paid into a bank account can evidence ongoing dealing by a defendant charged with offences of possession of drugs with intent to supply.

If pleas are negotiated in a potential POCA case it is also important that there is clarity as to whether the basis is accepted for both the purposes of POCA proceedings and the sentencing exercise. It is not uncommon for the prosecution to be in a position where a particular basis can be accepted for sentencing purposes, either because it would not make a material difference to sentence or because they could not prove the contrary in a *Newton* hearing beyond reasonable doubt, but where the evidential position would be quite different in the POCA hearing. Ideally, the basis of plea itself should make it clear if it also to apply to the POCA hearing or not.

THE SENTENCING HEARING

In straightforward cases, it may be possible to agree a benefit figure and confiscation figure at the sentencing hearing. A typical example will be a drug dealer, caught with drugs and some cash who was dealing to fund their personal drug habit. There is no suggestion that they have any other assets or prospect of assets other than the cash seized. An order is agreed detailing that the benefit is the value of the drugs and the cash, and the cash is the only realisable asset. When cash or other items seized are the only assets it can also be possible to deal with the financial aspect of the case by way of a forfeiture order under the Powers of Criminal Courts (Sentencing) Act 2000, s 143. This can have the advantage to a defendant of there being no prolonged financial enquiry, and no outstanding benefit figure. The advantage to the police is that they receive the entirety of the proceeds.

In more complex cases it will be necessary to set a timetable for a subsequent POCA hearing. The POCA, s 14 allows the proceedings to be postponed for a period of up to two years. Although the POCA, s 14(11) states that a confiscation order will not be quashed by reason of a procedural defect, it remains important for the prosecutor to apply for the postponement of the hearing and for the timetable to be set *before* the judge proceeds to sentencing. In sequence dates need to be set for:

(a)   the provision of financial information by the defendant (POCA, s 18);

(b)   the prosecution statement (POCA, s 16);

(c)   a defence response (POCA, s 17);

(d)   a further response from the prosecution; and finally

(e)   a hearing date. It is usually sensible to have a hearing date with the case listed for mention with a view to possible agreement rather than with for a full hearing.

There are practicalities to bear in mind regarding the first stage. Any defence advocate should ensure that ample time is allowed for the defendant to provide information about their finances. The client is likely to be starting a prison sentence. They will have limited access to their bank accounts and other financial documents. It can often be difficult to secure appointments with clients once they begin custodial sentences. It is not unheard of for defendants to be moved repeatedly from one prison to another, without their solicitors being informed, with the result that they turn up for a conference at one prison only to be told that their client is now elsewhere.

It is also important to advise the defendant that the information provided must be as full and accurate as possible. A defendant who blithely asserts in a POCA, s 18 statement that they have no assets, only for the prosecution to subsequently uncover an ISA or pension they had 'forgotten' about, will have little chance of being believed by the judge at a later stage if there are issues that are reliant on their unsupported evidence. Conversely, a defendant who has clearly engaged throughout has some prospect of overcoming judicial scepticism.

If the POCA hearing is postponed at the sentence hearing the judge shouldn't be asked to make any other financial orders such as for compensation or costs. These should also be postponed until the POCA hearing.

THE HEARING

As with any other type of hearing, there can be no substitute for careful and thorough preparation. However, this is particularly true for POCA hearings where, because of their very nature, detail can be important. Skeleton arguments will always repay the work you put into them. The judge will be thankful for the guidance and the clarification of the real issues. A good skeleton will also be a useful tool in negotiations. Your FIO will be invaluable in providing information; the POCA, s 16 statement and further responses will always be the basis of your submissions.

Any hearing, and indeed any negotiations will be focused on two issues: what is the defendant's benefit from criminal conduct, and what is the recoverable amount. It is in respect of the first of these that the assumptions under the POCA, s 10 apply if the defendant has a criminal lifestyle. In simple terms, anything owned, received or spent by the defendant in the last six years is assumed to be as a result of criminal conduct, and therefore a benefit of criminal conduct, unless the assumption is shown to be incorrect or there would be a serious risk of injustice if the assumption was made (POCA, s 10(6)).

It will be very dangerous to just rely on the defendant's uncorroborated account to try and rebut these assumptions. It is important at the preparation stage to garner as much documentary evidence, or at the very least supporting evidence from others, as can be found.

It is also important to scrutinise carefully the way the figures have been calculated by the prosecution. There is always a risk of double or even triple counting. By way of example: a sum of money is counted as benefit when it appears in a bank account. The money is used to buy a car. The car is then sold, and the proceeds paid back into the bank account. This might appear three times in the benefit figure when in fact it is the same money in three different forms.

A common issue in drugs cases is the extent of the defendant's benefit in relation to the value of the drugs involved. Often, the prosecution statement will include the entire value of the drugs as part of the benefit figure for each defendant. It may well be possible to argue that such an approach is not appropriate, for example for a defendant who was simply a courier, on the basis that they did not obtain the property in the sense of having a power of disposition or control, see *R v May, R v Ahmad: R v Fields.*

The second part of the calculation is assessing what is the recoverable amount. The burden is on the defendant to demonstrate that it is not the same as the benefit figure (see POCA, s 7(2)). The prosecution will often allege that a defendant has hidden assets. Making a judge believe otherwise will need as much independent evidence as possible as well as trying to guide a defendant through giving as coherent an explanation as possible for where the money has gone.

Tainted gifts (see POCA 2002, s 77) are also an issue that can have serious implications for a defendant. Thorough preparation to try and demonstrate that any alleged gifts were either exchanged for proper value or that there is now no realistic prospect of retrieving them will be vital.

R v Waya ruled that there was an overriding requirement of proportionality in POCA hearings. The decision is now reflected by the POCA, s 6(5), which states that an order for the recoverable amount should only be made if, or to the extent that, it would not be disproportionate to do so. This provision is immensely useful at all stages of the hearing to found arguments that a particular finding, in respect of either the benefit figure or the recoverable amount, should not be made.

One final caution when negotiating in POCA hearings. Defendants are often prepared to accept higher benefit figures if concessions are made on the recoverable amount, meaning they pay less immediately. However, any outstanding benefit remains owing, and what are termed 'revisits', where the Financial Investigation Unit look again at a defendant's assets, are becoming more common. In years to come the prosecuting authorities are likely to become more sophisticated in their information gathering techniques, (perhaps being automatically notified whenever a defendant with an outstanding benefit figure receives an inheritance for example). A high or inflated benefit figure should not be ignored or presumed to only be a hypothetical debt that will have no real impact on a defendant in due course.

Sentencing: key points

DO

- Be able to set out the salient facts when prosecuting, including of relevant previous offences.

- Be very familiar with sentencing guidelines and guideline cases.

- Check that the VPS complies with the rules.

- Be clear about the factual basis on which any sentence is being passed.

- Structure your mitigation carefully but be prepared to react to judicial intervention.

- Consider whether additional material such as references may make a difference.

- Put your best points forward with realism but also conviction.

- Remember every defendant is an individual and every sentencing exercise unique.

- Consider if there is a mental health aspect to the sentence at any early stage.

- Draft or ask for drafts of ancillary orders well in advance of sentence.

- Prepare a skeleton argument for any POCA hearing.

DON'T

- Try to obtain any particular sentence when prosecuting or shoe-horn it into the top bracket.

- Be put off if initially you can't think of anything to say in mitigation: if you talk to the defendant and plan your remarks, there will always be something to say of importance, however brief.

- Spout clichés: the judge will stop listening.

- Think you can delegate your role to a probation officer or psychiatrist.

- Allow for any ancillary orders to be made 'on the nod' without proper thought first.

Part IX

Appeals

Chapter 28

Appeal against conviction and sentence

Grace Flynn and Nick Lee

Key references

- *Archbold: Criminal Pleading, Evidence and Practice 2020*, 2-95, 2-108, 2-114, 2-133, 2-141, 2-143

- *Blackstone's Criminal Practice 2020*, D29.3, D29.4, D29.6, D29.14, D29.16

- *Banks on Sentence 2020*

- *Wilkinson's Road Traffic Offences* (29th Edn)

- Senior Courts Act 1981, ss 48, 74 and 79

- Magistrates' Courts Act 1980 (MCA 1980), ss 108 and 122

- Youth, Justice and Criminal Evidence Act 1999

- Road Traffic Offenders Act 1988

- Criminal Justice Act 1967

- Firearms Act 1968

- Dangerous Dogs Act 1991 (DDA 1991)

- Criminal Procedure Rules 2015, SI 2015/1490 (CPR 2015), Part 34 (Appeals)

- Criminal Practice Directions IX (Appeals)

Case law

- *Croydon Crown Court ex parte Bernard* [1981] 1 WLR 116 DC

- *Knutsford Crown Court ex parte Jones* [1985] 12 WLUK 197

- *R (Hayes) v Chelmsford Crown Court* [2003] EWHC 73 (Admin)

- *R (Khalif) v Isleworth Crown Court* [2015] EWHC 917 (Admin)

- *R v Croydon Crown Court, ex parte Clair* [1986] 1 WLR 746

- *R v Hayward et al* [2001] EWCA Crim 168

- *R v Isleworth Crown Court, ex parte Irvin* [1992] RTR 281

- *R v Northallerton Magistrates' Court, ex parte Dove* [2000] 1 Cr App R (S) at 140

APPEALS IN THE CROWN COURT

Overview

This chapter deals with advocacy in the Crown Court in its appellate capacity (ie appeals from the magistrates' court). Such hearings are something of a hybrid between summary justice and the Crown Court and have their own rules and conventions.

Appeals can feel rough and ready compared to other proceedings in the Crown Court. There is no digital case system by which everyone can navigate the evidence, you are more likely to encounter an appellant in person, papers may have been mislaid, there are three people to address (and confuse) on the bench, and case management can be lacking. The secret to advocacy in appeals can sometimes be just to get everyone on the same page.

Starting the appeal and bail

Everyone convicted or sentenced in the magistrates' court (including as a youth court) has a right of appeal to the Crown Court.

Appeal can be against sentence, or against conviction *and* sentence. In an appeal against conviction, you should be prepared to open/mitigate sentence as well. The appellant cannot appeal only conviction. If he is unsuccessful, he risks a more onerous sentence.

Provided the appeal notice is served within 21 days of sentence being passed or deferred, no special permission is needed. Standard templates for appeal notices are on the Ministry of Justice (MOJ) website.

If the notice is served out of time, it must include a written application to extend the time limit. This will be considered by Crown Court on paper, taking into account the length of delay, the reasons for it, the apparent strength of the case and the practicalities of a re-trial. There is no right to make oral representations if permission is refused, although the Crown Court may allow the case to be listed for further representations.

If you are representing the appellant (previously: the defence), your instructing solicitors will normally have served the appeal notice before you are briefed.

However, it may be useful to know that a defendant who has been convicted by the magistrates and sent for sentence to the Crown Court can still appeal his conviction, even after he has been sentenced. An appeal notice should be served as soon as possible.

Under the CPR 2015, in an appeal against conviction, the respondent (previously: the prosecution) must serve a notice in response to the appeal notice within 21 days of it being served. In reality, this is often overlooked. However, they can be useful for case management, even out of time.

A defendant who pleaded guilty in the magistrates' court can appeal to the Crown Court against his or her conviction. The Crown Court will conduct an investigation into whether the plea was equivocal and, if satisfied that it was, remit the case to the magistrates.

An application for bail can be made pending the appeal (as can an application to suspend a driving disqualification). The Bail Act 1976 does not apply, so there is no right to bail. The appellant should specify on the appeal notice whether he wants the bail application to be considered by the magistrates or the Crown Court. If refused by the magistrates, the appellant can apply to the Crown Court.

Abandoning an appeal

An appellant can abandon the appeal by serving a signed notice on the magistrates' court, the Crown Court and every other party. There is a template notice on the MOJ website.

Provided the notice is served before the Crown Court has started hearing the appeal, its permission is not needed, although both the magistrates' court and the Crown Court can impose costs for an abandoned appeal. The Crown Court cannot reinstate an abandoned appeal unless satisfied the abandonment was a nullity.

Appeals are quite often abandoned at the door of the court when the appellant receives some stern advice from his advocate for the first time. Try to present this to the court in such a way that no (or minimal) costs are incurred.

Once the Crown Court has started hearing an appeal, it can only be abandoned with the court's permission, which will be granted only in exceptional circumstances. However, where an appellant seeks to abandon an appeal against sentence after the case is called on and the appellant identified, but before further progress, permission should only be withheld exceptionally.

THE APPELLANT'S FAILURE TO ATTEND

The appellant is entitled not to attend his appeal and his absence cannot be treated as abandonment. As in the magistrates' court, where the appellant's legal representative is present and able to represent him, he is treated as being present.

See the MCA 1980; s 122 interpreted in *R v Croydon Crown Court, ex parte Clair*.

When the appellant is unrepresented or his representative does not have sufficient instructions to represent him, the court may face a difficult decision about whether to proceed in his absence. When applying to do so, the respondent may wish to draw on both the MCA 1980, s 11 (the presumption that cases will proceed in the defendant's absence in the magistrates' court) and *R v Hayward et al* (the factors considered by the Crown Court before deciding to proceed in their absence).

The court may be more inclined to hear an appeal against sentence than an appeal against conviction in the appellant's absence, but if witnesses have attended (having previously attended trial in the lower court) that will often be a persuasive reason to hear an appeal in the appellant's absence. Ultimately, it is a case-by-case decision, but even if the appellant's absence appears to be entirely cynical, it cannot be treated as abandonment; see *R (Hayes) v Chelmsford Crown Court*.

THE CONSTITUTION OF THE COURT

The appeal will be heard by a legally qualified judge (usually a Circuit Judge or a Recorder) and two justices of the peace (JPs), neither of whom heard the case in the lower court. The judge determines matters of law, and all three decide the facts. The judge can allow the appeal to proceed in front of only one JP, if the start of the hearing would otherwise be unreasonably delayed, or if the hearing began with a full complement but one JP has become absent (eg through illness), see CPR 2015, r 34.11(2).

Where the appeal is from the youth court, there should be one male and one female JP, both of whom are authorised to sit in the youth court.

It can be tempting to focus your attention on the judge. However, do not ignore the JPs. They can out-vote the judge on the facts, and they are often more familiar with the kind of case under appeal than the judge, who may not have dealt with an exceptional hardship argument for decades. Addressing them as 'your honour and your honour's colleagues' is an inclusive approach.

The full re-hearing

Once the appeal gets underway, it is a full re-hearing.

Appeals generally proceed in the same order as other cases in the Crown Court. Appeals against sentence begin with the respondent opening the case before the appellant mitigates, whereupon the court retires to reach its decision. Appeals against conviction begin with the respondent opening the case, calling their evidence and closing their case, before the appellant calls their evidence and closes their case, and the court hears closing submissions. Legal applications are heard at the appropriate moment. Again, the court will retire to reach a verdict.

Each party is entitled to call new evidence which was not presented in the lower court, and to put their case in a different way. The appellant should have indicated on the appeal notice which prosecution witnesses are required, and whether he will call any witnesses.

LEGAL APPLICATIONS

The Crown Court cannot amend the charge on which the appellant was convicted by the magistrates, nor can it reverse an amendment made in the lower court. Beyond that, each party can renew any legal applications (bad character, etc) made in the lower court, or make new applications. The appellant should indicate which applications will be made on the appeal notice (including any new applications). When you are instructed by the appellant and decide that legal applications are needed but the appeal notice has already been served, you would be sensible to notify the respondent and the court in good time, even if you do not serve the applications until later.

When you are instructed by the respondent in a case which calls for legal applications or in which you intend to call new witnesses, but no respondent's notice has been served, you might consider serving that notice (even out of time) as a tool for case management. Doing so will help to keep a grip on a messy case, keep the court updated and show that you are dealing with the appellant fairly. You will also be better placed to resist any complaints around 'ambushing'.

If you realise that, due to new witnesses or new legal applications, the time estimate for the appeal is unrealistic, notify the other party and the court in good time with a proposed new time estimate. Going part-heard when JPs' diaries have to be taken into account is best avoided.

Just as in the magistrates' courts, where the tribunal of law is also the tribunal of fact, you might wonder whether the court will *really* be able to put a failed but prejudicial character application from its mind when deciding the case. You might consider requesting a 'preparation for appeal hearing' if concerned that such an application will prejudice your client. Either party can request a hearing where it is necessary to give directions for the effective determination of the appeal, or where it is required to set ground rules for questioning a witness or appellant. However, be aware that circuit judges and JPs consider themselves more than capable of 'putting from their minds' an adverse ruling!

The Crown Court's powers on appeal are limited to the powers originally available to the magistrates' court. As regards applications to stay proceedings as an abuse of process, this appears to limit the court to hearing applications based on the so-called 'first limb' of that doctrine (the impossibility of a fair trial), as magistrates' courts are prevented from hearing applications under the 'second limb' (that trial would offend the integrity of the criminal justice system).

POWERS ON APPEAL

The Crown Court's powers on appeal are set out in the Senior Courts Act 1981, s 48. Its main powers are to quash or uphold a conviction, and/or vary the sentence imposed by the magistrates. Crucially, this includes the power to increase sentence. The court is obliged to give reasons for the decision it makes. Please note that it has no power to vary a costs order imposed by the lower court, however unfair it seems (see MCA 1980, s 108; *R v Northallerton Magistrates' Court, ex parte Dove*). As mentioned previously, the court does however have the power to impose further costs should the appeal be unsuccessful.

APPEALS AGAINST CONVICTION

When acting for the respondent, read your papers as soon as possible and double-check that nothing is missing:

i)   Have all required witnesses been warned to attend the appeal? Do you need the OIC, and have they been warned?

ii)   Do you have all the statements and exhibits (eg CCTV)?

iii)   Are there legal applications to be made, and do you need to draft them?

iv)   Was the police summary of the interview agreed with the defence (the 'Preparation for Effective Trial' (PET) form will provide clues)?

v)   Are any special measures required? Have applications been made?

vi)   Is an interpreter needed?

vii)   If the appellant is in person, will court appointed counsel be required to cross-examine the witnesses (under the Youth, Justice and Criminal Evidence Act 1999, s 36)?

viii)   Do you have the unused material schedule?

ix)   Was there a defence statement in the magistrates' court?

x)   Were written legal applications served in the magistrates' court?

xi)   Has there been any correspondence between the parties?

xii)   Is anything new raised in the appeal notice?

xiii)   Has a respondent's notice been served?

Special measures must not be overlooked. Appeals frequently include allegations of domestic violence. The complainant will expect the same measures again, so ensure that an appropriate application is made. Equally, arranging court-appointed counsel for cross-examination or an interpreter will take time. Do not leave it too late for these essential arrangements to be made.

When representing the appellant, you will need all of the above material, as well as statements from defence witnesses, the pre-sentence report, and any attendance notes from the lower court. Be proactive in checking that defence witnesses have confirmed attendance, that any missing evidence your solicitors could obtain is tracked down, and if the disclosure looks inadequate, make the respondent aware immediately.

If you need to advise the appellant that his appeal is hopeless and he is risking a higher sentence (possibly custody; does he need to bring a bag to court?), a conference in advance may be a better place to do so than outside court. Whatever the case, warn the appellant that the Crown Court will impose further costs if the appeal is unsuccessful.

If there are defence witnesses, check that their full names, dates of birth and addresses have been provided to the respondent and the court well in advance of the appeal. The prosecution will ask for these on the day anyway. You will also want to know if your star witness has three convictions for perverting the course of justice, rather than finding out on the day.

Remember that an appeal against conviction also re-opens sentence. You will need to take instructions and prepare to mitigate in case the conviction is upheld. A copy of the pre-sentence report (PSR) will help. If a driving disqualification is probable, ask your solicitors to remind the appellant not to drive to court. They will be banned with immediate effect if the appeal is unsuccessful.

Whatever the offence, and whether acting for the respondent or the appellant, ensure that you know the elements that must be proven, who bears the burden of proving them, and the test that the court needs to apply. Be ready to summarise it in a nutshell. You will become very familiar with appeals under the Road Traffic Offenders Act 1988, s 172 but some circuit judges will not be. An effective tactic for getting everyone on the same page is to prepare a bundle including a short summary of the law and the key cases which can be handed to the court at the outset of the case or before your closing submissions. Ensure that you print enough copies for everyone, including the appellant. Judges and justices will not appreciate leaning over to share papers.

You want to make the hearing as straightforward as possible. If there is a confusing background, consider preparing a chronology. Identify what the issues are and streamline the appeal as much as possible by preparing a set of agreed facts under the Criminal Justice Act 1967, s 10. You don't need to call witnesses to bring the case to life as you may consider doing for a jury; the more you can reduce the evidence to agreed facts, the more clearly the real issues will shine through.

When appearing for the respondent, the same rules apply on speaking to witnesses at court as they do in trials. A more challenging scenario arises when you are dealing with an unrepresented appellant. This is not uncommon. You are expected to speak to the appellant before the hearing:

(i)   Introduce yourself and your role as prosecutor;

(ii)   Explain the procedure in court and that it is a fresh hearing where the judge and justices have no prior knowledge of the case;

(iii)   Confirm that the appellant is content to proceed without representation today; if not, explain that this will need to be raised with the judge;

(iv)   Check that they have received all the evidence and statements;

(v)   Provide them with a copy of any exhibits, proposed agreed facts and other papers that you will be presenting.

Be mindful of what you say and the ethics of the situation. You should *not* let slip your view of the appellant's prospects of success or informally provide them with legal advice. You should have a keen awareness of your own professional responsibilities. Sometimes an appellant will have no desire to speak to you at all, perceiving you as the enemy out to trick them. Accept this with good grace and confirm to the judge that you have complied with your duty, but the appellant preferred not to discuss matters with you.

An appellant in person may not be aware of various technical defences. It is not your job to give legal advice to an appellant, but the appellant should be aware what the offence actually consists of. If you can see a prima facie defence that has not been raised, you should make the judge aware so that the judge can ask appropriate questions, or suggest that the appellant gets legal representation.

In terms of the hearing itself, those representing appellants should be aware that the judge may be less restrained in questioning your client than if there were a jury present, especially if your opponent's cross-examination is underwhelming. Be mindful of follow up questions you can ask to put an unattractive answer in context, or whether you just need to move on as quickly as possible.

Whichever side you act for, your advocacy should be tailored to an audience which has more experience of criminal proceedings than the average juror. Clarity and succinctness will be appreciated; sowing confusion, less so. Signposting at the start of your submissions where you are heading ('I have three main points, which are x, y and z, and I will address each in turn') can help the court to follow your argument. Summarise your best points again at the end. Your submissions don't have to be dry, but they will probably be most effective if restrained, focussed and succinct.

Be flexible in your closing submissions. Respond to any steers from the judge (eg 'we only need to hear from you on these points'). It usually means they have already decided the other points in your favour.

If the appeal is unsuccessful, the court will usually proceed to the sentencing exercise but it can order a PSR if one doesn't yet exist and it is thought necessary.

APPEALS AGAINST SENTENCE

As the respondent, your preparation for an appeal against sentence will be very similar to preparing to open a case for sentence. Your appeal bundle should include the memorandum of conviction. This will confirm the sentence handed down in the magistrates' court.

If you are representing the appellant, it may be sensible to have a conference ahead of the hearing date if possible. You will need to explain that the sentence could be increased on appeal and that, if you are unsuccessful, the prosecution are likely to make an application for costs. Identify exactly what it is about the original sentence that is said to be excessive or unfair. Closely analyse the sentencing guidelines and, if relevant, locate case law from a source such as *Banks on Sentence*. It is vital to obtain a copy of the PSR, if you know that one exists. The probation office at the Crown Court will often be able to print you a copy if you ask nicely, should your solicitors be unable to locate the original.

An appellant may wish the court to reconsider:

(i)   The length of their custodial sentence;

(ii)   Whether a community sentence or suspended sentence should have been imposed instead of immediate custody;

(iii)   Making the requirements of a community or suspended sentence order less onerous (eg too many hours unpaid work, or an excessively restrictive curfew);

(iv)   The imposition of ancillary orders (eg a restraining order, or a criminal behaviour order);

(v)   The length of a driving disqualification;

(vi)   The level of compensation to be paid;

(vii)   What level of credit for guilty plea was given;

(viii) Any other aspect of their sentence with which they take issue (except costs, which cannot be appealed).

Much of what has been said earlier in this chapter regarding appeals against conviction applies to appeals against sentence as well, particularly when dealing with an appellant in person. Follow the guidance above and provide the appellant in person with a properly edited copy of any victim personal statement and a copy of the sentencing guidelines. Explain where you say that the offence falls on those guidelines and that he will have his opportunity to explain his points and circumstances to the judge. Do not give legal advice!

If you will be applying for costs, explain this, and let the appellant know that the sentence is 'at large' (ie the court can move it up or down). Do not say anything that could be construed as advising them to abandon their appeal: it is up to them, but perhaps they may want to ask the judge further questions or seek legal advice?

Should the appeal concern a driving offence, particularly if the number of penalty points handed down might lead to disqualification, check that you have the DVLA record. When responding to an appeal, print sufficient copies of all relevant materials for you, your opponent/the appellant in person, and the judge and the JPs.

Whatever the nature of the offence, ensure that you have the appellant's PNC record. Do any minimum sentences or mandatory disqualifications apply as a result of previous offences? Confirm whether you should be applying for (or opposing) any application for ancillary orders. If orders were made in the magistrates' court, were their terms suitable? Any new applications should be served in advance of the hearing.

The appeal will usually follow the same structure as a sentencing hearing in the Crown Court. Technically, the entirety of the sentence is re-opened by the appeal, but the appeal notice may specify that it only relates to a specific aspect of the sentence. For example, the appellant may be arguing against the imposition of unpaid work instead of a curfew, due to childcare commitments. When opening, you can flag to the court that the appeal is on a narrow issue. The judge may give you a steer on what you need to address. Do not be offended if the judge does not need to hear from you in such a case. However, before opening in this manner you should confirm with the appellant that he takes no issue with the rest of the sentence.

When responding to an appeal from an appellant in person, it is particularly important to remember that your duty is to the court, and that all of the facts which may have an impact on sentence should be before it. This includes pointing out any mitigating factors which are apparent to you but which the appellant may not be able to articulate.

In an appeal against sentence, the court asks whether the lower court imposed the right sentence. To answer this question, it should consider sentence afresh. If the court arrives at a sentence which is significantly (rather than triflingly) different from that passed by the magistrates, it should be varied accordingly – either upwards or downwards.

The court's sentencing powers are limited to those of the magistrates, and sentence cannot be increased to reflect the court's view that the magistrates ought to have sent the case to the Crown court in the first place. Although the appeal is a re-hearing, the court should not ignore an appellant's legitimate expectations as to sentence (for example, if he was told by the magistrates on entering his plea that he would not receive custody, but was subsequently sentenced to custody by a different bench).

Where an appellant disputes the factual basis for sentence, but this was not raised before the magistrates and they heard no evidence on it, the Crown Court should follow the process set out in *Newton* to decide whether it needs to hear evidence on the disputed issues. If it does, authorities suggest that the trial of issue should also take place in the Crown Court. If the magistrates already heard evidence and ruled on the factual basis for sentence, the Crown Court will adopt those findings.

Where a basis of plea was entered before the magistrates but they decided it was unnecessary to hear evidence on the matters in dispute before sentencing, and the appellant then appeals his sentence, the Crown Court is not bound by the previous decision and may decide that it does need to hear evidence before deciding the appeal. The consequences of this in terms of credit could be significant.

SPECIALIST APPEALS

Road traffic offences

Road traffic law is not to be underestimated in its complexity. You cannot go far wrong if you have access to a copy of *Wilkinson's Road Traffic Offences*, the key practitioner text in this field. Appeals against sentence frequently concern 'Special Reasons' for a court not to impose penalty points/disqualification and 'Exceptional Hardship' to avoid a 'totting' ban. Obtain a copy of an appellant's DVLA record as part of your preparation.

Firearms licence

Anyone who has their firearms licence or shotgun certificate revoked or cancelled has the right to appeal the decision to the Crown Court (see Firearms Act 1968, s 44). The appeal is listed as being against the relevant Chief Officer of Police. The notice of appeal must be served within 21 days.

The appeal is not a review of the initial decision, but a fresh look at the case on its merits. The judge can either dismiss the appeal or issue further directions about the certificate or register. Bear in mind that the normal rules of evidence are more flexible in firearms appeals. The court can consider any evidence put forward by the appellant (including hearsay) regardless of whether it was available when the decision was taken (see Firearms Act 1968, s 44(3)). You must ensure that you are familiar with the guidance issued under the Firearms Act 1968, s 55A that is relevant to the appeal.

Dangerous dogs

A magistrates' court has the power to order the destruction of a dog whose owner has been convicted of certain offences. Most common is the offence under the DDA 1991, s 3 of being in charge of a dog dangerously out of control in a public place. The aggravated version of the offence is committed if the dog bites someone in public. The power also applies to section 1 of the Act (possession of a prohibited dog).

There is a statutory presumption in favour of the destruction of a dog following conviction for a DDA 1991, s 1 or an aggravated s 3 offence, unless the court is satisfied that the dog is not a danger to public safety. This is the test that will be at the forefront of the court's mind. The court must consider the temperament of the dog, its past behaviour and whether the owner or person in charge at the time is a fit and proper person. The court may also consider 'any other relevant circumstances'.

As an alternative to a destruction order, the court has the discretion to impose a Contingent Destruction Order ('CDO') under the DDA 1991, s 4A. You might think of this as the canine equivalent of a suspended sentence, albeit with fatal consequences for falling short. Conditions are attached to the order setting out rules that the owner must abide by. Typically, this will include:

(i)   muzzling;

(ii)   being on a lead in public places;

(iii)   banning from certain locations;

(iv)   a male dog being neutered;

(v)   attendance at dog behavioural classes.

Appeals to the Crown Court will often turn on this issue – whether the court will be willing to replace a destruction order with a CDO. Clients will generally be emotional, and you will need to be mindful of this. Your task when appealing a destruction order is to satisfy the court that the dog is not a danger to public safety, and that appropriate conditions can be imposed to manage its behaviour. To establish this, you will need to advise your instructing solicitor and clients to obtain whatever evidence they can to assist your arguments. Some suggestions include:

(i)   A report from an expert dog behaviouralist is vital; they will carry out an assessment of the dog's ability to behave appropriately around strangers and in public. Ask the expert to come to court to give evidence, preferably with video evidence of the assessment. Visual proof of how well-behaved the dog was when being assessed can be very persuasive.

(ii)   Certificates – any dog behavioural classes attended since the incident to show that proactive steps have been taken to prevent future incidents.

(iii)   References – anyone who can speak to the dog's temperament, eg neighbours who also own dogs, dog groomer, dog kennels, the veterinary clinic.

The court also has the power to disqualify an offender from having custody of a dog. This can also be the subject of a Crown Court appeal. The test that the court must apply in this situation is 'whether the offender is a fit and proper person to have custody of a dog'. As with the above, references will assist, and the appellant may wish to give evidence on oath to the court about their dog handling ability. The court can consider:

(i)   any relevant previous convictions, cautions or penalty notices;

(ii)   the nature and suitability of the premises that the dog is to be kept at (can it escape?); and

(iii)   any relevant previous breaches of court orders.

Part X

Final word

Chapter 29

The Good Advocate

Andrew Langdon QC

Key references

• Bar Standards Board Code of Conduct, Part 2B Bar Standards Board Code of Conduct; Core Duties & Guidance

---

Case law

• *R v Farooqi and others* [2013] EWCA Crim 1649

Some advocates believe that ethical conduct is instinctive and that there is no need to learn about how to behave by studying any prescribed code of conduct. Whereas the essence of what it takes to behave well may be instinctive, it is a serious mistake to think that professional ethics need not be learnt.

On the contrary, it is probably the most important part of our professional education. Though some frequently encountered ethical problems have routine answers, others are more complex and may not be easy to resolve.

Experienced and respected practitioners and even judges will sometimes disagree upon what you should do/should have done. An advocate who is never troubled by ethical questions is probably one who does not see where they arise. A good set of barristers' chambers fosters a culture of sharing and discussing the ethical problems that you will encounter. That is how best we learn.

Ultimately your strength as an advocate depends upon high ethical standards. In pursuing them, you will also be contributing to a wider public interest. As Lord Neuberger has said:

> '... the earlier and more effectively we train and encourage potential professional lawyers and advocates to appreciate and understand the importance and nature of their ethical duties, the stronger a legal profession we will have, and the stronger the rule of law will be.'[1]

---

1   The Lord Slynn Memorial Lecture 2016 'Ethics and advocacy in the twenty-first century'

The Bar's Regulator sets out our professional duties and some guidance on how best we deliver them: https://www.barstandardsboard.org.uk/the-bsb-handbook.html.

The Bar Council has provided an invaluable 'Ethics Hub', with practical guidance on a whole range of regularly encountered problems; absconding clients, change of plea, client incapacity, defence statements, documents disclosed to you by mistake, witness preparation and comments to the media, to name but a few: https://www.barcouncilethics.co.uk.

In addition the Bar Council provides a popular confidential Ethical Inquiry Service: 020 7611 1307 and ethics@barcouncil.org.

What is the effect of the professional code of conduct on how we perform as advocates? Does adherence to our ethical duties reduce our efficacy? The answer (of course) is no; partly because all advocates are bound by the same rules, but mainly because the rules have, at their heart, the object of ensuring fair and just outcomes. The result is that if you have at your command a good understanding of your ethical duties, you will become a better advocate. The court craft displayed by such advocates is invariably more attractive.

Judges, opponents and even jurors can be astute in their detection of an advocate whose conduct is questionable, and the clients of such advocates are thereby at a distinct disadvantage. No one wants an impeachable advocate.

Under our code of conduct your first duty as an advocate is to the court and the administration of justice (Core Duty:1). It overrides all other duties.

Whilst you must also act in the best interests of your client (Core Duty:2) where there is a conflict, your duty to the court prevails.

Sometimes, in the heat of battle between adversaries, an advocate may in their exertions on behalf of their client, forget their wider duty to the court. For example, they might sense an opportunity which has suddenly presented itself to advance their client's cause, but they can only take advantage of it by asserting or implying some fact which, if they paused to think, they would realise they know to be untrue. Such conduct is often reckless rather than deliberate: but it amounts to a serious breach of your duty to the court. The Bar Standards Board Code of Conduct rules are specific: 'you must not knowingly or recklessly mislead or attempt to mislead the court' (r C3.1) and that includes the obligation not to make submissions, or put facts to witnesses 'which you know or are instructed are untrue or misleading'. (r C6.1).

So if, for example, your client has confessed to you, or conceded to you some fact that you believe the opposition may have difficulty in proving, you cannot mislead the court by presenting a case that runs contrary to that confession or concession.

Some advocates misunderstand this duty not to mislead and try to use it to take shelter from having to advance an unattractive or implausible case. This is a mistake. It may commonly be the case that your client's instructions strike you as implausible, but if they disclose a defence, you are not only permitted but obliged to advance those instructions. That is so, even if you hold a strong suspicion or belief that your instructions contain assertions of fact that are untrue. Were it otherwise, you would yourself be acting as judge and jury and our adversarial system could not function. Furthermore, you may be wrong, and an injustice may thereby be risked.

Your duties are of course wider than merely ensuring you do not mislead the court. Whilst acting in the best interests of your client, neither should you abuse your role as an advocate, for example by making serious allegations about a witness when you have not given the witness a chance to answer the allegation in cross-examination (r C7.2). Such conduct is a good example not only of what is unethical but also unattractive advocacy.

Similarly, you must not make any serious allegation against any person unless first, it is relevant to your case to do so and second, you have reasonable grounds for making the allegation (rC7.3). Here you must use objectivity. It is no defence to insist you are merely acting on instructions, if those instructions do not provide you with reasonable grounds to make what is in effect, a public accusation against someone who is not on trial.

These are examples of things you must not do, but you will be unsurprised to find that most of the time most advocates are trying to behave well. We all care about our reputations and we try to win the respect of people we respect. Becoming excellent at advocacy and winning respect cannot be achieved by anyone who has not, as part of an honest endeavour to do the right thing, grappled with ethical issues that arise in practice. Up to a point you will get help from opponents and judges, but often your duty of confidentiality to your client (Core Duty:6) prevents you from explaining the issue to them. You should always ask for time to consider and to take advice from others. Remember, most judges will have stood where you stand and they will see the fact that you are grappling with an ethical question as a sign of your professionalism and quality.

Good judges want good advocates to succeed, but a good advocate is not one who is overly compliant. You may be required to submit that the judge is going about something in the wrong way. In doing so you are simultaneously performing your duty to your client and to the administration of justice. On the other hand, personal attacks on your opponent or on the judge are never going to be good advocacy, let alone in accordance with your professional obligations. An extreme illustration of an advocate behaving badly in that and many other respects and being roundly criticised for doing so, is the case of *R v Farooqi and others*. It's rather a grim read, but an educational one.

Do not view our code of conduct as something which fetters your ambition to flourish. On the contrary it is in certain respects, empowering. Subject only to your duty to the court, your duty to act in the best interests of your client expressly requires you to promote those interests 'fearlessly and by all proper and lawful means' and 'without regard to your own interests or any consequence to you' and 'without regard to the consequences to any other person' (r C15). When faced by a judge or opponent who looks askance at the position you have adopted, the fact that you are not only immune from informed criticism, but more than that, are to be congratulated for performing your duty fearlessly, may serve to reassure you. To the rest of us, it can be inspirational. The availability of fearless representation, independent of the state and the judiciary, is integral to our confidence in civil liberty.

Crown Court advocacy requires each side to distil and advance its case within the boundaries of law and procedure. Fundamental to becoming a good advocate is an understanding of how to do so ethically. A really good advocate begins to flourish when high ethical standards become the minimum objective. If you consider yourself not bound by your duties as an advocate, but empowered by them, really good will become excellent.

Index

[All references are to page numbers]